Immunitas

Immunitas

The Protection and Negation of Life

Roberto Esposito

Translated by Zakiya Hanafi

polity

First published in Italian as *Immunitas* © Giulio Einaudi Editore S.p.A, 2002

This English edition © Polity Press, 2011

Polity Press
65 Bridge Street
Cambridge CB2 1UR, UK

Polity Press
350 Main Street
Malden, MA 02148, USA

ISBN-13: 978-0-7456-4913-9
ISBN-13: 978-0-7456-4914-6(pb)

A catalogue record for this book is available from the British Library.

Typeset in 11 on 13 pt Sabon
by Toppan Best-set Premedia Limited
Printed and bound in Great Britain by the MPG Books Group

The publisher has used its best endeavours to ensure that the URLs for external websites referred to in this book are correct and active at the time of going to press. However, the publisher has no responsibility for the websites and can make no guarantee that a site will remain live or that the content is or will remain appropriate.

Every effort has been made to trace all copyright holders, but if any have been inadvertently overlooked the publisher will be pleased to include any necessary credits in any subsequent reprint or edition.

For further information on Polity, visit our website: www.politybooks.com

The translation of this work has been funded by SEPS
SEGRETARIATO EUROPEO PER LE PUBBLICAZIONI SCIENTIFICHE

Via Val d'Aposa 7 - 40123 Bologna - Italy
seps@seps.it - www.seps.it

Contents

Introduction

1.

The news headlines on any given day in recent years, perhaps even on the same page, are likely to report a series of apparently unrelated events. What do phenomena such as the battle against a new resurgence of an epidemic, opposition to an extradition request for a foreign head of state accused of violating human rights, the strengthening of barriers in the fight against illegal immigration, and strategies for neutralizing the latest computer virus have in common? Nothing, as long as they are interpreted within their separate domains of medicine, law, social politics, and information technology. Things change, though, when news stories of this kind are read using the same interpretive category, one that is distinguished specifically by its capacity to cut across these distinct discourses, ushering them onto the same horizon of meaning. This category, as the title of this book makes apparent from the outset, is immunization. I will take a more detailed look at the semantic origins of this term and the mechanism by which it functions in the next section. But at a purely phenomenological level of discourse, a rough outline can immediately be traced out in an obvious analogy: in spite of their lexical diversity, all these events call on a protective response in the face of a risk. Whether we are talking about the outbreak of a new infectious

[handwritten margin note: interpretive framework]

[handwritten margin note: risk response]

disease, a dispute over established legal prerogatives, a sudden intensification of migratory flows, or an instance of tampering with large-scale communication systems—not to mention a terrorist attack—what is presented in any case is the rupture of a previous equilibrium and the consequent need for its reconstitution.

Up to this point, though, we are still dealing with a generic formulation of the category. It takes on a more nuanced connotation when we pass from mentioning vague situations of danger to identifying their specific characteristics. What becomes immediately obvious is that in each of the above examples the risk has to do with trespassing or violating borders. Whether the danger that lies in wait is a disease threatening the individual body, a violent intrusion into the body politic, or a deviant message entering the body electronic, what remains constant is the place where the threat is located, always on the border between the inside and the outside, between the self and other, the individual and the common. Someone or something penetrates a body—individual or collective—and alters it, transforms it, corrupts it. The term that best lends itself to representing this dynamic of dissolution—thanks precisely to the semantic polyvalence that places it at the crossroads of biology, law, politics, and communication—is "contagion": what was healthy, secure, identical to itself, is now exposed to a form of contamination that risks its devastation. Naturally, a threat of this type is constitutionally inherent to every form of individual life, as it is to all forms of human aggregation. But what lends particular importance to the need for immunization, making it the symbolic and material linchpin around which our social systems rotate, is the accelerating, generalizing character that this contagious drift has taken on for some time now. When we count the number of people in Africa dying from AIDS as more than two million per year, with a forecasted mortality rate of one-quarter of the total population; or when we calculate that the potential number of immigrants to European countries from territories in the Third World, whose populations are growing at dizzying speeds, is in the tens of millions, we are only arriving at a macroscopic view of a phenomenon that is actually much more diffuse and articulated. What frightens us today is not contamination per se—which has been viewed as inevitable for some time now—as much as its uncontrolled and unstoppable diffusion throughout all the productive nerve centers of our lives.

2.

Take the apparently marginal case of the computer. The diffusion power of viruses transmitted by email is not only immeasurably faster than that of the viruses once introduced by floppy disk, but because it is practically coextensive with the space occupied by the Internet, it is also potentially unlimited. The instant the infected document is opened by the user, it is immediately multiplied through all the contacts in the user's address book, who then go on in their turn to replicate it in an exponential fashion. If we consider that roughly a hundred new types of viruses are discovered each day, the enormous sums of money set aside by governments to come up with antivirus programs capable of stopping them becomes understandable (in the United States, four times as much as what is allocated for AIDS).

It might at first seem arbitrary to group this together with the legal controversy on the immunity of certain political figures, but the phenomenology is structurally analogous. The question needs to be framed in terms of the relationship between the law of an individual state—with all the ensuing prerogatives for the members of its government and diplomatic staff as well as for its members of parliament—and the law that is currently taking shape as a new form of international justice. Now, as holds true for all forms of boundary-breaking, it is clear that each time a judge puts forward an extradition request for a foreign subject who is protected by immunity, this creates a wound in the body of national sovereignty, one that is bound to be transmitted sooner or later to other organs of the state as well. This is what was really at stake in the legal battle against Pinochet's immunity (against Milosevic's as well, but for other reasons): not only his eventual conviction, but the contagious consequences that his conviction would give rise to in a world order based substantially on the mutual independence of sovereign states. Not surprisingly, Amnesty International hailed the sentence of the House of Lords and the later decision by the British Home Secretary Jack Straw, both condemning the ex-dictator, as the first breach to be opened in the heart of immunity law in favor of something that could be defined as "common law": if it is true that a crime committed by any tyrant affects not only his or her own people but all the citizens of the world, then the implication is that the crime may be prosecuted by anyone, in any place. It implies that there exists an instance of justice that goes beyond the territorial borders of the law and law itself as a form of territorial delineation. Is this not the same concept of extranational justice that illegal immigrants or refugees stripped of their civil rights tacitly appeal to when they are expelled by the state police forces and taken back to the other side of the border that they violated?

What initially appeared as heterogeneous events begin to take on the shape of interdependent polarities of a single figure. If we consider the continual lexical slippage between one and the other as yet another effect of the contagion, affecting language itself, there can be no better confirmation. The multiple dimensions of the immigration phenomenon, spanning social, political, and legal realms, is familiar to us. But in addition to constituting a threat to the public order, immigration is also commonly presented by the media as a potential biological risk to the host country, according to a model that pathologizes the foreigner, the roots of which lie in the European imaginary of the last century. It is thus perfectly understandable that the type of terrorist attack most feared today, precisely because it is the least controllable, is a biological one: germs of smallpox, Ebola, even the plague, released into the air, the water, the food. The epidemic emergency that the major infectious diseases represent in their turn has precise economic, legal, political, and even military implications. A recent CIA report that envisages the possibility of revolutions, genocides, and the establishment of dictatorships as a consequence of demographic collapse in various parts of the Third World ranks AIDS in the top five out of seventy-five destabilizing factors on a planetary level. When we consider on the one hand the explicitly medical, even epidemiological, vocabulary adopted in the battle against computer viruses—also feared as a potential vehicle for international terrorism—and on the other hand the expressly military terminology used in the scientific world to describe how the immune system responds to environmental threats, we come full circle. The more life is hounded by a danger that circulates without distinction throughout all its practices, the more its response is concentrated into the mechanisms of a single device: as risk of the common becomes increasingly extensive, the response of the immune defense becomes increasingly intensive.

3.

But if the notion of immunity only takes form against the backdrop of meaning created by community, how are we to characterize their relationship? Is it a relation of simple opposition, or is it a more complex dialectic in which neither term is limited to negating the other but instead implicates the other, in subterranean ways, as its necessary presupposition? An etymological analysis goes some way to answering these questions. Latin dictionaries tell us that the noun *immunitas*, with its corresponding adjective *immunis*, is a negative or privative term whose meaning derives from what it negates or lacks, namely, the *munus*. The meaning of *immunitas* can be arrived at by examining the predominant meaning of its opposite: where *munus* refers to an office—a task, obligation, duty (also in the sense of a gift to be repaid)—by contrast, *immunis* refers to someone who performs no office ("*e contrario immunis dicitur qui nullo fungitur officio*"). Whoever is *muneribus vacuus*, *sine muneribus*, disencumbered, exonerated, exempted (think of the Latin term *dispensatio*) from the *pensum* of paying tributes or performing services for others, is defined as immune. Those who are immune owe nothing to anyone, in terms of both *vacatio* and *excusatio*: whether referring to an originary autonomy or the later release from a previously contracted debt, what counts in defining the concept is exemption from the obligation of the *munus*, be it personal, fiscal, or civil.

That said, our definitions up to this point are still too general to bring us any closer to answering the question with which we began. To do so, we must bring into view another vector of the concept that has remained in the shadows until now.

→ exemption & privilege

Immunitas, as we have said, is an exemption. But, based on both ancient and modern definitions, it is also a privilege. The most fertile connotation of the term lies precisely where these two meanings overlap or intersect; immunity is perceived as such when it occurs as an exception to a rule that everybody else must follow: "*immunis est qui vacat a muneribus,* **quae alii praestare debent.**" The stress belongs on the second part of this sentence. In addition to being privative, immunity is also an essentially comparative concept: its semantic focus is more on difference from the condition of others than on the notion of exemption itself—so much so that the true antonym of *immunitas* may not be the absent *munus*, but rather the *communitas* of those who support it by being its bearers. In other words, if the privation—that which lacks—is the *munus*, the point of contrast against which immunity takes on meaning is the *com* through which the *munus* becomes generalized in the form of the *communitas*. This is also borne out by another even more pointed definition: "*immunis dicitur, qui civitatis, seu societatis officia non praestat; qui vacat ab iis societatis officiis,* **quae omnibus communia sunt.**" Compared to a generality of this sort, immunity is a condition of particularity: whether it refers to an individual or a collective, it is always "proper," in the specific sense of "belonging to someone" and therefore "un-common" or "non-communal." The official definition of ecclesiastical immunity in the canon law of the Roman Catholic Church expresses the same condition: "*jus quo loca, res vel personae ecclesiasticae a communi onere seu obligatione liberae sunt et exemptae.*" This is where its anti-social, or more precisely, anti-communal character comes to the fore: *immunitas* is not just a dispensation from an office or an exemption from a tribute, it is something that interrupts the social circuit of reciprocal gift-giving, which is what the earliest and most binding meaning of the term *communitas* referred to. If the members of the community are bound by the obligation to give back the *munus* that defines them as such, whoever is immune, by releasing him- or herself from the obligation, places himself or herself outside the community. In doing so, they become constitutionally "ungrateful": "*immunes ingratos significat, quemadmodum munificos dicebant eos qui grati et liberales exstitissent.*"

immunitas ≠ communitas

Proper (Privilege)
Particularity

immunitas interrupts

4.

Although the most evident vector of meaning in the idea of immunity is expressed in its primal juxtaposition with community, this oppositional relation does not exhaust its significance. To fully understand the term, we must follow another semantic trajectory that does not entirely coincide with the first: rather, it intersects it as part of a complex figure. This second meaning originally derived from the biomedical aspect that little by little began to take its place alongside the legal one we have been discussing. From this point of view, what is meant by immunity is the refractoriness of an organism to the danger of contracting a contagious disease. In reality, even this definition is an ancient one, since an early instance is to be found in Lucan's *Pharsalia*, referring to the resistance of an African tribe to snake poison. But what makes it significant for the purposes of our reconstruction is the turn it takes within its own field between the eighteenth and nineteenth centuries, first with the discovery of a measles vaccine by Jenner, and then with the experiments by Pasteur and Koch, the birth of medical bacteriology proper. The passage that most interests us is the one leading from natural to acquired immunity—in other words, from an essentially passive condition to one that is actively induced. The basic idea that came into play at a certain point was that an attenuated form of infection could protect against a more virulent form of the same type. From here came the deduction, proven by the effectiveness of the various vaccines, that the inoculation of nonlethal quantities of a virus stimulates the formation of antibodies that are able to neutralize pathogenic effects at an early stage.

In the following chapters we will be exploring this phenomenon in greater depth from a biological perspective; for now we will limit ourselves to a more general observation on the effects of meaning that it creates with regard to the immunitary paradigm as a whole. The first thing to point out is that the immunitary paradigm does not present itself in terms of action, but rather in terms of reaction—rather than a force, it is a repercussion, a counterforce, which hinders another force from coming into being. This means that the immunitary mechanism presupposes the existence of the ills it is meant to counter, not only in the sense that

disease makes it necessary (it is the risk of infection that justifies
the prophylactic measure) but also, in even stricter terms, that the
immune mechanism functions precisely through the use of what
it opposes. It reproduces in a controlled form exactly what it is
meant to protect us from. The relationship between the protection
and negation of life that is the subject of this book thus begins to
take shape: life combats what negates it through immunitary protection, not a strategy of frontal opposition but of outflanking and
neutralizing. Evil must be thwarted, but not by keeping it at a
distance from one's borders; rather, it is included inside them. The
dialectical figure that thus emerges is that of exclusionary inclusion or exclusion by inclusion. The body defeats a poison not by
expelling it outside the organism, but by making it somehow part
of the body. As we were saying: the immunitary logic is based
more on a non-negation, on the negation of a negation, than on
an affirmation. The negative not only survives its cure, it constitutes the condition of effectiveness. It is as if it were doubled into
two halves, one of which is required for the containment of the
other: the lesser of two evils is intended to block the greater evil,
but in the same language.

Of course, this homeopathic protection practice—which
excludes by including and affirms by negating—does not consume
itself without leaving traces on the constitution of its object: not
only because of the compensatory mechanism of subtraction that
thereby balances out the increase in life, but because this increase
takes the form of a subtraction. Instead of something good being
acquired, something bad has been taken away. Or better, it has
been shifted, diverted, deferred. If life—which in all its forms is
the object of immunization—cannot be preserved except by placing
something inside it that subtly contradicts it, we must infer that
the preservation of life corresponds with a form of restriction that
somehow separates it from itself. Its salvation thus depends on a
wound that cannot heal, because the wound is created by life itself.
For life to remain as such, it must submit itself to an alien force
that, if not entirely hostile, at least inhibits its development. It
must incorporate a fragment of the nothingness that it seeks to
prevent, simply by deferring it. This is where the structurally aporetic character of the immunitary process is to be located: unable
to directly achieve its objective, it is forced to pursue it from the

[margin notes: "key", "self separation", "a wound that cannot heal because the wound is created by life itself."]

inside out. In so doing, it retains its objective in the horizon of meaning of its opposite: it can prolong life, but only by continuously giving it a taste of death.

5.

This antinomy, one might say, traverses all the languages of modernity, leading them to their outcome in dissolution. This book attempts to reconstruct the lexical shifts involved in this event, but also its deep genealogy, through a series of figures that, purely for the sake of explanatory convenience, we can trace back to different disciplines—law, theology, anthropology, politics, and biology—because, in point of fact, their tendency is to overlap. As we have said, this occurs along the *clivage* that at the same time juxtaposes and connects immunity and community, making one not only the contrasting background for the other, but also the object and content of the other. From this point of view, it is important not to lose sight of the fact that immunity, as a privative category, only takes on relief as a negative mode of community. Similarly, when viewed in a mirror image, community appears to be entirely immunized, attracted and swallowed up in the form of its opposite. Immunity, in short, is the internal limit which cuts across community, folding it back on itself in a form that is both constitutive and deprivative: immunity constitutes or reconstitutes community precisely by negating it.

This negative dialectic takes on particular prominence in the sphere of legal language or, to be more precise, in law as the immune apparatus of the entire social system. If, as Niklas Luhmann claims, starting in the eighteenth century, the semantics of immunity have progressively extended to all sectors of modern society, this means that the immune mechanism is no longer a function of law, but rather, law is a function of the immune mechanism. The German sociologist tends to present this crucial transition in its most neutral and, thus, most ideologically loaded wording, but in actuality it constitutes the point of precipitation of an otherwise sharply aporetic path that has its origin in the structural relation between law and violence. Far from being limited to the role performed by the law of immunizing the community from the violence that threatens it, violence actually comes to characterize the immunitary procedures themselves: instead of being eliminated, violence is incorporated into the apparatus it is intended to repress—once again, violently. This is the short circuit that Walter Benjamin recognizes in the ambivalent figure of *Gewalt*, understood as the inseparable intertwining of law and force. Held within this vise grip—to which Benjamin attributed the mythical traits of an unavoidable fate—every possible form of "right," or "common" life, is sacrificed for the mere survival of its bare biological content.

The basic reason for such a reduction of life to simple living matter is traced by Simone Weil to the inherently private, and privative, nature of all law, including that which defines itself as public. Law, or right, in its historically constituted form, always belongs to someone, never to all. This is the source of its contrasting principle with the community which it is ordered to protect— but in a form that reverses its most intrinsic connotation: to be common, in the modern legal order, is only to lay claim to what is one's own. Whence the necessary recourse to force, which constitutes both the transcendental precondition of law and the guarantee of its effectiveness. This is the conclusion, from another perspective, that René Girard also comes to in an analytical framework that places along the same genealogical track both the persecutory violence of the victimage mechanism and the legal type of repressive apparatus meant to secularize it, but which precisely for that reason also ends up reproducing it. That law is essential for protecting all types of shared life from the conflicts that traverse them does not detract from the core of violence that the law brings with it, lodged squarely at its origins but also at the very heart of its process. As was expressly stated in the ancient definition of the first *nomos*—which was sovereign over life *and* death—law is located at the point of indistinction between the preservation and exclusion of life. Life is preserved inside an order that excludes its free development because it is retained within the negative threshold defined by its opposite. The same claim of the law to provide for all acts that may contradict life, by penalizing them, places it in an anticipatory position, with the result that life is both protected and prejudged.

6.

This particular persistence of the negative in the form of its containment is the vector of meaning that in categorical terms connects the language of law with that of theology. I am not thinking especially, or exclusively, about the inevitably legal character that all religious dogmatics assume when passing from the phase of the prophetic word to its ecclesiastical codification, even though the significance of this phase, necessary to any religion wishing to endure over time, is a defensive self-immunization against the heretical tendencies threatening its stability. But what ties the form of the *religio* even more profoundly to the semantics of immunization is the overlap between the two prevailing vectors of meaning that are present from the time of its origins: one is salvific—in the biological sense of something that is healthy or keeps healthy—and the other is normative in character. The meaning created by their intersection is traceable to the idea that the survival of life, whether bodily or spiritual, depends on the performance of a ritual, but also on the observance of a prohibition, which must not be violated. This means that its unfolding, or its preservation, here at least, depends on submission to a foreign power that is not born of it, but which constitutes both its condition of existence and its intended outcome.

The simultaneous presence of development and restraint, opening and closing, positive and negative—typical of the immune paradigm—is represented in exemplary fashion by the enigmatic figure of the *katechon*: whoever its historical and political bearer may be, it still embodies the principle of defense from evil through its preliminary internalization. In biological terms it could be compared to the antibody that protects the Christian body through assimilation of the antigen. Or, in more legal terms, to the *nomos* that counters anomia, itself in an antinomic form, by taking on its language. Its most obvious scope of application, inasmuch as it refers to the legitimizing point of union between a plane of immanence and a plane of transcendence, is the category of "political theology." Whether the plane of transcendence refers directly to God or to His earthly representative, one or the other is entrusted with the role of the unification of Christianity—which itself lies suspended between the religious sphere of the *corpus mysticum* and the secular although still theologically justified body politic. This is where the same terminology of *corpus* and "incorporation," which early on took the place of *carne* and "incarnation," mark the closure of the Christian vocabulary within an institutional framework intended to neutralize the anarchist and apocalyptic tensions that marked its beginnings. What soon emerged in response to these tensions was the normative reference to an order defined by divergence between the unfolding of existence and its ultimate meaning. Based on the assumption of this divergence, evil, inevitably at work throughout the course of history, can also be subsumed and overcome by its opposite. When this dialectic was later used—by the Christian community, it was originally intended to legitimize—in order to justify God, now personally accused of the evils of the world, the immunitary paradigm acquired the compensatory traits of a theodicy: no evil, no matter how intolerable its effects may appear, can cancel out the good that not only accompanies and compensates for it, but also, when viewed from a broader perspective, even ensues from it.

7.

It is not surprising that, as secularization has been established in the modern age, the category of *compensatio* has once again taken on central importance in the discipline known as "philosophical anthropology." Starting out with an economic and legal meaning, the term gradually extended its reach first to the language of cosmology, then to psychoanalysis, until it acquired an even more general field of application: regardless of the sphere involved, compensation occurs when a lack—damage, a debt, a defect—is balanced by restoring the initial condition of equilibrium. But for this compensatory dynamic to take its place at the heart of the anthropological lexicon, a further conceptual shift was required to nudge it in an explicitly immunitary direction: namely, the passage of meaning from a simple equality between negative and positive to a positive functionalization of the negative. This is the route German philosophical anthropology took when it identified the original lack or insufficiency of human nature as man's greatest resource. As Herder grasped, it is the failure of our organs to achieve the sort of specialization proper to other animal species that has put us in the position of having to artificially construct our experience in any environment we come to inhabit. This means that in order to preserve itself, human life must transcend itself—no longer in a sphere that is external to it, as theology would have it, but inside itself. It must objectify itself—and therefore exteriorize itself—in forms beyond its simple coming into being.

When Max Scheler recognizes the power of spirit as residing in its alterity with respect to the flow of life; when Helmuth Plessner searches for the intersection between power and survival in the human capacity to split ourselves off from the immediacy of our natural condition; when, finally, to an even more radical degree, Arnold Gehlen identifies the possibility of compensating for the morphological delay of animal-man in our exemption from instinctual excess, all three, in different ways, tie the preservation of life to the construction of an artificial order that distances life from itself. Whether this takes the form of a social ritual meant to safeguard the distance between individuals, as Plessner conceives it, or an institution able to stabilize otherwise destructive dynamics as in Gehlen, what remains is the anticommunal outcome that anthropological immunization seeks to prevent: the community as such is literally unsustainable. To allow the community to withstand the entropic risk that threatens it, and with which it ultimately coincides, it must be sterilized of its own relational contents. It must be immunized from the *munus* that exposes it to contagion using that which, coming from within it, goes beyond it. To this end are ordered the forms—roles, rules, institutions—by which anthropology divides life from its common content. What remains in common is nothing but mutual separation. This is where the intensely nihilistic aspect that philosophical anthropology absorbs from the immunitary dialectic is made explicit: the only protection against the nothingness underlying human nature is nothingness itself. And, indeed, a nothingness that is even more profound than the natural one because it is artificially created in view of its containment.

8.

But the excess of institutional mediation envisaged by philosophical anthropology is only one of two prevailing ways through which the immunitary paradigm relates to the collective dimension of life. There is another which must be added—or more often, which overlaps onto it—which seems to run in a symmetrically opposite direction. I am referring to the set of phenomena, or better, the regime of meaning, that at least since the appearance of Michel Foucault's last work has come to be known as "biopolitics." The contrast arises from the fact that while the anthropological model tends to separate life from itself by accentuating the formal elements, on the contrary, the biopolitical apparatus tends to eliminate any mediation. When politics takes life as an object of direct intervention, it ends up reducing it to a state of absolute immediacy. In this case, too, as in the previous one, any "form of life," even the possibility of a "right life" or a "common life," is excluded. Rather than deriving from an excess of form, though, its exclusion comes from life being crushed into its nude biological content. It is as if politics needed to deprive life of any qualitative dimension, to render it "only life," "pure life," or "bare life" in order to relate to it.

This is where the decisive importance attributed to the semantics of the body originates. Contrary to a widespread theory tying the immunitary dynamics of modernity to a procedure of gradual marginalization or emptying of the individual and social body, the biopolitical register is actually built around its renewed centrality. The body is the most immediate terrain of the relation between politics and life, because only in the body does life seem protected from what threatens to harm it and from its own tendency to go beyond itself, to become other than itself. It is as if life, to preserve itself as such, must be compressed and kept within the confines of the body. This is not because the body, both individual and collective, is not exposed to processes of involution and dissolution: what has more experience with the bite of evil than the body? Rather, it is because this risk is precisely what sets off the mechanisms of alarm, and therefore, of defense meant to protect it. It is true, then, as Foucault himself maintained, that the living being begins to enter onto the horizon of visibility of modern knowledge the moment its constitutive relationship with what continually threatens to extinguish it emerges. Sickness and death make up the cone of shadow within which the life sciences carve out their niche.

Biopolitics, one might say, simply takes this presupposition to its point of extreme radicality, where it is also productively turned inside out. By placing the body at the center of politics and the potential for disease at the center of the body, it makes sickness, on the one hand, the outer margin from which life must continually distance itself, and, on the other, the internal fold which dialectically brings it back to itself. The key figure in this passage is the classic one of the *pharmakon*, understood from the beginnings of the philosophical tradition in the double sense of medicine and poison, but in this context more specifically interpreted as an antidote needed to defend life from the dissolutive possibility of its being "put in common." This immunitary significance is what lies behind the remarkable longevity of the "body politic" metaphor, not only in early modern treatises on governance where it appears in explicit form, but also subsequently, when the metaphor seems to eclipse itself simply because it is "realized" in the actual body of the people. In order for it to become an object of biopolitical practice, it had to be brought back to the same vocabulary of the "body politic" through which first the King and then the State had long been represented in the form of sovereign power. But this had to take place within a framework that inverts the relations of dominance between power and life. The threshold of transformation from the paradigm of sovereignty to that of biopolitics is to be located in the time when power was no longer the subject of inclusion (as well as of exclusion) of life but instead, life—its reproductive protection—became the ultimate criterion for legitimizing power. This explains the process of medicalization that has invested the entire gamut of social interaction over the last two centuries. It explains also, more generally, the hypertrophy of the security apparatuses that are increasingly widespread throughout contemporary societies. The blind spot that their development seems to arrive at can be seen precisely in this hypertrophy, since this self-protective syndrome ends up relegating all other interests to the background, including "interest" itself as a form of life-in-common; the effect it creates is actually the opposite of what is desired. Instead of adapting the protection to the actual level of risk, it tends to adapt the perception of risk to the growing need for protection—making protection itself one of the major risks.

9.

The relation between protection and negation also re-emerges out of this dynamic: life can be protected from what negates it only by means of a further negation. Even though this is the bottleneck our entire contemporary experience seems to funnel into, the intention of this book is not limited to describing it. Rather, I pose a fundamental question that puts its phenomenology into a more ambiguous light: is there a point at which the dialectical circuit between the protection and negation of life can be interrupted, or at least problematized? Can life be preserved in some other form than that of its negative protection? Naturally, I have tried from the outset to avoid the temptation of an immediately affirmative response, one that situates the development of life in a horizon that is radically external to the one defined by the paradigm of immunization. There are two reasons for this. First because, as I have stressed repeatedly, the category of immunity is inseparable from that of community: as its inverse mode, it cannot be eliminated. This is borne out by the fact that there is no community without some kind of immunitary apparatus. And second, because to negate the negation through which immunity in its turn negates what threatens life would mean to repeat the same procedure. The route to be taken can only pass through the same object that it intends to deconstruct; not by negating it, but rather by deepening the internal contradiction. For these reasons, I have sought the answer to the question with which I began at the very heart of the protective mechanism that has progressively extended itself to all the languages of life—namely, on the biological plane, in the immune system that ensures the safeguarding of life in the body of each individual. Not because the biological immune system is a neutral or original object compared to the derivative or metaphoric nature of other forms of social immunization. On the contrary, more than any other thing, we might say that its functioning has been the object of an excess of meaning that threatens to erase, or at least confuse, its distinctive traits. The whole history of immunological theory, not only in its popularized offshoots, but also in its scientific formulation, is the most evident proof of this. A reading of the most widely used immunology manuals, even when focusing purely on the lexicon used, provides solid confirmation of this. The immune system is actually described as a military device, defending and attacking everything not recognized as belonging to it, and which must therefore be fended off and destroyed. The most striking feature is the way a biological function is extended to a general view of reality dominated by a need for violent defense in the face of anything judged to be foreign. Whatever the ideological origin this stereotype responds to, what emerges is its objectively nihilistic tone: the relation between "I" and "other"—between the immune and the common— is represented in terms of a destruction that ultimately tends to involve both the contrasting terms. The impulse toward self-dissolution appears to be more than metaphorical in illnesses labeled appropriately as autoimmune diseases, in which the warring potential of the immune system is so great that at a certain point it turns against itself as a real and symbolic catastrophe leading to the implosion of the entire organism.

However, more recent study of the structure and functioning of the immune system seems to suggest another interpretive possibility, one that traces out a different philosophy of immunity. Without concealing its constitutive antinomy, even calling attention to it, this new interpretation situates immunity in a nonexcluding relation with its common opposite. The essential point of departure, recently adopted by such widely divergent thinkers as Donna Haraway and Alfred Tauber, is a conception of individual identity that is distinctly different from the closed, monolithic one we described earlier. It has been made possible, even inevitable, by advances in genetic and bionic technologies: rather than an immutable and definitive given, the body is understood as a functioning construct that is open to continuous exchange with its surrounding environment. Moreover—this is the argument (a problematic one, to be sure) put forward in the concluding section of this work—the immune system may very well be the driving force behind this exchange. Immune tolerance, understood as a product of immunity rather than as an unraveling or a deficiency of the system, is one of its first expressions. The figure of the implant, whether an artificial prosthesis or a natural implant like fertilized eggs in the mother's womb, provides the most striking case in point. The fact that the genetic heterogeneity of the fetus rather than its genetic similarity is what encourages the mother's immune system to accept it means that the immune system cannot be reduced to the simple function of rejecting all things foreign. If anything, the immune system must be interpreted as an internal resonance chamber, like the diaphragm through which difference, as such, engages and traverses us. As we were saying: once its negative power has been removed, the immune is not the enemy of the common, but rather something more complex that implicates and stimulates the common. The full significance of this necessity, but also its possibility, still eludes us.

*

We have spoken about how the concept of immunity is divided into two different lexical fields, one legal and political, and the other biomedical. This entire inquiry is directed toward probing the margin that simultaneously separates and joins these two categories. The question arises whether there are any historically contiguous segments in which these two meanings of immunity overlap in the same practice. I believe that one of the most significant cases, probably because it is the first, can be found in the right to immunity granted practicing physicians in Imperial Rome. The background and circumstances of this event are made hazy by the complex social position of Roman doctors. What immediately strikes the eye is an apparent inconsistency between the high level of income, but also power, that the medical profession attained versus the lack of consideration given to most of its members, except in rare cases, partly because of their humble origins. Based on statistics gathered from the inscriptions, the number of *medici ingenui* (free Roman citizens) is absolutely miniscule compared with *medici servi*, *liberti* (freed Roman slaves), or *peregrini* (immigrants from the provinces).[1] To this already perplexing set of circumstances—a real "social puzzle," as it has been described[2]—the issue of immunity adds a further interpretive problem. How are we to explain and understand the granting of a particular privilege to a profession that often (in Pliny, for example) had derogative connotations associated with greed and even dishonesty? In reality, the granting of immunity was itself a far from peaceful process.[3] To begin with, as we learn from Ulpian (*Digest*, 50.13.1.2–3), and especially from Modestino (*Digest*, 27.1.6.8–11), after Caesar had granted Roman citizenship to physicians practicing medicine in Rome starting in AD 46, the status of immunity granted to doctors by Vespasian, and then reaffirmed around AD 117 by Hadrian, involving exemption from certain civil and tax obligations, did not apply only to physicians but also to the other intellectual profession: philosophers, rhetoricians, and grammarians. Immunity was further tied to specific conditions, such as that of practicing in one's hometown, and, of course, the *probitas morum* and the *peritia artis*. Despite these restrictions, as emerges from a text on a constitution by Commodus, *immunitas* was further limited by Hadrian's son, Antoninus Pius, who fixed the number of doctors allowed to practice at five in small towns, seven in medium-sized towns, and ten in big cities (except Rome). All later attempts to pass measures extending these privileges were always accompanied by controversy and steps backward.[4]

Why so much vacillation on an issue that, all in all, was of such minor importance? Bowersock traces the cause back to some sort of incompatibility with the economic prosperity of the provinces where the exemption was in effect.[5] But as Nutton points out, the question remains murky.[6] How could a few privileges granted to no more than ten physicians put the economy of the entire province into crisis? I believe the answer should be sought elsewhere, or at least in other explanations as well: namely, in the ambiguous and vacillating status of immunity itself. An observation by Mario Vegetti points in the same direction when he stresses that *immunitas* "has a socially ambiguous meaning, because it excludes whoever enjoys it from the obligations that come with *honores* and *munera*, but also from the high prestige they confer."[7] Given that some of the exemptions included in immunity involved very important social *munera civilia*, like building and priestly functions or the protection of widows and orphans, in addition to the *sordida munera*, it becomes clear why the acquired privilege is negative, and thus, constitutively ambivalent: it consists in the privation of a *munus*, which, together with the weight of the *onus*, also includes the dignity of an *officium* that is prestigious because it participates in the public sphere. This privation is what explains the contradiction of a highly remunerative but socially unimportant position. It is no coincidence that the immunity granted to physicians falls under the purely private conception—in the sense of "being deprived of something"—of Roman medical practice. As Vegetti notes, this is precisely what differentiates the legally immunized doctors from those who were salaried state employees in Hellenistic times: while the salaried doctors had the obligation—the *munus*—to provide their services free of charge to all citizens and to the poor in particular, the private practitioners were exempt.[8] Accordingly, they received potentially unlimited private honorariums but no public salary. Even in AD 386, under Valentinian II, when a college of fourteen public *archiatri* was set up, one per district, the members were paid in kind (*commoda annonaria*), to which they could add revenue from private sources, rather than being given a state salary. This explains the inherently equivocal status of Roman physicians: they were financially privileged, since there was no limit to how much they could charge for their services, yet socially disparaged. In other words, they were remunerated, but they were immune from the obligations and honors that were common to the rest of the free citizens.

I

Appropriation

1. *Ius proprium*

The immune function that the law performs for the community is immediately obvious, and as such is universally recognized even outside the legal literature. From the outset, it was prescribed to preserve peaceful cohabitation among people naturally exposed to the risk of destructive conflict. Even before being put into codified forms, therefore, law is necessary to the very life of the community. This is the primal, radical sense of the immunizing role it performs: just as the immune system functions for the human organism, law ensures the survival of the community in a life-threatening situation. It protects and prolongs life, snatching it from the jaws of death. This comparison with the biomedical lexicon reveals a more complex and disturbing meaning of legal immunization, however. The immunity created by law for the community, just like the immunity created by the human body, does not operate directly and affirmatively, so to speak, in attaining its goal. On the contrary, it is forced to adopt an indirect, twisted, or even, literally, perverse method to reach its objective, one that is only attainable through an instrument that contradicts it (albeit only partially or temporarily). This is because it contains an element of the same substance it is intended to defend against.

There is an antinomy implied in the very wording we began with: when it is stated that the primary goal of law is to immunize the community, its negative character is assumed in advance. As becomes apparent from the contrastive coimplication of the two terms, law does not seek to shelter the community from a risk external to it, but rather from something that is originally inherent to it, which constitutes it as such. To grasp this point, we need only turn our attention to the most radical significance of *munus* from which "community" derives its own meaning:[1] law seeks to protect the common life from a danger that can be seen in the relation that makes it what it is. Common life is what breaks the identity-making boundaries of individuals, exposing them to alter-ation—and thus potential conflict—from others. Also, because the community brings its members together in a common relationship that is necessarily one of reciprocity, it tends to confuse the bound-aries between what is proper to each individual and what belongs to everybody and hence to nobody.

The law responds to this unsustainable contamination by reconstituting the limits threatened by the connective power of the *munus*. This is where the aporia we spoke about earlier is to be found. Since the relationship and the alteration are not pathological possibilities but the originary forms of community, by immunizing it, law turns community into its opposite. From this perspective, the negative connection that binds community and law together is finally clarified. Although, as we have seen, law is absolutely necessary for the community to survive, it actually relates to the community through its inverse side: to keep community alive, it tears it away from its most profound meaning. By protecting it from the risk of expropriation—expro-priation being community's most intrinsic, natural inclination—law empties community of its core meaning. One could even go so far as to say that law preserves community by making it destitute. Law constitutes community through its destitution. It does so, by extreme paradox, exactly insofar as it seeks to strengthen its identity, to ensure its mastery over its own identity, to return the community to what is "proper" to it—assuming that what is "proper" is exactly what is not "common." By striving to make community more proper to itself, law necessarily makes it less common.

This aporetic dialectic between common and proper, implicit in the legal form, is central to the work of Simone Weil. When she juxtaposes "rights" to "obligations," she is actually reasserting an idea of community that is entirely faithful to its original meaning of "law in common." The obligation she speaks of is none other than the *munus* that the members of the *communitas* share, moving in a direction from inside to outside, from the one to the other, and from the proper to the common. This is not to exclude the possibility of using the notion of rights, but in a form that is complementary and subordinate to the notion of obligation, that is, regarding those to whom each individual is obligated: "A man, considered in isolation, only has duties, amongst which are certain duties towards himself. Other men, seen from his point of view, only have rights. He, in his turn, has rights, when seen from the point of view of other men, who recognize that they have obligations towards him. A man left alone in the universe would have no rights whatever, but he would have obligations."[2] What Weil seeks, in short, and what she means by "justice," is to end the nonreflexive relationship between subjectivity and rights. No one is a direct subject of rights, in first person; solely of obligations, which only indirectly transmute themselves objectively into rights for those who are benefited by them. But to say that we are subjects of an obligation—or, more precisely, that we are subject *to* an obligation—means that we are subjects of nothing but our own expropriation: an expropriation of what is proper to us, beginning with the subjective essence. This is ultimately the fulfillment of one's own obligation: its translation into a common benefit. This expropriative dynamic, in which the community recognizes the deep sense of its *munus*, is what legal immunization responds to by way of contrast. It re-establishes the direct passage between rights and subject that is cut off by the ridge of obligation: rather than "seeing as I have obligations, then *others* must have rights," "seeing as *I* have rights, others must have obligations." This passage takes place through the idea of the "legal person." If the *communitas* necessarily refers to something "impersonal," or even "anonymous," as Weil specifies, the immunitary principle of law places the person as the sole bearer of rights back into the picture: "The notion of rights, by its very mediocrity, leads on naturally to that of the person, for rights are related to personal things. They are on that level."³ If we recall that in the same years she was writing her *Prelude à une declaration des devoirs envers l'être humain*, Maritain's *Declaration des Droits de l'homme* appeared in New York, and Mounier prepared a *Declaration des Droits des personnes et des communautes*, the terms of the alternative become crystal clear. On the one hand, there is the absolute impersonality, the subjective anonymity, the constitutive impropriety of the "human being" to whom the infinite obligation of each finite existence is addressed: "The object of any obligation, in the realm of human affairs, is always the human being as such. There exists an obligation towards every human being for the sole reason that he or she *is* a human being, without any other condition requiring to be fulfilled."⁴ On the other, there is the individuality of a subject—man or woman, person, community—who is only granted the enjoyment, or even better, the property/propriety [*proprietà*] of certain rights. This is because in its immunizing function, the law—*of* the community and *from* the community—takes on the same form as the *proprium*, regardless of whether we are talking about private or public law: in either case it is proper, in the sense that it "belongs" to the subject, public or private, who claims to be its bearer.

This is a truism that has characterized the legal form since its origins: even when the law is general or a generalization is called for, it always remains essentially particular, or even personal, because it concerns a legal person. The dimensions of this person may vary, from the discrete entity of a single individual to the institutional magnitude of a state, but the way it deals with all other legal persons does not: always and forever through comparison, negotiation, and contention. What this implies, in addition to its mercantile qualities, is its opposition in principle to the concept of community. Laws are always partial, never for everyone: the all, like nothingness, is a matter of justice. It is logically impossible to extend a right to all without emptying it of meaning as a right. If it were extended to everyone, it would no longer even be perceived as such. Not being proper to anyone, it would no longer be a right, but perhaps, at most, a fact [*fatto*]. It would lose the faculty that differentiates those who possess it from the status of those who are deprived of it, namely, its immunitary sense of privilege or privation. How can something be made common that is in essence private? Or how can a privilege be shared without losing it? "To the dimmed understanding of our age," writes Weil, "there seems nothing odd in claiming an equal share of privilege for everybody—an equal share in things whose essence is privilege. The claim is both absurd and base; absurd because privilege is, by definition, inequality; base, because it is not worth claiming."[5]

Yet it is precisely in this contradictory demand—the generalization of what is particular—that the law exercises its immunitary value. The legal form safeguards the community from the risk of conflict through the fundamental rule that things are completely available to be used, consumed, or destroyed by whoever can legitimately claim to possess them, without anyone else being able to interfere. But in this way it reverses the affirmative bond of common obligation into the purely negative right of each individual to exclude all others from using what is proper to him or her. This means that society is legally governed and unified by the principle of common separation: the only thing in common is the claim to whatever is individual, just as the object of public law is precisely the safeguarding of that which is private.[6]

The fact, however, that the content of private law requires the formal guarantee of public law reveals a precondition, so far unremarked, that legal immunization is a generalized form of bringing the common back to the proper. As Nietzsche already explained, it can only work under one of the following conditions: either there is a substantial balance of powers behind the sharing of what is common (but society is by definition an imbalance of powers); or there is a power that prevails so strongly over the others that it imposes an unequal exchange. "Justice in this initial phase is the goodwill among people of about equal power to come to terms with each other, to come to an understanding again by means of a settlement, and with regard to the less powerful, to *compel* them to agree among themselves to a settlement."[7] It is precisely the passage that leads from law to force, or rather, that makes force the logical and historical precondition for law. Weil frames this question with utter accuracy. If legal rights are nothing but a "sharing out," they can never exist without force: "The notion of rights is linked with the notion of

sharing out, of exchange, of measured quantity. It has a com-
mercial flavour, essentially evocative of legal claims and arguments. Rights are always asserted in a tone of contention; and
when this tone is adopted, it must rely on force in the background, or else it will be laughed at . . . rights are by their nature
dependent on force."[8] In this context, the law appears as an
internal passage to legal immunization which seems to reduplicate
it: to be able to immunize the community from its self-destructive
tendencies, the law needs to protect itself first. But, according to
the immunitary dialectic we have learned to recognize, it may do
so only by relying on the same principle it seeks to dominate, on
the same force it must keep at bay. All of human history—from
ancient Rome to the Absolutist State of the early modern period,
to twentieth-century totalitarianism—is interpreted by Weil as a
tragic confirmation of this inexorable dialectic between rights and
force. This holds true both at the level of individuals and in the
relationship between each individual and the community, because
the subordination of law to force is joined to the subordination
of individuals to the collective to which they belong. The more
individuals seek to defend from others what is proper to them,
the more they must allow themselves to be appropriated by the
collectivity intended to defend their defense. This metaphysics of
appropriation—first the thing, and then the person who claims
possession—is deeply entwined around the juridical heart of
Western civilization. Was it not precisely a "human property"
that the Romans contested in the Hebrew God, understood as a
property owner of slaves in his own right? "It is singularly mon-
strous that ancient Rome should be praised for having bequeathed
to us the notion of rights. If we examine Roman law in its cradle,
to see what species it belongs to, we discover that property was
defined by the *jus intendi ed abutendi*. And in fact the things
which the property owner had the right to use or abuse at will
were for the most part human beings."[9] Truth be told, what else
is a sovereign right, as conceived in the modern era, if not a form
of decision over life that is governed by the principle of its violent
appropriation? "A sovereign right is the right of property according to the Roman idea, or any other essentially similar to it."[10]
Here the relationship between *ius* (law, right) and *communitas*
contracts in all its antinomy. It would appear that to ensure

common life, law is forced to put something inside it that maintains it beyond itself: to make it less common or not common—in other words, immune. But by immunizing life from community, law ends up sacrificing the intensity of life to the need for its preservation.

*

We know the partial, even partisan, nature of the interpretation Simone Weil provided of the Roman paradigm when she identified it as the root of twentieth-century totalitarianism. It brings the *antirömische Affekt* circulating in European culture at the time to an apex, almost an excess of signification, beyond any seen before. Yet the close connection between *ius*, property, and violence that she sees at the root of the Roman *ordo* does hit on an essential trait of Rome and *its* notion of law. Or to spell it out: law can be understood as a specifically Roman language. When Martin Heidegger, who shared in the "anti-Roman" tradition, connects *ius* to the injunctive force of *iubeo*, dragging the Roman *iustitia* into a distant semantic field juxtaposed to that of the Greek *dike*,[11] he is only addressing one aspect of the question. Its full scope is addressed, however, in a work that is a true monument to the greatness *aere perennius* of Roman law. I am referring to the *Geist des römischen Rechts* by Rudolf von Jhering. In situating Roman law before religion rather than after it, he grasps that its dominant character lies in its absolute orginarity. Since Rome extracted and excavated everything out of itself—no reference is made to anything that lies outside the lines of its own genesis, nothing stands behind Roman law other than its own founding force. Jhering expresses this in no uncertain terms: while other peoples have used some kind of mythic, religious, or moral mantle to cover up the blood and sweat lying pooled at the source of their legal system, Rome lays them bare. At the root of the Roman legal order there is nothing but the force of those who imposed their order by means of violence on those who had to submit to it: "The world is a part of personal force, the individual bears the foundation of his *ius proprium* within himself, and by himself must preserve it: this is the quintessence of the way life was understood in ancient Rome."[12]

That this force is "personal"—not rooted in the objective order of the state, but rather arising directly out of the subjective will of the individual who is capable of exercising it—brings us back to the kernel of the question later taken up again by Weil, although for diametrically opposing reasons: right is rooted in the original form of *ownership*. It always belongs to someone: it is both the object and mode, the content and form, of a possession. Originally, there "were" no rights, they were something you "had"; and they were in any case subjective, in the rigidly determined sense of belonging to whomever had the force to tear them away from others and make them their own; because if right has the form of subjective property, then property is always the fruit of appropriation. It is not transferable and cannot be transmitted. It cannot be inherited and cannot be transferred: it is *taken*. As we might expect, the transfer of ownership, what will later be called the right of succession, was unknown in ancient Roman law. Property can never be passed along. It is originary, because there is nothing behind it except the violent act of appropriation, the same act the Romans used to procure women by force, tearing them away from other peoples at swordpoint. Jhering discovers this in the primary meanings of the three verbs *capere*, *emere*, and *rapere*: the fact that plundering is not a crime means that taking, grabbing and tearing away are at the root of legal ownership, or what is legally proper. When Gaius (4.16) observes that the prototypical form of legitimate property is the right of plunder— *maxime enim, sua esse credebant, quae hostibus cepissent*—he is giving us a strong indication to this effect: for the Romans, whatever is *manu captum*, *mancipium*, or taken by the force of arms, becomes proper or one's own. Jhering goes even further, etymologically linking *praeda* to *praedium*:[13] the fact that territorial land is also connected to the dynamic of the *preaedatio* rather than to the static state of possession clears away any doubts as to the origin of Roman law as well as to the Roman origin of law. Although Gaius does not mention it, the founding relationship between property and plunder is witnessed to by the symbol that stands for property: the auction in the expression used to refer to public sales: *sub hasta vendere*. Like Simone Weil, and even more bluntly than her, Jhering locates the origin and meaning of the Roman legal system in the tip of the lance.

2. Violence against violence

The idea of law as a violent form of control over life was explored most fully by Walter Benjamin. When he writes that "all violence as a means is either lawmaking or law-preserving,"[14] his intention is not simply to reiterate the connection between law and force that is seminal to the great tradition of Realism running from Pindar to Nietzsche, passing through Thucydides, Machiavelli, and Pascal. What attracts his attention is not only the support that the use of force provides to the law, or even the legitimacy that the law provides to the use of force, because in both cases the relationship is founded on two distinct terms: "laws" and "arms" in Machiavelli, "justice" and "force" in Pascal. The radically new point of view that Benjamin offers is his recognition of them as modes, or figures, of the same substance: *Gewalt*, which takes on meaning precisely at the point they overlap. This allows him to distance himself from both the conception of natural law and that of positive law: because he looks at law neither from the perspective of its origins (as does natural law) nor from that of its outcome (as does positive law); neither from the perspective of nature nor that of history. Rather, he starts from where they intersect in myth and destiny: namely, from the point where history is seized once again by its previous natural origin and forced to perpetually retrace its contours. Rather than being limited to coming before or after law, violence actually accompanies it, or rather, violence constitutes law throughout its trajectory, in a pendular movement that swings from force to power and back again from power to force. Within this circuit, three distinct yet linked stages can be distinguished: 1) law is always founded at the beginning by a violent act (one that is legally unfounded); 2) once established, it excludes any other violence external to it; 3) but this exclusion can only be carried out by means of further violence, no longer to institute but rather to preserve the established power. In the final analysis, this is what law is: violence against violence in order to control violence. The immunitary function it performs for the community is all too evident: if violent means such as the police apparatus or even the death penalty are used to exclude violence external to the legitimate order, the legal system works by adopting the same thing it aims to protect against. And, in any case, what is the exclusion of an external element if not its inclusion? Benjamin is very clear about this. When it comes to violence that is external to the legal order, what law seeks to eliminate is not the violence, but the "external"; in other words, to convey it to the inside:[15]

> one might perhaps consider the surprising possibility that the law's interest in a monopoly of violence vis-à-vis individuals is not explained by the intention of preserving legal ends but, rather, by that of preserving the law itself: that violence, when not in the hands of the law, threatens it not by the ends that it may pursue but by its mere existence outside the law [*durch ihr blosses Dasein ausserhalb des Rechts*].[16]

What is threatening to the law is not violence, therefore, but its "outside": the fact that such a thing as "outside the law" exists at all, that the law does not encompass all things, that something evades its grasp. From this point of view, when we commonly refer to violence as being "outlawed," this should be understood in an entirely literal sense: the illegitimacy of violence does not stem so much from its content as it does from its location.[17] Violence clashes with the law not *because* it stands outside the law, but rather, *as long as* it does so. When violence is simply moved from outside to inside the law, it ceases to be at odds with the law and actually ends up coinciding with it. This is not to say that the "outside," the originary exteriority of violence, its naturally extra-legal character, must be done away with: in this case the coercive power of the law, the sovereign power of the sword, would be done away with at the same time. Or better yet, the "outside" we are talking about must be situated inside while continuing to be an outside, introjected as such, in a form that simultaneously eliminates and maintains the outside by leaving it external to that which it is nevertheless inside. Based on this line of reasoning, law can be defined as a process of interiorization of that which remains exterior to it: its making-itself-internal [*il suo farsi interno*]. The outside includes not only their point of indistinction but the line where they overlap (as Hobbes grasped intuitively when he preserved the natural right of the sovereign precisely at the instant he took it away from someone else). We can just as reliably assert that violence is nothing but a passage inside law, its black box, so to speak, and that law is nothing but a passage inside violence, or its rationalization. For Benjamin, these two perspectives converge and ultimately coincide. There is no such thing as two histories, one of law and one of violence. There is only one history: that of violent law *and* legal violence. As already noted by Giorgio Agemben,[18] this irreducibly antinomic structure of the *nomos basileus*, founded on the interiorization, or better, the "internment" of an exteriority, is particularly evident in what is referred to as a "state of exception," precisely what Carl Schmitt located in "the outermost sphere" of law.[19] But it is reproduced in relation to each case in which the law refers to itself in its generality. Something is a law if it is able to prevent any event that can possibly take place, any accident that can go beyond it. Only in this way—by legislating on what still evades its control—can it immunize against becoming: it does so by making *becoming* into a "state," a "given," an "already-become" [*un divenuto*]. The law holds every "maybe" in the iron grip of the "already" and the "still," the "forever thus" and the "thus forever."

It is in this repetitive, cyclical pattern that Benjamin identifies the mythical core of law. It consists in violently retracing any moment in historical development back to its initial stage, in crushing the entire history into the tracing of its nonhistoric origin. Only the constant return of the past can assure the present in the face of the uncertainty that bears down on it from the future. This reassuring figure is the most meaningful expression of legal immunization: what else does immunity imply if not assurance against a future risk, paid for by taking preventive, sustainable doses? But the specific object that law exercises its coercive control over also refers to the semantics of immunization: namely, life itself. Life is the event, the situation, which by definition tends to escape its own confines—it tends to break down its own limits and turn itself inside out. The mandate of law is to immunize life from its irresistible impulse to overcome itself, to make itself more than simple life, to exceed its natural horizon of biological life (or as Benjamin expresses it, "bare life," *das blosse Leben*) so as to take on a "form of life" such as "right life" or "common life." This gap in life is what law seeks to fill by continuously bringing it back inside its biological confines. Only in this way, by prohibiting every self-transcendent act, anything that tears it away from itself, can the law keep all its infinite cases under control. To do this, to fully normalize life, it must be judged by the law in such a way as to prevent any possible infraction, any possible offense.

This is precisely what appears impossible to achieve at first glance. How are we to anticipate something that has yet to happen? How are we to control something that in itself escapes all control? How are we to provide for a crime that has not yet been committed? The only solution is to decide on a guilty verdict in advance, regardless of the actual crime; to always regard life as guilty, even before and beyond the fact that the offense has or has not been committed; to assign the punishment (in German, *strafe*)—or better, the expiation (*sühne*)—regardless of whether the circumstances merit it. What comes of this is not only anticipation, but also a logical reversal between guilt and condemnation: guilt is the outcome rather than the reason for the condemnation. Life is not condemned because it is guilty, but rather *in order to make it* guilty. This is the function that the law inherited from the demonic stage of human existence that preceded it and shaped its violent procedures: the function of condemning life to perpetual guilt. Life is not judged because it is guilty; life is made guilty so that it can be judged—and condemned. Released from will and choice, guilt converges entirely with fate. Law is what crushes life against the bare wall of fate: "Fate shows itself, therefore, in the view of life, as condemned, as having essentially first been condemned and then become guilty. . . . Law condemns not to punishment but to guilt. Fate is the guilt context of the living."[20]

As we know, this mythical, fateful conception of law is not restricted to Benjamin: in spite of all the variations on the theme, it is an integral part of a line that runs, with countless interruptions, from the Greek tragedians to Kafka.[21] For the Greeks, fate was the power that struck the hero above and beyond any subjective guilt; while for Kafka, the violence of law is all one with the senselessness of its persecutory procedures. But in Benjamin's essay, both these themes are knit together in a form that reveals their specific immunitary significance. We have already seen that the stated aim of law is to preserve life. And also that life can be preserved only if held in the fold of an inexorable anticipation that judges life to be guilty even before any of its acts can be judged. This means that preservation is not painless. On the contrary, it requires a preventive condemnation of what it seeks to save: by being condemned, life is reduced to pure material, it is subtracted from any form of right life or shared life. It is precisely this formal possibility that is sacrificed to the reproduction of the biological stratum of life, to the perpetuation of simple survival. Benjamin traces this sacrificial mechanism to the distinction between the sphere of "bare life" and the sphere of "the living"— of he who removes himself from the objectivity of life to make himself its subject. This is the person the violence of the legal apparatus is unleashed on: its immune system consists in perpetuating life through the sacrifice of the living. This means that to preserve life something needs to be introduced into it that at least in some aspect negates it to the point of suppressing it. The relationship between life and death comes back into play: life only maintains itself in relationship with its opposite. And in any case, is the "first" law—sovereign law—not the right to life *and* death? "In the exercise of violence over life and death more than in any other legal act, law reaffirms itself."[22] Not only because it *decides* (from L. *decidere*, *de-* "off" + *caedere* "cut," thus cuts, separates) life from death, but, more profoundly, because it unites them in a bond connecting life to death, to the extent that it makes death the instrument for the preservation of life. Is "survival" not the prolongation of life beyond the limit of death? The only life that can last beyond its natural end is one that presupposes death. This is the meaning of the myth of Niobe that Benjamin places at the origin and very heart of the legal form. When he stresses the fact that the violence that rained down on Niobe from the sphere of fate "is not actually destructive" since, having brought "a cruel death to Niobe's children, whom it leaves behind, more guilty than before through the death of the children,"[23] he is saying that the mother's life is saved not despite death of the children but *because* of it. This connection, in reality, is what she is guilty of: to be saved from death, which she invokes in vain, through the contagious contact with the blood of those who died in her place. Here, "the mythical ambiguity of laws"[24] is revealed in all its unearthly meaning, represented by the storm of arrows that fall around Niobe, enclosing her in a life of stone, a life that cannot end because it issues from and contains death: it is the line that both separates and unites life and death. Life is preserved by its proximity to death, with death settled on the horizon of life.

*

It has been said that the relation between law and force in Machiavelli is that of a relationship between implicit but distinct terms. If so, the force *of* the law that was later fully brought to light by authors such as Nietzsche, Weil, Benjamin, and Derrida would be left in the dark.[25] In reality, these supposed limits of Machiavelli's thought are only applicable up to a certain point. As Thomas Berns argues, there is a vector of meaning in Machiavelli's writings that somehow pushes beyond these limits.[26] It will come as no surprise that the thematic horizon in which the vector takes on importance is once again constituted by the Roman legal order, and more precisely, from the way it is related to the violent time of its foundation. The specificity of Machiavelli's point of view lies in the distance he explicitly takes from those who condemn the initial event—the fratricide of Romulus—precisely because they lose sight of its positive consequence for future republican institutions. They are wrong not because they condemn the "act"—the murder of Remus—but because they fail to connect it to its "end" or "effect": "For although the act condemn the doer, the end may justify him; and when, as in the case of Romulus, the end is good, it will always excuse the means" (*Discourses*, 1.9).

Machiavelli's reasoning has traditionally been interpreted as arguing in favor of the autonomy of politics from ethics; or for the technical accommodation of means to ends—the end justifies the means. But it must be questioned from another angle, concerning the very structure of law, and what could paradoxically be defined as its retroactive effect. I say "paradoxically," because this is exactly what the law *cannot*, or at least *should not*, have, but which, on the contrary, somehow always defines its functioning; because it is true that normally the ends of the law are geared to the future, but to a future that is always *prior* [*anteriore*]. Its function is to legitimize *a posteriori* the extrajudicial, and antijudicial, moment from the past that made the institution possible. On no account, then, should Romulus be condemned: not simply because when the act was committed there was no legal order prohibiting it; but because it *would have been* precisely that order that would claim that act as its condition of existence. In this instance, the law reveals its constitutively antinomic structure: it has the form of a postponement decided in advance [*posticipazione anticipata*]. This is not simply due to the fact that the instituting power—always somehow violent because torn from the fabric of historical continuity—cannot be subject to the laws it establishes, but rather because it is the established power that in its turn grants legitimacy to the instituting power. Derrida has shown how this retroactive effect is at work in every constitutive process, such as the American Declaration of Independence: the signature at the bottom of each constitutive document presupposes it; just as the document presupposes the act to which it seeks to grant legitimacy.[27]

But the presuppositional structure of the law does not end here—or, better, it must be viewed from another angle as well, which, in addition to making it a postponement decided in advance [*posticipazione anticipata*], also makes it a postponed advance decision [*anticipazione posticipata*]. Its circularity is recognizable in a passage from the *Discourses* analyzed by Berns: "Nor can we reasonably pronounce that city ill-governed wherein we find so many instances of virtue; for virtuous actions have their origin in right training, right training in wise laws, and wise laws in these very tumults which many would thoughtlessly condemn" (I,4). The most explosive element in Machiavelli's text, as we know, is his reversal of the normally negative opinion of "tumults": the "wise laws" that gave long life to the Roman Republic. This dynamic confirms the need of a founding force for the constitution of the established order. What requires our attention, however, is the other side of the coin, the assumption this presupposition is based on: for initial violence to have ordering effects rather than destructive ones, it must be preceded and shaped by "instances of virtue" and "right training," which derive, in their turn, from "wise laws." In short, wise laws may be the positive effect of social conflicts only if such conflicts were *already* contained within the limits set by the laws. In order to put into effect what it is founding, the founding act must be founded, in its turn, by the act. It therefore presupposes that which presupposes it—it presupposes its own presuppostion. This might very well be the false bottom of the origin that we must delve into in order to penetrate the enigmatic Machiavellian figure of the "return to principles" as the only salvation for a state in decline. The return to principles is to be viewed as the remembering of the original contents of the constitution; but even more so as the reference to something that precedes all content because it coincides with the very form of the precedence. This is precisely the point where law and force overlap with each other in the antecedence of one over the other—continually chasing after each other in the illegitimate temporality of the future anterior.

3. Double blood

Does the presupposition of the law grasp the whole horizon of life in its retroactive fold—or is there a point of escape, a lever, that makes it possible to break the circuit? Is it still possible to shield the community from that sacrificial paradigm to which it seems destined, or has this possibility, too, already been prejudged? These are the questions the work of René Girard has been exploring for years, bypassing both the messianic perspective and the cyclical-fate perspective. What in Benjamin is still "a residue of the demonic stage of human existence"[28] for Girard is rooted in the clear-cut and determined order of history. Not only the period of law—which will constitute the definitive secularization of history—but the period of sacrifice belongs to the time of reason as well. Since Girard considers myth to be the unconsciously rational method through which the community removes itself from the endlessly threatening risk of extinction, history is revealing even if expressed in the language of myth. This is the case even though both sacrifice and law speak the language of violence. As in Benjamin, and perhaps to an even greater extent, violence occupies the entire represented framework because it controls the very order of representation. It is both the object and the subject of desire, in the specific sense that it is not the object of desire that provokes violence, but violence that awakens the giddiness of desire: "violence becomes simultaneously the instrument, object and all-inclusive subject of desire . . . the signifier of ultimate desire."[29] When Girard explains it in terms of the reciprocal mimetic system—A desires B because C also desires B—it perfectly captures the "communal" aspect involved: if each person wants what everybody desires—precisely because everybody wants it— then violence is not something that strikes the community from the outside, but is rather something that comes from inside it. Violence is actually community's most intrinsic expression. We might even say that violence is the inside of the community that has grown to the point of destructively boiling over outside itself. The community is filled up with itself to the point of overflowing all barriers and confines, left to its own absoluteness, to its "absolutely communal" being: without limits, separations, or differences. Not surprisingly, violence is always connected to figures of indifferentiation: that of brothers, perfectly symmetrical; or of twins, perfectly the same, generated through the scissiparity of the form of the One. Because violence is actually the identity, or continuity, that flows through the veins of the community, "gluing it" to its own skin. For Girard, this is where its most authentic character lies, its root and premise, its double and its "squared": its double doubled. The violence of violence does not reside so much in its arbitrariness, or even specifically in its intensity, so much as in its communicability: "From the outset of this study . . . I have regarded violence as something eminently communicable."[30] What it brings to mind, more than a solid—a striking boulder or a penetrating tip—is the pervasiveness of a flowing liquid, which insinuates itself and seeps into the world until it is reduced to a sponge, or a boggy marsh, like at the time of the universal flood. Something that *contaminates* above all, following a logic familiar to Simone Weil: "Contact with the sword causes the same defilement whether it be through the hilt or the point."[31] Nothing renders its infinitely *circulatory* character better than blood: "When men are enjoying peace and security, blood is a rare sight. When violence is unloosed, however, blood appears everywhere—on the ground, underfoot forming great pools. Its very fluidity gives form to the contagious nature of violence."[32]

Girard repeatedly describes violence in terms of infection and blood—the germ that spreads like a wildfire, first to the objects of desire and then to its carriers, causing disasters "just as a slight cut can prove fatal to a hemophiliac"[33]—in order to introduce the prophylactic procedure intended to prevent it or, alternatively, to treat it. Here we get a closer glimpse of the point that interests us: if the community has managed to rescue itself from the current to which it is continually exposed by its own violence, it is because an immunitary device capable of diminishing its devastating effects has been put in place from the very beginning. This is not to suppress the violence—the community itself, which is inseparable from it, would be extinguished along with it—but to take it in nonlethal forms and doses: "The physician inoculates the patient with a minute amount of the disease, just as, in the course of the rites, the community is injected with a minute amount of violence, enabling it to ward off an attack of full-fledged violence."[34] Although Girard is hesitant to translate into the language of modern epidemiology something utterly primordial that apparently predates any forms of modern medicine, he cannot help but call attention to the astonishing similarities it holds with our immunitary discourse:

> The analogies abound. "Booster shots," for instance, correspond to the repetition of sacrificial rites. And of course, in all varieties of "sacrificial" protection there is always the danger of a catastrophic inversion: a too virulent vaccine, a too powerful *pharmakon* can promote the illness it was supposed to prevent.[35]

Getting the quality and quantity of the *pharmakon* right is as important for the sacrificial victim as it is for immunization treatment. To curb the violence that pervades and engulfs the social body, it must be internal and external, contiguous and distinct, similar and different. But most important, it must allow the three neutralizing vectors of polarization, diversion, and differentiation to be activated simultaneously. All the violence initially directed to the community as a whole must be attracted magnetically to the sacrificial victim in a form that diverts its natural course, and in such a way as to separate the situation of the victim from that of the aggressors: "The victim . . . is a substitute for all the members of the community, offered up by the members themselves. The sacrifice serves to protect the entire community from *its own* violence; it prompts the entire community to choose victims outside itself."[36] To sterilize itself from its own contaminating power, the community is forced to "operate on itself": to divide itself from itself; to separate off a point inside itself on which all collective evil will converge in order to distance it from the rest of the body.

From this point of view, it would appear that the community is deferred violence—which differentiates from itself by redoubling itself into *another* violence: the gap that opens for an instant in the heart of violence—then immediately closes like a pincer around the victim. It is a shift of violence from same to other. From all to one. All *minus* one. One *in place of* all. Even when the community takes a nonviolent form, when it appears to yearn for peace, it is the hidden fruit—a concession and product—of violence: "Nonviolence appears as the gratuitous gift of violence; and there is some truth in this equation, for men are only capable of reconciling their differences at the expense of a third party. The best men can hope for in their quest for nonviolence is the unanimity-minus-one of the surrogate victim,"[37] because violence cannot be eliminated; at the most, it can be "tricked," deceived, given the runaround, as in the symbolic circle of the duel. It can be turned upside down: transformed from "common" to immune. It can be immunized against the virus that carries it and makes it what it is: in other words, disinfected, or disinfested, through a ritual that substitutes the impure, clotted, encrusted blood of disease and collective death with the pure, fresh, crimson blood of the surrogate victim. In this transformation from the common to the immune, what remains constant, however, is the reign of blood: blood that has been made double, however, in its dual powers of destruction and salvation. And indeed—as is typical of the immunitary procedure—it is salvific for the all *inasmuch as* it is destructive to a part. It has the capacity to cleanse *just as* it is meant to soil. It generates life *because* it causes death. "Blood serves to illustrate the point that the same substance can stain or cleanse, contaminate or purify, drive men to fury and murder or appease their anger and restore them to life."[38]

This is the homeopathic double bind that for Girard is the origin and very condition for civilization: the self-sacrificing frame without which civilization would not have had the strength to survive itself, but that continues to shape its entire development along an evolutionary line that runs from a level of "prevention" to one of "cure." Even if modern culture is not always aware of this—indeed, precisely because it is not, because we continually tend to forget about or dismiss it—we are caught in it and ruled by it much more than we are able to exert our control over it. Thus, immunization becomes not only the instrument but also the form of Western civilization. Like ancient civilization, but to an even greater extent, modern society is the product rather than the source or the subject of violence and the immune mechanism it requires as its *enhanced limitation*:

> Neither primitive nor modern man has yet succeeded in identifying the microbe responsible for the dread disease of violence. Western civilization is hindered in its efforts to isolate and analyze the causes and to examine them in any but the most superficial manner because it has enjoyed until this day a mysterious immunity from the most virulent forms of violence—an immunity not, it seems, of our society's making, but one that has perhaps resulted in the making of our society.[39]

The immune protection Girard speaks of here is essentially the law. The law replaces rather than eliminates the sacrificial rite that lies within its own logic; namely, revenge, which the law not only takes into its own hands but actually perfects into a form that connects prevention and cure: "our judicial system rationalizes revenge and succeeds in limiting and isolating its effects in accordance with social demands. The system treats the disease without fear of contagion and provides a highly effective technique for the cure and, as a secondary effect, the prevention of violence."[40] While the sacrificial rite prevents revenge by substituting a victim who cannot be revenged with one that can be, the judicial system takes care of the revenge itself; but starting from a point that is out of reach for further revenge. What changes in this case is not the object but the subject of revenge, who is made abstract and general like an institutional mechanism rather than a concrete individual. It is as if, once the revenge has been taken, it folds up into itself and is exhausted. As if it were put into practice by dissolving itself, or dissolved itself by being put into practice. This auto-immunizing process is what the rationalization of judicial revenge consists in: rather than randomly striking some innocent person, as in the sacrificial order, now the truly guilty person is stricken. The blow is struck, however, not by the person who first suffered the wrong, nor by his group, but by a third figure—the judge, the court, the State—in an asymmetrical space with regard to the position of the person who receives the sentence, making it outside the scope of anyone wanting to take revenge.[41]

It is as if the law, having taken violence within itself—or rather, having penetrated itself within its own perimeter—then dragged violence outside the community it simultaneously strikes and immunizes. The dynamic that Girard reconstructs is thus twofold: first, the law internalizes violence; second, and at the same time, the law moves to a theater external to the one where it will actually perform. Rather than simply incorporate what lies outside itself (namely violence) the law places itself in a different dimension from the social body onto which it perpetrates the violence. From this perspective, the judicial "cure"—the sentence and the penalty—appear both immanent and transcendent: the transcendence of an immanence. This translation, or transfer [*traslatio*], transcendental to what is in every respect immanent, is what reveals the character of judicial secularization as theological in the final analysis, the shadow generated by its own rationalistic "enlightenment":

> This obscurity coincides with the transcendental effectiveness of a violence that is holy, legal, and legitimate successfully opposed to a violence that is unjust, illegal, and illegitimate. In the same way that sacrificial victims must in principle meet the approval of the divinity before being offered as a sacrifice, the judicial system appeals to a theology as a guarantee of justice.[42]

But this "ideological" mechanism of a mirrorlike projection of the internal onto the external is neither perfect nor eternal. It is doomed to seize up or break up, precisely because of its immune load; at a certain point and beyond a certain limit, it is destined to turn on itself with a self-destructive force directly proportional to the introjected violence. And not only because, reminiscent of atomic power plants, when "decontaminating the installation . . . accidents can always happen."[43] More to the point, this self-destructive recursion occurs because, to the extent that modern civilization emancipates itself from the sacred, or immunizes itself against the original immunization principle, it reconverts the sacred into the very power it seeks to curb and contain. Once again, it seeks to curb by containing, as when the preceding epochal cycles came to their end, but even more, by fighting violence with violence. It does so by transforming violence into violence against violence until this violence ricochets back on itself, threatening to unloose onto the community the same forces it was intended to save it from:

> With the founding mechanism absent, the principle of violence that rules humanity will experience a terrifying recrudescence at the point when it enters its agony. . . . This means that the violence, having lost its vitality and bite, will paradoxically be more terrible than before its decline. As the whole of humanity makes the vain effort to reinstate its reconciliatory and sacrificial virtues, this violence will without doubt tend to multiply its victims, just as it happened in the time of the prophets.[44]

*

Girard exemplifies the ever-impending threat of sacrificial crisis through two tragedies, Euripides' *Heracles*, and *The Women of Trachis* by Sophocles,[45] which we will focus on first. Nessus the centaur, mortally wounded by an arrow from Heracles, before dying offers Heracles' wife Deianira a shirt smeared with his own poisoned blood, telling her that she can ensure her husband's eternal fidelity by having him put it on. But when Heracles dons the shirt, the poison is activated by coming into contact with the fire he had lit to celebrate the rites of a sacrificial purification. After smashing the servant who had brought him the shirt, Lichas, against a rock, Heracles dies, provoking Deianira to commit suicide for having unwittingly caused his death. In this entropy-laden dynamic, Girard sees the same catastrophic reversal that takes place in the first tragedy. In the work by Euripides, after Heracles has killed the usurper Lycus who had captured his wife and children, he confuses his family with his enemies and kills them, too. As in *Women of Trachis*, here too the sacrificial logic creates an excess that he is incapable of mastering and which ends up overwhelming the individual who set it in motion. What is shattered is the symbolic and material dividing wall between pure

violence—directed against the "legitimate" object of sacrifice—
and impure violence, which is undifferentiated and unstoppable,
striking anyone who wanders onto its path. Prior to this shift,
there is a fragile balance between continuity and distinction, one
that must exist between the victim and the rest of the society who
sacrifice him. If the surrogate victim is too different from those he
is meant to replace, a danger exists that he will fail to draw all
the communal violence to him; if he is too similar, he may drag
them along with him to the same end. This is exactly what happens
in the Sophoclean tragedy: when the dividing wall between one
(the victim) and the others is broken down, Heracles' violence is
unleashed on the very people it was supposed to protect. For
Girard, this is the essential point: contrary to or even in agreement
with other possible types of psychoanalytic or sociological interpretations, what matters is that violence overflows beyond its
established limits. In the face of this general truth, there is nothing
to be added by the mythological theme of Nessus's shirt: it "joins
company with all the acts of violence that Heracles carries on his
back."[46]

But is this really how things stand? Or does the antagonism
between Heracles and the centaur bring something else inside that
makes sense based precisely on the dialectic between community
and immunity? I am thinking particularly of Giambattista Vico's
interpretation of the Hercules myth in *The New Science*. In this
work—as in the *De constantia iurisprudentis*—Hercules, a political hero par excellence, symbolizes the beginning of order in the
extralegal world that preceded it. By slaying the Hydra and setting
fire to the Nemean forest, with an act of purification he puts an
end to the reign of the formless created by the universal flood and
the monsters it had generated. Against the chaos and dispropor-
tionality of a world without form, Hercules sets up the bulwarks
and boundaries that channel undifferentiated violence. Hence,
after the original *turbatio sanguinis*—the sharing of women and
confusion of human seeds—came the distinction necessary for the
institution of political authority. Gennaro Carillo has recently
noted that the oppositional line between these semantic fields corresponds to the one dividing *communitas* and *immunitas*.[47] While
the first term is used by Vico to refer exclusively to the extralegal
situation, prior to any law whatsoever whether natural or positive,

the second is the result and simultaneously the precondition of political form. Only when men are immunized from the contagion of a relation without limits can they create a political society defined by the division between the goods of each person. But the establishment of the proper marks the end of the common. Since that moment, all of human history unfolds in the unresolved dialectic between the two opposing poles of chaos and order, identity and difference, community and immunity: each time "popular freedom" prevails—in Republican Rome as in modern Europe— some of the extralegal qualities of the community return, with all the potentials but also the risks that they bring with them. Whence the need for a restraint—religious, legal, social—capable of containing the dissolutive drive of the *communitas* with a counterthrust.

In Vico's view, Hercules is the hero of this resistance, but also of the antinomy that he brings inside. With his labors, he erects a protective barrier between the feral world and the world of humans. He marks a boundary between inside and out. He puts an end to the mixing of genera, signaling the dominance of the strong. In so doing, he inaugurates the political struggle whose aim is to cast doubt on this dominance. The clash with the centaur expresses this contradiction in its most extreme form. The element that adds a further layer of meaning to the one Girard sees in the myth (not an alternative one) is the fact that Vico places Nessus on the other side of the semantic divide: if Hercules is the hero of political *immunitas*, the centaur represents feral *communitas*. While Hercules represents limits and difference, the body of the centaur conveys the fusion, or the confusion, between two different natures. The encounter between the two must perforce be fatal. Striking the monster dead, Hercules comes into contact with his blood and is inevitably contaminated: "Finally Hercules breaks into a fury on being stained by the blood of the centaur Nessus, the same plebeian monster of two discordant natures mentioned by Livy, that is, in the midst of civil fury he extends connubium to the plebs and is contaminated by plebeian blood and so dies."[48] The significance of Hercules' death, within and beyond the sacrificial crisis described by Girard, is to be found in this contrast. If his poisoned arrow brings the community contagion to an end, Nessus's shirt responds with an additional, final contagion: it com-

municates to whomever comes into contact with it a contagion
that is impossible to be immunized against, because it is the poisoned product of immunization itself.

4. Legal immunization

The catastrophic outcome that Girard envisages for an entire cycle
of civilization radically questions the immunitary logic that characterizes it. Leaving aside the "evangelical solution" that has come
to the fore in his most recent work, we are still left with the question most pertinent to our own query: how can law immunize the
community from violence without at the same time being sucked
up into it? And, furthermore, is it possible to imagine a community
that lacks legal protection from the destructive powers that traverse and tear at its fiber? The only way to escape the insolubility
of these types of questions is to refute the premises of their terms.
This is what Niklas Luhmann has done, drastically altering the
lexical and conceptual framework of the problem by relocating it
in the functional perspective of systems theory. The basic assumption he put into question, one from which the whole interpretative
tradition sprang, was first and foremost the relationship between
law and community—in other words, the idea that it really is a
relationship between external entities that are present to one
another. If this were true, law would be located outside society,
and for this reason would affect and be affected by it in a causal
fashion. This is precisely what Luhmann disputes: law can neither
influence nor be influenced by society because it is itself a system
of social communication that arose out of differentiation from a
larger system, which it helps to perpetuate and reproduce through
its specific function.

What this function may be is explained in such clear terms that
it would appear to validate and conclude our entire inquiry thus
far: Luhmann's intention, he says, is to "argue that the legal
system serves as society's immune system."[49] Indeed, while preserving and even intensifying the category of immunization we
have examined in the previous thinkers, Luhmann's reformulation
of the concept, which he rotates 180 degrees around its semantic
axis, is highly relevant. When he writes that the immune function

of the law is to "secure the autopoiesis of society's communication system as much as possible against as many disturbances produced" within the system as possible he is explictly arguing against the notion that immunization and communication can be opposed:[50] not only does immunization serve to protect communication from potential risks, it actually overlaps it, in the final analysis, to the point of fully coinciding with it. Of course, in order to arrive at a conclusion of this sort, Luhmann has to perform a strategic move that removes him from the tradition of legal sociology in two respects. First as regards the scope of the communicative sphere, which ends up occupying the entire systemic horizon. This point he stresses with unusual emphasis, considering his notoriously sober style of writing:

> In spite of all the political borders that exist within it, today there is only one world society: and this is because universal communication has been realized, because we have become aware of the fact that there is a common world, that everyone's experience is contemporary, because a common death has become possible.[51]

Luhmann goes so far in this direction as to claim that "only communication is necessarily and inherently social; action is not."[52] It is social only to the extent that it presupposes communication.

This statement on the fundamental importance of communication for social systems should not, however, lead us to believe that Luhmann's thinking leans in the direction of a Habermasian theory of communicative action: from a systems theory point of view, it is not the subjects who communicate, but communication itself. This means that the social system communicates only within its own limits, and in fact only communicates this limitation:

> Observing themselves, that is communicating about themselves, they cannot avoid using distinctions that differentiate the observing system from something else. Their communication observes itself within its world and describes the limitations of its own competence. It never becomes self-transcending.[53]

This is exactly what we were saying about how communication coincides with an immune device that, far from being its categorical opposite, constitutes both its condition and effect.[54] This is not to say that first there exists communication (or community) and then its immunization. Or that the community, or communication, immunizes itself to defend itself from something that comes from outside it, or even inside it. This is the classic scheme that Luhmann's critique takes as its point of departure. For him, communication is *already of itself* immunization. Or, in complementary fashion, immunization is the very form of communication: its *non*-communication of anything other than communication, that is, once again, immunization. This is the same conceptual passage that makes opening and closing overlap. Luhmann's gambit is based from the outset on replacing the theory of closed systems with a theory of open systems: the system only lives in relation to the environment from which it draws the stimulus toward increasing complexity, which it reproduces in continually more developed forms. But this relationship is a closed one, since systemic communication with the environment is, in principle, impossible, other than through a progressive inclusion of its exteriority. This means that the system is open only to its own closure; or that closure is a condition for any form of openness: "the concept of autopoietic closure has to be understood as the recursively closed organization of an open system. The new insight postulates closure as a condition of openness."[55]

It is not that communication differentiates itself from some primeval indifferentiation. Communication expresses itself specifically and exclusively in differentiation from what is not part of the system: communication thus necessarily creates a separation through differentiation. "What is uttered is not only selected, but also already a selection—that is why it is uttered."[56] This is how we are to understand the statement that the system "includes all exclusions."[57] This is not meant in the sense that the inclusion causes an exclusion, or that the exclusion is the result or residue of an incomplete inclusion; these would still constitute an oppositional relation, or at least a dialectical one, between communication and immunization. It is meant in the sense that inclusion is the same mode as exclusion and vice versa. In the system and with respect to the system, one is included by exclusion and excluded by inclusion. When it comes to systems, one is included by excluding, united by separating, and joined by differentiating. It is true that the social system always refers to its exterior—subjectivity, life, the community—but understood as environment. And thus as nonsystem, as other-than-system. The environment is thus simultaneously included and excluded. It is excluded in the form of interiority and included in the form of exteriority.

It cannot escape the leap in quality that is generated as a consequence within the immune paradigm. This no longer takes shape as some thing, a device or strategy, which is deployed on the social system to defend it from the other or from itself; it is rather the only way to be for a system coinciding with the inclusive exclusion, or exclusive inclusion, of its environment. Now the law is precisely the locus—the subsystem—where this coincidence is secured. Its function is not at all one of bringing men back to an order given in nature; nor is it to determine the greatest possible number of legitimate acts, as the respective interpretations of natural law or positive law would have it. True, it also has the task of producing certainties for non-evident expectations, but this is precisely the role that makes it society's immune system, since the law produces certainties not by way of affirmation, not through the use of "yeses," but through the use of "nos": "The system does not immunize itself *against the no* but *with the help of the no.* . . . Or, to put this in terms of an older distinction, it protects through negation against annihilation."[58] It is true that for Luhmann the neurophysiological analogy with organisms can only be taken so far, since they function through a process of biochemical selection, while social systems operate through a process of meaning selection.[59] But meaning, referring to everything that is possible, also includes the possibility of its own negation: there is no sense outside the possibility of another sense or even nonsense. Law functions exactly on the basis of this binary code, transforming certain cognitive expectations into normative expectations; namely, into the type of attitude that, instead of limiting itself to experiencing disappointment, faces it with the threat of a penalty until the expectation is fulfilled. Only if the disappointment is envisaged can it be formulated and thus neutralized. This is precisely how law immunizes the social system as a whole: substituting uncertain expectations with problematic but secure expectations. That is to say, not by eliminating instability, but by establishing a stable relationship with it: better foreseeable uncertainties than insecure certainties.

This passage opens the gate to the final, and most radical, split from a more traditional concept of legal immunization. If the only way to secure oneself against the disappointment of expectations is to prepare oneself to deal with them in terms of rejection, the immune system of the law would no longer have the task of protecting the community *from* conflicts, but, on the contrary, *through* them: "Law is not only a means for resolving conflicts, it enables them and even creates them."[60] From this point of view, Luhmann leaves behind the classic oppositional dichotomy between order and conflict—conflict as that which hinders order, and order as that which eliminates conflict—which the Hobbesian paradigm of order was based on, and as Talcott Parsons still intended it.[61] While for Parsons, the primary problem of the social system is how to maintain the equilibrium threatened by an excess of contradictions, for Luhmann the problem becomes how to produce enough contradictions to create a valid immune apparatus: "[Contradictions] serve as alarm signals, which circulate within the system and can be activated under specific conditions."[62] This means that they are an integral part of the system that produces them in view of its own self-reproduction. Here the theory of self-reflexivity, in which the system is constituted of the same elements that it constitutes, reaches a point of singular coincidence with the new cellular immunology. The specific function of contradictions—of sustainable contradictions—is to create a selective memory capable of protecting the system even without the stress of external stimuli:

> Contradiction permits reaction *without cognition*. . . . This is why one can invoke an immune system and coordinate the theory of contradictions with an immunology. Immune systems also operate without cognition, knowledge of the environment, or analysis of disturbing factors; they merely discriminate things as not belonging.[63]

In biomedical terms, you could say that the system does not require external antigens to produce antibodies. Or that the antibody is all one with the body it serves to protect; that it is the selfsame body that differentiates from itself in order to better self-identify itself through a movement that goes simultaneously from the inside to the outside and from the outside to the inside. And indeed, that preemptively eliminates this distinction between inside and outside, making the outside the springboard for the reproduction of the inside, and the inside the absorption filter for the outside. The outcome of strengthening, or rather doubling, legal immunization that this discourse brings about is quite clear. Compared to its classic form, legal immunization is immunized, in its turn, against the violence implicit to its homeopathic process. For Luhmann, the immune system of the law does not imply violent repression of the community as Benjamin viewed it, or the sacrifice of a victim, as in Girard's model. It does not spill blood and is no longer covered in blood because there is nothing and no one outside it to which it can apply itself: the system cannot communicate, immunizing with its own components, except by immunizing them. From Luhmann's perspective, then, the outside *is* the inside, conflict *is* order, and the community *is* immunity. If everything is communication in our social systems, then everything is also immunization. Hence, immunization is not only the protective shield for something that precedes it, but the object itself of protection: self-protection. It is at once subject and object, form and content, part and whole of itself. Not surprisingly, Luhmann emphasizes that "certain historical tendencies stand out, indicating that since the early modern period, and especially since the eighteenth century, endeavors to secure a social immunology have intensified."[64] Immunization has progressively extended itself from the legal sphere to politics, economics, and culture until assuming the role of system of systems, the general paradigm of modernity.

From this perspective, we can no longer say that the immune system is a function of law, but if anything that law is a function of the immune system. And therefore it no longer has need of violence in order to pacify violence, because in this generalized immunization, extended to all communication and coinciding with it, there is no place left for violence. Unless in this coextension we see an even greater violence: one that seeks to eliminate the community's violence by eliminating the community itself, by identifying it with its preventive immunization. Truth be told, this reappropriation of the common has always been a goal of legal immunization. Luhmann does nothing but draw to its ultimate conclusion a logic that Weil, Benjamin, and Girard had recognized in its negative potential. What distinguishes his perspective is the positive (or neutral) value he assigns that negative. But the neutral affirmation of a negative is equal to a double negation: in Luhmann's world, the community is unassailable by the disease that threatens it because it no longer exists, or never has existed, as such. Community is simply the interface of its own immune system, the margin without depth along which immunity folds self-reflexively back on itself.

II

The *katechon*

1. *Sacer* and *sanctus*

In an essay expressly devoted to the topic of religion, Jacques Derrida introduces the theme of immunity on the very first page.[1] Although immunity is only one of the various terms whose origins can be found in the semantics of religion—the sacred, the holy, the healthy, the saved, the unscathed and, obviously, the immune— Derrida assigns it a seemingly privileged role. Not only does it reappear in other parts of the essay, it also furnishes the interpretive key for the relation he traces out between the spheres of religion and "technoscience." Contrary to what one may expect, there does exist a connection of mutual implication between the two spheres, expressed in a dialectic of acceptance and refusal, incorporation and rejection. On the one hand, religion, especially Christianity, has universalized itself through the spectacular forms of media provided by contemporary communication technologies; on the other hand, in order to protect its principles from their destabilizing effects, it maintains an attitude of cautious reserve toward technological thinking [*ratio*], when not rejecting it outright.

> The same movement that renders indissociable religion and tele-technoscientific reason in its most critical aspect reacts inevitably

to itself. It secretes its own antidote but also its own power of auto-immunity. We are here in a space where all self-protection of the unscathed, of the safe and sound, of the sacred (*heilig*, holy) must protect itself against its own protection, its own police, its own power of rejection, in short against its own, which is to say, against its own immunity. It is this terrifying but fatal logic of the *auto-immunity of the unscathed* that will always associate Science and Religion.[2]

Following this line of reasoning, resurgent fundamentalist movements can also be understood as compensatory forms reacting to the globalization that religion has embraced for some time now. Fundamentalist movements are certainly related to the process of uprooting engendered by the generalization of the technoscientific paradigm, and indeed, constitute its counterfactual outcome, its rebound effect: like a backward wave that in an attempt to immunize the community from the process of generalized immunization "spreads death and unleashes self-destruction in a desperate (auto-immune) gesture that attacks the blood of its own body."[3]

Still, this is hardly sufficient to resolve the question of religious immunity. The entropic dialectic we have just described would itself appear to be the final outcome of a much more ancient process, one whose beginnings have been preserved in the original semantic stratification of the religious phenomenon. To unearth them, we must revisit Emile Benveniste's etymological studies on the concept of the sacred, also cited by Derrida but without their implications being fully explored.[4] After noting that there is no common term for religion in the Indo-European area, possibly because religion had been separated from the other social practices with which it was traditionally associated only a short time earlier, Benveniste remarks that in more than one language it tends to have dual meanings, along two vectors of meaning that run close to each other but never overlap. What is more, not only is it impossible to transfer these pairs from one language to another with any exactitude, the terms within the pairs themselves are situated on different planes. This is the case for the Greek terms *hieros* and *hagios*, but also for the Latin *sacer* and *sanctus* and for the Avestic *spenta* and *yaoždāta*.

Despite this preliminary cautionary observation, Benveniste's study can still provide us with a hermeneutic perspective that makes it possible to tie all these pairs to a single, basic bipartite term. On the one hand, the sacred signifies a state of fullness as well as vital expansion that is bestowed on the person. It refers to a growth of divine origin, with all the attributes of power [*potenza*], prosperity, and fertility implicit to this sort of development. The idea of salvation has the same meaning, also and primarily associated with a biological and bodily sense of health, soundness, physical vitality, and thus, with that of protection or healing from all kinds of disease. This is where we glimpse the first immunitary trait of the religious phenomenon: religion is what keeps us, at once, safe and sound. It is a guarantee and reassurance in the face of a deadly peril. If we then look at the act of libation to the gods expressed by the Greek *spendo* and its derivatives, this protective, reassuring aspect takes on an even greater role: both in Homer and Herodotus "the libation accompanies a prayer which aims at obtaining security" or it is offered "at the moment of beginning a dangerous enterprise."[5] Man asks the god to keep him alive, to safeguard him from harm, and to transmit to him the divine force: "By its very nature divinity possesses this gift which is integrity, well-being, good fortune, and it can bestow this on men in the form of physical health and by omens of good fortune."[6]

In apparently contrasting terms to this first positive, affirmative, expansive side of the sacred—in the Greek *hieros*, but also in the Germanic *heilig*, English *holy*, Slavic *cělǔ* and Baltic *kails*—there is another semantic chain that expresses its negative side. The Greek *hagios* and the Latin *sanctus* (although not equivalents) and, finally, the Avestic *yaoždāta*, allude to something that is forbidden to human contact, and in broader terms, to the law sanctioning this separation. According to the definition in the *Digest* (1.8.8)—*sanctum est quod ab iniuria hominum defensum atque munitum est*—it is everything that is defended and protected from the injury of man through the threat of a sanction or penalty: "In the expression *legem sancire*, the *sanctio* is properly that part of the law which lays down the penalty which will be inflicted on the person who transgresses it; *sanctio* is often associated with *poena*."[7] This is exactly where the negative aspect—a force that prohibits, forbids, excludes—is to be located; not only is it dissimilar in form, it is also semantically opposed to the vital, affirmative side of the sacred. Benveniste also takes pains to stress this difference: "*Sacer* and *hieros*, 'sacred' or 'divine', are used of a person or a thing consecrated to the gods, whereas *hagios*, like *sanctus*, indicates that the object is defended against all violation, a negative concept, and not, positively, what it is charged with the divine presence, which is the specific sense of *hieros*."[8] In point of fact, *sanctum* does not mean what is sacred, or even what is profane, but more precisely, what distinguishes the two by placing an insurmountable barrier between them. What it refers to, actually, is precisely this barrier: the line of enclosure, or even the fencing itself, which isolates and separates off what-ever cannot, must not, be approached. "What is *sanctus* is the wall and not the domain enclosed by it, which is said to be *sacer*. What is *sanctus* is what is defended by certain sanctions. . . . One might say of the *sanctum* that it is what is found on the periphery of the *sacrum*, what serves to isolate it from all contact."[9] A similar meaning, similarly negative, defensive, excluding, is expressed by *hagios* and *yaoždāta*: both refer to a rigid normativ-ity that removes something sacred from a possible violation or forbidden proximity.

Let us try to draw the threads of the argument together. The concept of the sacred bifurcates into two horizons of meaning— one type primarily organic, and the other basically juridical— which seem to be mutually exclusive, or at least difficult to place in the same semantic space, unless we conceive of them as inte-grated or complementary. By doing so, the category of immuniza-tion that Derrida only hints at or takes in another direction is ushered back into the foreground, but under a new light: the intrinsically immunitary character of religion lies precisely in the functional overlap between these two aspects of the sacred and the holy. Benveniste suggests just as much when he sees in *hieros* and *hagios* two sides of the same coin: "on the one hand what is animated by a sacred power and force, on the other hand, what is forbidden and placed out of bounds to human beings. This is how these two qualities are distributed in the vocabulary of each language and illustrate the two aspects of the same notion: what is filled with divine power and what is forbidden to human contact."[10] In other words, the immunizing effect of religion is

inscribed at the point of intersection between the biomedical paradigm and the juridical paradigm. More precisely, it is seen in the
way one acts as a function of the other. This is clear in the relation
that exists between the two corresponding Indo-Iranian roots of
the Latin *ius*, the Vedic *yoḥ*, and the Avestic *yaŏs*: once again,
while the first refers to "prosperity," "happiness," and "health,"
the second alludes to a normative "purification," to be carried out
in observance of the rites prescribed for oblation by the particular
religion. Only this condition, in the broadest juridical sense, makes
it possible for the sacrifice to have a salutary effect. This is where
Benveniste draws his "immunitary" conclusion from: "In this way
we can better understand the Vedic *yoḥ*; it is not happiness as
enjoyment, but the state of 'integrity', i.e. of physical perfection
as yet unaffected by misfortune or disease."[11] Rather than an
intrinsic, full, absolute state of health, what we have here is a state
of immunity that blocks evil by setting up an impassable limit.
This means that the negative—the prohibition, the interdiction,
the law—is not only the opposite of the affirmative, the expansive,
or the vital; rather, it is its very condition of existence. The negative is the point of resistance that allows life to last, as long as it
submits to that which protects it. It is the limit, the order, the law
by which life can remain as it is, only by bending itself to the
power that goes beyond it.

   To escape from the extreme risk of annihilation, life must take
inside itself a fragment of the nothingness that threatens it from
outside. It must partially and preventively incorporate what
negates it. Benveniste comes close to this conclusion when discussing the *vexata quaestio* of the two probable etymologies of the
term *religio*: Cicero's, connecting it to *relegere* ("to collect again,
to reunite") versus that of Lactantius and Tertullian, which associates it instead with *religare* ("bind, reunite"). Benveniste concludes, opting for the first, that *religio* is a hesitation that holds
back, a scruple, and not a feeling that urges someone to take
action or incites them to religious practice.[12] The positive significance of salvation is not diminished, but it remains within a
framework that makes it dependent on the presence of a restraint,
a block, a closure: an opening that is maintained through the
incorporation of a closure or an immanence bound by a transcendence. Fundamentally—as Derrida also notes[13]—this element of

conjunction is what subterraneously connects rather than juxtaposes the two etymons of *relegere* and the *religare*: the "re-," repetition, reply, reiteration. Religion, we might say, is the impractibility of the *novum*, the impossibility of man to be a beginning for himself, his continual reinscription within a predefined framework that makes every beginning a re-beginning, a taking up again of something that is always already taken up in what precedes and predetermines it. Like a gaze that is continually drawn to look backwards, or a voice that is duplicated in its own echo, its vital power is not diminished, but only on condition that it submits itself to the pressure of that which counters it. If you link this perspective to the deadly semantics of sacrifice, as Benveniste does, it can be inferred that religion saves—or heals—life through the absorption of something that binds it to its opposite, that draws life from death or includes death in life: Why is it, he wonders, that sacrifice, "although it properly means 'to make sacred' (cf. *sacrificium*) actually means 'to put to death'?"[14] Why does sacrifice necessarily involve a death sentence? The answer is quick to come. As all the studies on sacrifice have shown us, but especially the ancient juridical figure of the *homo sacer*, it relates to the fact that sacralization involves crossing over a threshold of indistinguishability between the preservation of life and the production of death: "To make the animal 'sacred', it must be cut off from the world of the living, it has to cross the threshold which separates these two universes; this is the point of putting it to death."[15]

2. The restrainer

This aporetic node of life and death, of momentum and restraint, of opening and binding, is inherent to all religions. It actually constitutes the necessary precondition for religion, something recognized by all the classical interpretations, both sociological and philosophical in approach. If Max Weber already identified the law governing the religious phenomenon in the oscillation between prophecy and priesthood, grace and norm, mysticism and dogma,[16] Bergson goes even further in the direction that interests us by bringing this essentially juridical dynamic back to its original biological roots. What results is a balanced movement of neutralization and development—and indeed, development by neutralization—clearly attributable to the immunitary logic:

> It is none the less true that the certainty of death, arising at the same time as reflexion in a world of living creatures constructed to think only of living, runs counter to nature's intention. Nature, then, looks as if it is going to stumble over the obstacle which she has placed on her own path. But she recovers herself at once. To the idea of inevitable death she opposes the image of a continuation of life after death; this image, flung by her into the field of intelligence, where the idea of death has just become installed, straightens everything out again.[17]

For Bergson, then, the role of religion is to counteract the draining effect that the intelligence produces against the flow of life through the idea of the inevitability of death. Religion restores life to health, healing the wound inflicted by an awareness of its irremediable finitude, and relaunches it beyond itself by promising it immortality. It opens up a salvific space of survival beyond the natural boundaries of life. But the decisive factor, in terms of immunization, is that this opening is included in the same circle that it is meant to break. It uses the same poison it must protect itself from, namely, the intelligence: "We postulate a certain instinctive activity; then, calling into play intelligence, we try to discover whether it leads to a dangerous disturbance; if it does, the balance will probably be restored through representations evoked by instinct within the disturbing intelligence; if such representations exist, they are primary religious ideas."[18] The vital battle against intelligence takes place within its own perimeter; intelligence is pitted against itself. Religion is the antidote intelligence uses against its own destructive potential, and which it creates itself: not an action, therefore, but a reaction on the part of life to the fear that restrains it and which therefore also acts in the form of restraint: "a feeling which pulls us up, turns us aside or pushes us back."[19] It participates, therefore, in the life force, but in negative terms: as that which restrains the restraint, curbs the curb, interrupts the interruption.

When Niklas Luhmann attempts to analyze the religious experience in functionalist language—hence, from a perspective seemingly opposed to Bergsonian vitalism—the conclusion he arrives at is not much different. To understand the uniqueness of religion in the transformation of an "indeterminable world, since it is not circumscribable toward the outside (the environment) or toward the inside (the system), in a determinable world,"[20] he recognizes the same neutralizing function identified by Bergson. Moreover, he situates it along a sliding arc that reproduces, albeit in different terms, the same dialectic that Bergson described between static religion and dynamic religion. The task Luhmann attributes to religion in its archaic forms is to absorb uncertainty through a reassuring mechanism designed to mitigate its effects. In segmentary and stratified systems, however, the function of religion is to be found in the activation of a new contingency. What is more contingent, after all, than the idea of divine creation? As long as it is kept below a tolerable threshold, that is. Once again, religion "works" by producing that from which it must be cured—or cures from that which it itself produces. "Religious ritual, by producing anxiety," Walter Berkert notes, "manages to control it."[21] Even the dogmatic construct that every religion must necessarily formulate in order to preserve and transmit itself to future generations is interpreted by Luhmann from the same perspective: it is the mode of self-identification through which religion directs toward its own body the function of selective determination that it exercises with respect to external contingency. Religion, therefore, cannot immunize anything from what appears to be indeterminate except by immunizing itself, in its turn, from its own indeterminateness—by consolidating itself in ways that appear to restrain its own original impetus, but at the same time allow it to last over time.

This is why all attempts to oppose the two facets of religious experience—those based on interpretation or on historical development—are not very convincing in their methodological approach and often result in questionable hermeneutics. Religion does not exist, or at least it is unthinkable, outside of its dual source: dynamic and static, universal and particular, communitary and immunitary. It is always both things at once; indeed, one is always inside and through the other. This is why the alternative put forward by Emmanuel Levinas, between a natural religion based on the Greek and Roman notion of the sacred, and a spiritual

religion based on the Hebrew notion of the holy,[22] is very problematic, since, as we have seen, the sacred is not the opposite, but
the complementary reverse of the holy. But it also creates serious
problems in identifying a precise turning point in Christianity
between the open and fluid formulation of the evangelic message
and its dogmatic institutionalization. The fact that this point is
always pushed further and further back in time—from the Scho-
lastics to political Augustinianism, to Paul, back to Christ's
sermons—means that there is no phase, not even at the dawn of
Christianity, when the Christian word coincided with its pure
inner truth, when it was free from the need for a doctrinal formulation.[23] Despite what Franz Overbeck might have thought, there
is no Christianity apart from historical Christianity, since history—
as event *and* duration, as the duration *of* the event—is the horizon
of the original meaning of the whole Christian language. Secularization, in the literal sense of relationship with the *secolo* or
"century," is entirely intrinsic to the Christian reality, unless we
drastically bend Christianity toward some kind of Gnostic view
that would inevitably end up renouncing it, taking away its very
object of salvation. But even Christ never thought of abandoning
the world to its end, of *not* saving the world. Otherwise, he would
not have chosen Peter as his legitimate successor. He would not
have permitted, indeed, required *his* church to be built "upon this
Rock." He would not have united his followers in his name; he
would not have even assumed a name to begin with. But that is
not what happened: despite how radically different he was compared to all the other "saviors" who came before and after him,
despite the deep wedge he placed between eternity and time, his
intention was to open, not close, the world, even to that which
exceeds it. He did indeed come to separate, but also to unite; to
make hungry, but also to feed; to rend, but also to heal: to safeguard and protect the same human beings he had decentralized
by exposing them to their otherness. There is no Christianity
outside the promise of redemption—at least if it is still to be conceived as a religion and not as a philosophical sect devoted to
self-destruction. Also because, if it were, if Christianity really had
taken that path of no return, there would be no trace of it now.
To be coherent, it would have had to annihilate itself in accordance with a perspective that is actually not at all foreign to

Marcion and other heretical movements with Manichean leanings: "The Christian Church," writes Martin Buber, "did not follow Marcion: it knew that if creation and redemption were separated from each other, the bases for its influence on the world order would vanish."[24]

From this point of view, and certainly with his own peculiar characteristics, Paul acts perfectly in coherence within the contradiction opened up by Christ. He did not choose, he did not cut the knot that Christ himself had tied through his incarnation: Paul was neither Peter nor John. He was the man of antinomy: he carried on his shoulders the tragic weight of two-in-one and neither-one-nor-the-other in the form of an unresolvable *complexio oppositorum*. He did not misrepresent or betray with a conciliatory attitude something unambiguous and "decisive" that came before him. This is because the need for self-preservation responded to a historical or, worse, political necessity of the Christian community, as well as to the fact of it being such: *a community* among others, albeit with the ambition to conquer all the others (in the sense of love, but also of war). Thus, Paul's opposition to the law is still in the name of the law: it is the law that separates itself from itself into its other—into love, and therefore in conjunction with what is also separated. So even though Paul broke the limited circle of the synagogue, he did in any case build an *ekklesia*, which can be universal only to the extent that it unifies and incorporates all particularities: the Greek as much as the Jew, and the Jew as much as the Gentile,[25] because it connects and does not discriminate among Athens, Jerusalem and Rome. It is true, as Karl Barth sustains, that Paul broke with every positive political theology, with all orders or powers of this world.[26] But it is also true, as Jacob Taubes shows, that this break with the world turned into a negative political theology that was just as effective as others, or more so, precisely to the extent that it subverted the existing law—the ethnic, natural law of the Hebrews as well as the juridical, imperial type of the Romans.[27] Although he established its foundations in heaven and not on earth, Paul also founded an order made to last over time, to delay the end, to meld its members into one body: "For as in one body we have many members, but all the members have not the same office: So we being many, are one body in Christ, and every one members one of another" (*Rom.* 12.4–5).

The Pauline analogy between the individual body and the body of Christianity brings us back to our basic problem. As Christ became *incarnate* for us, so we, through the Church, share in his *body*. The direction goes from multiplicity to unity, from dispersion to identity: from the many and different that we were, we become one single body. It may be the body of Christ, but it is still "a body"—*one* and *body*—because the organic body is always one, as is clear from all the biological, liturgical, and political formulas that describe it. This presumed unification, inherent to the very notion of body, hermetically seals tight what the original semantics of incarnation seemed to leave open and indeterminate: "This people of God," observes Taubes, "is not conceived by Paul as a theocracy but as the constitution of a social body that he imagines as a 'body in Christ'. . . . The medium of this knowledge of God is the congregation as the body of Christ, the union-covenant [*Ver-Bund*] as 'corporation'."[28] This is the crucial point: Paul conceives the "cum-" in the universalistic sense: as a donation, an expropriation, a disruption of any particular identity. But interpreting it according to the organismic metaphor of the body and corporation, he inevitably destines it for the language of immunity. In other words, he submits it to the logic of its preservation through biological and legal rules that protect us from evil by incorporating the same principle: not only the specular dialectics of law and sin, that is, but also the homeostatic mechanism by which man's guilt, transmitted hereditarily in the human species, can and must be juridically compensated for by the sacrifice of an innocent. Once again: life through death, and death inside life. The well-studied *Epistle to the Romans* on the relationship between law and sin (7.7–25) is absolutely clear on this point: the law is that which simultaneously produces sin and its remedy; that which, by fighting it, reinforces it. The law injects within itself the death that sin brings to life, and thus brings life to death and death to life: "For without the law sin was dead. And I lived some time without the law. But when the commandment came, sin revived, and I died. And the commandment that was ordained to life, the same was found to be unto death to me" (7.8–10).

The Pauline figure that expresses this immunitary logic more than any other is the *katechon*, spoken about in a passage from the enigmatic second letter to the Thessalonians: "And now you

know what withholdeth [*to katechon*], that he may be revealed
in his time. For the mystery of iniquity already worketh [*ener-
geitai*]; only that he who now holdeth [*ho katechon*], do hold,
until he be taken out of the way" (*2 Thess.*, 2.6–7). Considering
that even Augustine says he has no idea what Paul is referring to
in this passage (*De civ.*, 20:19), its meaning remains obscure. For
some exegetes, it refers to a historical and political power: the
Jewish people who oppose the attempt of Caligula to occupy the
Temple of Jerusalem, or the Roman Empire committed to stopping the forces of dissolution. For others, it is a spiritual or divine
power, aimed at blocking the rise of evil. What is not in question
is its nature as a restrainer, its function of holding back. It is a
power *qui tenet*: "The Christian Empire as a Restrainer [Katechon]
of the Antichrist [*Das Reich als christliche Aufhalter*]" Carl
Schmitt entitled a section of the *Nomos of the Earth*,[29] alluding
precisely to the role assumed by the *katechon* in the time of the
respublica Christiana. It is the force of order, with great physical
power, which stops those who are about to plunge into the abyss,
echoes Dietrich Bonhoeffer.[30] It blocks the *anomos*, the principle
of disorder, rebellion, separation from the constraint of law. But
most important—for how it fits perfectly into the immunitary
paradigm of *religio*—is the way this takes place, the manner in
which evil is restrained: the *katechon* restrains evil by containing
it, by keeping it, by holding it within itself. It confronts evil, but
from within, by hosting it and welcoming it, to the point of
binding its own necessity to the presence of evil. It limits evil,
defers it, but does not eradicate it: because if it did, it would also
eliminate itself.[31] We could go so far as to say that the *katechon*—
its constitutive juridical principle—opposes the absence of law by
taking it up inside itself, and thereby, in some way, giving it form,
rule, and norm. The *katechon* antinomically assigns a *nomos* to
anomie, thus restraining its catastrophic unfolding. But in so
doing, in delaying the explosion of evil—this is the consequence,
clear not only to Schmitt but to all Christian apologetics throughout the first centuries—it also at the same time delays the final
victory of the principle of good. The triumph of evil is held in
check, true, but the divine *parousia* is also delayed by its very
existence. Its function is positive, but negatively so. The *katechon*
is exactly that: the positive *of* a negative. It is the antibody that

protects the Christian body from what threatens it. By containing iniquity, the *katechon* forbids its annihilation, removing it from the final battle: the *katechon* nurtures and is nurtured by iniquity, just as the body is nurtured by the antidote necessary to its survival.

*

The most striking aspect in the debate on the meaning of the *katechon* is the indecisiveness that separates authors from each other, but which also seems to affect their interpretations. Typical in this respect is the hermeneutic vacillation of Carl Schmitt, who, starting from a clearly negative definition of the term in his essays from the early 1940s, gradually began to assign it a positive valence, solidified in the *Nomos of the Earth* written in 1950.[32] Why so much uncertainty? What makes it so hard to come to an opinion on the restraining power of the *katechon*? And why such caution in arriving at a definition, starting as far back as Augustine? Surely it is due to the apparently counterfactual status of the verb in question: to oppose by preserving, to confront by incorporating. But it probably also has something to do with the nature of the object on which it exerts its action: the *anomie* from the Pauline letters that, according to a widespread translation, we have so far rendered simply as "evil" or "iniquity." Is it possible that a writer like Paul would use the terms *anomia* and *anomos* in such a generically negative way, after subjecting the complex semantics of the *nomos* to such a critical analysis? Giorgio Agamben, in a radically messianic reading of Paul, has proposed a particularly interesting exegesis that casts new light on the whole question of the *katechon*.[33] Comparing all the passages in the *Epistles* where the word *nomos* appears, he concludes that Paul, rather than limiting himself to opposing the term with *pistis* (faith) or *epaggelia* (promise), actually ties them together, splitting its meaning into two different figures of law: one that is normative and the other promissive. While the first meaning, related to works (*nomos ton ergon*, in the words of *Rom.* 3.27–28), is rejected as negative, the second, inherently free from any implementation, coincides with the law of faith, which Paul sees as the revolutionary force of the Christian message.

But how do you define a law not subject to the principle of work, and of what does it consist? At the heart of his inquiry, Agemben places the verb *katargein*—composed of *argos*, in turn derived from *ergos* in its deprivative form: *a-ergos* is what is not-at-work, inoperative, inactive. *Katargeo*, in short, indicates a deactivation, a suspension of effectiveness, a taking away of the *energeia* of works. When referring to the law, as Paul uses it, this verb does not lead to its suppression, but rather to an internal reversal that identifies the fulfillment of the law no longer in the form of an act, but in the form of potential *(potenza)*, and therefore in the direction of weakness *(astheneia)* rather than strength. While in the law of works the effect is measured by the execution of its precepts, in the law of faith the effect is demonstrated by its inactivity. Here, precisely, lies the weak power of the messianic word: the impossibility of executing the law is the measure and sign of its fulfillment.

Going back to the *katechon*: where does this hermeneutic path lead in terms of arriving at a definition? To begin with, it entails the fact that what the *katechon* opposes and restrains—opposing by restraining—is not a generic iniquity, and not even a pure absence of law, so much as precisely that peculiar deactivation of the law that fulfills it in the messianic mode. Whence its constitutive antinomy, binding it to that which it opposes, and opposing it to that which it binds. The *katechon*, one might say, more than simply deferring *anomie*, is what keeps enchained its two possible expressions: one that translates the meaning of the law into work, and the other that frees it from the compulsion to work. Transposing this conceptual alternative into the binary opposition between community and immunity, we immediately note how homogeneous the semantics of the *katechon* are with the lexicon of immunity. Superimposing satanic *anomia* onto messianic *anomia*, making one the exact double of the other, the *katechon* subjects the community to the power of a law that simultaneously reproduces and enslaves it. That fact that this law is the law of works opens up a prospective horizon, yet to be developed to be sure, on the possible meaning of an "inactive" [*inoperosa*] or "inactivated" [*inoperata*] community. What is a community governed, not by the law of works, but by the messianic principle of its deactivation? What would its status be? But the answer to this

Immunitas

question presupposes another preliminary one: is it possible to conduct a political inquiry of our time through the category of messianism? Or does messianism, precisely because of its deactivating mode, speak the silent language of the Impolitic?

3. Political theology

If this is the objective function of the *katechon*, who is its subject? Who incarnates the *katechon* in what is still our age? Who is the *katechon* of our time? For some, as we have said, it is the political institution that guarantees order: the State, in all its forms. For others, it is the Church, which has always been committed to defending the *nomos*, both divine and human, from the powers of antinomy that besiege it. But perhaps the most convincing answer to this question is that the categorical epicenter of the *katechon* is located precisely at the point of intersection between politics and religion: in the horizon defined as "political theology" according to all the various meanings of the term.[34] Without going into detail on the topic, political theology can generally be said to refer to a relationship between the sphere of theology and the sphere of law and politics, expressed in the form of a structural analogy—and therefore, exclusively in a hermeneutic key—or, more instrumentally, as a function of the religious legitimacy of power.

Despite this basic distinction, however, it must be said that the boundary line between these two ways of using the notion is not clear enough to exclude possible ambiguities of interpretation or objectively overlapping elements. Suffice to say that it was precisely its most neutral formulation, in terms of apologetics provided by Carl Schmitt beginning in the 1920s, that set off a long polemic, initiated by Erik Peterson, against any "political theology" that misuses the Christian message to justify a particular political situation.[35] Having located the source of this misuse in the functional parallel introduced by Bishop Eusebius of Caesarea between Christian monotheism and the Roman Empire based on the symmetry of "*unus deus, unus rex,*" Peterson traced back the principle that would have made political theology structurally impossible to the Trinitarian formula established earlier by Gregory of Nazanzius and then, finally, by Augustine. The fact that Carl Schmitt responded a few decades later[36] that even the doctrine of the Trinity is not exempt from being used in a similar fashion with regard to certain political models (for example, those of the triumvirate or the mixed State)—since even the negation of political theology has a political importance in the final analysis—means that the question of the relationship between the religious lexicon and the political lexicon is far from resolved. In other words, far from being attributable to any particular legitimizing purposes, it winds up being inextricably intertwined with the theological and legal-political constitution of our civilization.

The intrinsically juridical character of historical Christianity, especially Roman Catholicism, is too well established to merit a re-examination of the question here. As Carl Schmitt has shown, not only the external organization of Catholicism but also Catholic dogma is based on a semantics that bears a clear legal imprint: accusation, confession, retribution. Theology tends to "normalize" life by submitting it to procedures intended to control events, including the word of Christ, subject from the beginning, for normative purposes, to doctrinal interpretation: "Catholic argumentation is based on a particular mode of thinking whose method of proof is a specific juridical logic and whose focus of interest is the normative guidance of human social life."[37] What calls for our attention here, though, because it is the exact equivalent of the immunizing principle of the *katechon* in the sphere of political theology, is the inverse phenomenon: not so much, or not solely, the juridical and political purpose of religion, as the religious foundation of political sovereignty. It passes through a complex process of incorporating the sacred core, conducted in parallel with the incarnation of Christ. According to the originally Pauline formula, later transferred to the entire Patristic and Scholastic tradition of the *corpus mysticum*, just as Christ unites all Christians who identify in him thanks to his dual nature, similarly, the physical and institutional person of the monarch concentrates the unifying principle of the body politic, thereby preventing its fragmentation and disintegration. Of course, this transfer involves a very lengthy and complex process, both in terms of its lexicon as well as its historical and institutional profile. As is clear from the work by Henri De Lubac, as indispensable as ever,[38] the term

corpus mysticum was initially used only in relation to the consecrated host, while both the Church and Christian society were
represented by the expression *corpus Christi*. Only in the Caro-
lingian period, during the controversy on the Eucharist that for
years pitted Radbertus Paschasius against Ratramnus, was there
a sort of semantic exchange that led to defining the host as the
corpus Christi and the Church, or Christianity as a whole, as the
corpus mysticum. This took place in response to two different
needs that oddly intersected: on the one hand, the need to defend
against the spiritualistic theories of Berengar of Tours and other
heretical sects on the real character of the two natures of Christ;
on the other, the need to counteract the secularization of the
Church, increasingly inclined to emphasize its institutional and
administrative character, by providing a mystical interpretation of
its office. It goes without saying that the logical–semantic shift was
made possible by the presumed identification between the body of
Christ and the body of the Church, whose head was also represented by Christ, officially proclaimed in Boniface VIII's *Unam
Sanctam* Bull. Indeed, it was only through the Church that the
flesh of Christ, after his resurrection, took the form of a collective
body that could gather into it all the members of Christianity.
Now, the political organization was built on exactly this same
pattern of incorporation. That this final stage has proved anything
but peaceful—resulting in a grim struggle between Church and
Empire, and then with the individual nation-states—demonstrates
rather than detracts from the homogeneity of the foundation on
which both bodies rest and due to which, for this very reason,
they compete with each other: one body cannot have two heads.
The fact remains that, like the Church, the State also needs a
sacred core around which to establish its legitimacy in a way that
goes beyond its historical origin and prolongs its life over time.

Once again the two vectors of religious immunization, biological and juridical, intersect in a salvific strategy that acts on two
levels: on the one hand, leading the community back into the
organic form of the body; and on the other, normatively subjugat-
ing it to a transcendental principle in order to guarantee its survival in time. As regards the first, it is known that the metaphor
of the body politic largely preceded its Christian formulation. Yet
the Christian formulation is what lent it the connotations most

properly allied with immunity: only if the monarch represents the dual nature (divine and human) of Christ in his own flesh can he save the body of the state from decay. This is the source of the splitting—analyzed with unsurpassed hermeneutic sophistication by Ernst Kantorowicz[39]—of the king's body into two, one physical, subject to error, disease and death; and the other instead of divine origin, immortal, and, therefore, intended to last through the continuity of the dynasty beyond the demise of the first body. Of course, because this figure is solidified later by the Elizabethan jurists of the sixteenth century, starting from Plowden's *Reports* that Kantorowicz uses to construct his argument, the mere meeting of the ancient organologic metaphor with the Christian liturgical tradition is not sufficient. It may give rise, to be sure, to the figure of the *christomimetes* king, bestowed by grace with the double persona that Christ was provided with by nature; or to the distinction between individual body and collective body within an organism whose head is the king and whose limbs are the subjects. But in order to arrive at the specific metaphor of the double royal body, one more decisive step needed to be taken: namely, the overlap of the biological lexicon of the body with the juridical principle of the perpetuity of the institution contained in the concept, both personal and impersonal, of *universitas*. It was only the need for the immortality of the empire, and then the kingdom, which led to the first mutual embedding between the subjects and the monarch, who "is incorporated with them, and they with him."[40] The transfer of this incorporation into the same body of the king came subsequently through a sort of vertical cut of what was already constituted horizontally: "That is, one constructed a body corporate whose members were echeloned longitudinally so that its cross-section at any given moment revealed one instead of many members: a mystical person by perpetual devolution whose mortal and temporary incumbent was of relatively minor importance as compared to the immortal body corporate by succession which he represented."[41] What resulted was a doubling, through internalization, of the incorporation already performed with respect to the subjects. Having to endure as head of the realm beyond his own death, the king was incorporated in himself, as expressed in a formula by Plowden that was later taken up by Francis Bacon: "There is in the king not a Body natural alone, nor a Body politic alone, but a body natural and politic together [*corpus corporatum in corpore naturali, et corpus naturale in corpore corporato*]."⁴²

What we clearly have here is one of the most powerful procedures to come out of political-theological immunization. A relationship of mutual functionality is established between the two bodies of the king: the individual body gives his mystical body its fleshy consistency, while the mystical body ensures stability and durability to the individual body. It makes his mortality immortal through a hereditary chain that plays the same role as the resurrection: it immunizes him through a separation from himself that makes his natural death the vehicle for his institutional survival: "*non enim potest respublica mori*," as Baldo had already ruled. Kantorowicz argues that the idea of a "*rex qui nunquam moritur*" is situated at the juncture of three interrelated factors: the perpetuity of the dynasty, the corporate character of the crown, and the immortality of royal dignity. But even more significant for the purposes of our discussion is the metaphorical relationship established by Bernard of Parma between the principle according to which "*dignitas non moritur*" and the symbol of the phoenix. The phoenix symbolized the *aevum* and *perpetuitas*, but also what is continually reborn from its ashes. From this point of view, the phoenix combines in its body the mortal individual and the immortal species. It is itself and other than itself (*eadem sed non eadem . . . ipsa nec ipsa*), as expressed by Lactantius and Tertullian. Or, as Ambrose described it, the phoenix is "heir to its own body": in the sense that it is born *from* and *of* its own death. The phoenix needs to live in order to die and die in order to live: "*Mortuus aperit oculos viventis* [The dead opens the eyes of the living]," said the proverb quoted by the jurist André Tiraqueau to elucidate the famous maxim of the French law of inheritance *Le mort saisit vif* [The dead seizes (with regard to the inheritance) the living].⁴³ What else did the cries of "The King is dead! Long live the king!" that rang out during the burial of the king in the Abbey of Saint-Denis mean, other than it is through death that sovereignty survives itself?

This aspect makes it possible to penetrate further into the exact functioning of the mechanism of political theology. As Marcel Gauchet writes, it is "the incarnation of the separation between men"[44] or, more precisely, "the power of negation wholly redirected toward accepting and renewing the established law,"[45] where the emphasis should be placed on the relationship between the negativity and permanence of order—the power, that is, both deadly and salvific, that comes of religion being imbricated into politics. Political theology does not stand by definition on the side of immanence or transcendence, union or separation, life or death, but rather, as the sovereign right "of life *and* death," exactly at the point of their conjunction. It lies in an immanence—the body—founded on a transcendence, in a unity sustained by separation: between Christ and the king, between the king and his kingdom, between the king and himself, in an infinite multiplication of the original duplication of flesh and spirit. The monarch is both the whole and the part, the body and its head, his body and all the bodies that are part of it in the form of limbs, like the frontispiece image of the first English edition of *Leviathan*: a macrobody formed by the interconnection of many bodies fitted together like plated armor. A body made immortal by the sum, or product, of infinite mortality; an order made to endure by the sacrifice of all those who are at the same time both its subjects and subjugated by it. This is how political theology accomplishes and perfects the ancient function of the *katechon*: by including the principle of exclusion or by normalizing the exception. Is this not the very same relationship that exists between sovereignty and law? Sovereignty can be seen as a creation of law, that is, as its non-legal origin, and law as *a posteriori* legitimation of the illegality that constituted it: law *of* exception. Nothing in modern politics, in democratic as much as absolutist politics, is understandable without reference to the political theology model in which, despite all its setbacks, we remain deeply rooted.[46] It is this categorical permanence that is therefore constitutive of our conceptual lexicon, much more than the so-called returns of the sacred[47] that hold us back in the time of religion, with respect to which Christianity has had and still plays an ambivalent role, if it is true that it is a "religion for departing from religion."[48] Christianity is the religion *of* secularization: and therefore *no longer*, but *still*, religion; religion that dialectically separates from itself to preserve itself as such. To immunize the community—as indeed all religions do—Christianity must immunize itself primarily through the assumption of its secular opposite.

*

Marc Richir, in a phenomenologically informed genealogy of the political, argues for the need to strictly distinguish between the semantics of incarnation and those of incorporation. Indeed, he goes on to trace out with great precision a series of inconsistencies and genuine misunderstandings that arise from the confusion between the two that invest our entire philosophical and political tradition.[49] Ernst Katorowicz's work is not spared from this confusion when he establishes a necessary connection between the notion of the king's two bodies—in other words, the symbolic perpetuity of royalty—and the Christian problem of incarnation, without being aware of the categorical gap separating these two concepts. Of course both lexical fields, those of the body and the flesh, have their roots in the horizon opened up by Christianity, but with a difference that is far from negligible depending on the interpretation that the Christian community gives of itself. While the metaphor of incarnation describes conditions in which the community is still free from hierarchical ties—with elements of anarchy and subversion toward the established powers present— incorporation conveys its gradual institutionalization into the rigidly codified forms of a true Church. As we have said, there can be no absolute separation between these two conditions in terms of chronology or theology. And yet a heterogeneity persists: placing the accent on the moment when Christ alters his divine nature to incarnate all the flesh of the world, the flesh of everyone and of each individual, is different from looking at the inverse movement in which the flesh of the world is symbolically *identified* in the body of Christ. In the first case, it is a matter of an extroversion of the one into the many; in the second, the many is reassumed into the one. The crucial point of the inversion lies, according to Richir, at the moment of the resurrection, in the empty tomb, when the flesh of Christ's body is symbolically transferred into the disincarnated body of the Church. This is when the way is opened for the next figural transfer, which we examined earlier, from the mystical body of the Church to the political body of the royal principle that both represents it and substitutes it:

> Church history is instituted symbolically through the disincarnation of the flesh-of-the-body of Christ . . . the same way the flesh of the political community, which likewise had no body or no corpse, *disincarnates itself* in order to embody itself or *incorporate itself* into the organic body instituted in the body of the community, and its head, the king.[50]

This is how the multiple, errant flesh of the original Christian community is closed within the theological-political confines of an ecclesiastical, state body.

So far, however, we are still in the realm of interpretation. Is there any textual evidence to be found in the sources? Based on the wide collection of texts presented by De Lubac in his book on the *corpus mysticum*, a cautiously affirmative response would seem to be in order. Of course, the terms used for body (*soma*, *corpus*) and flesh (*sárx*, *caro*) are sometimes used indistinguishably. Elsewhere, they are combined in a dialectic that makes one the function of the other, as is already clear in Augustine: "*Ut simus in eius corpore, sub ipso capite, in membris eius, edentes carnem eius* [that we may be in His body, in His members under Himself as head, eating His flesh]" (*In Joannem*, 27.1). Christ became flesh so that we could be reborn in his body. However, this does not eliminate a distinction that occurs too often to be insignificant: while *corpus* is the expression generally used to designate the Church as a whole—or the Sacrament of the Eucharist, but always in relation to the ecclesial representative—*caro* signifies the Eucharist as such; and in any case, with rare exceptions, never the Church, for which, from the dogmatic point of view, it appears to have lacked the proper credentials. It is true that over time we see a process of spiritualization of the "flesh," which thus becomes *caro invisibilis*, *caro intellegibilis*, *caro spiritualis*, but without ever becoming wholly devoid of its original meaning, inextricably tied to the materiality of the flesh intended for animal sacrifices under the ancient law. Hence the irreducibly antinomic element that continues to characterize the use which the Church fathers, beginning with Augustine, were well aware of: "*vocatur caro quod non capit caro, et ideo magis non capit caro, quia vocatur caro*" (PL, 35.1612). The flesh cannot comprehend the very thing (the Incarnation) that it designates. It exceeds its own meaning or has a meaning that exceeds it. There is something elusive about it: a plurivocality, and also an opacity, irreducible to a dogmatically univocal use.

On the other side of the semantic divide, *corpus* is fully adequate to represent the unity of the Church, and indeed the Church as the very principle of unity: "*in Christo naturaliter unum corpus efficimur*" (Radbertus Paschasius), "*Omnes christiani propter unitatem corporis Christi unum corpus sunt*" (Remigius d'Auxerre). That this unity comes from reference to the Eucharist only reinforces its internal consistency: "through the mediating term 'unity of sacrifice', this duality itself is restored to unity, the unity of the sacramental body."[51] What matters, in short, is "the organic unity, the totality that defines it: the body of the Church."[52] The body and the Church overlap exactly in the figure of the One: they are *all one*—the one in the form of the all. The conclusion De Lubac comes to is not far from the one presented earlier: "A 'body' is an organism, it is the exchange between members whose functions simultaneously differ and work together. It also represents plenitude."[53] What the flesh scatters and opens, the body unifies and closes. What the body identifies, the flesh alters. If flesh expropriates, the body appropriates. We might say that the body is to *immunitas* as flesh is to *communitas*.

4. Theodicy

In modern thought the immunization of Christian immunization, its auto-immunization, is called specifically by the name of theodicy. As we know, this term means the defense of God from the accusation of having created, or at least having allowed, evil in the world. In more technical terms, Kant expresses it as the defense of the Creator's supreme wisdom against the accusations that move the reason, starting from the consideration of what is contrary to it for the purpose of this wisdom.[54] How can a God who is both good and omnipotent tolerate the suffering of the innocent? There are two logical possibilities: either He is incapable of eliminating it, or He does not want to. If He does not want to, it means that He is not infinitely good; and if He cannot, then He is not omnipotent. But what kind of a God lacks the goodness or power to implement either? The question is anything but new, seeing as it resounded in Job's lament before being reformulated in a wide range of variations across all cultural traditions, none of which altered its essence: *si Deus, unde malum* (Lactantius, *De ira Dei*, 13.20–21).

What is decidedly modern, however, is the language in which the answer is expressed in the literary, apologetic genre inaugurated by Leibniz's *Theodicee*, in the form of replies to the skeptical, Epicurean objections of Bayle. It is the logical, or more precisely, the ontotheological language of the double principle of non-contradiction and sufficient reason: even though God is omnipotent, not only is He incapable of doing anything logically impossible, such as creating free men who are at the same time incapable of doing evil, He also demonstrates that He has adopted a criterion of maximization, inspired by the economic principle of marginal profit, by which the best possible order is made to coincide, in effect, with the necessary order. From this point of view, the created world was selected out of a wide variety of possible worlds for having the minimum number of defects along with the maximum perfection. If we do not grasp its logical necessity, this is because we imagine that everything in a perfect whole has to be perfect in every part, without realizing that every event decreed by God carries behind it a causal chain that is immutable except through the cancellation of the event. Moral evil is part of this series, which is headed by man's freedom. If evil fell away, so would freedom, necessarily.

However, despite being clearly connected to it, the peculiarly modern aspect of theodicy does not lie so much in the rationalization of the substance of faith, but rather, in its complete juridicization. The ancient ambivalence in religion between love and law, gift and prohibition, and *munus* and *immunitas* is decisively settled in favor of the second term. Odo Marquard has spoken in this regard of the "tribunalization of the reality in which we, as modern people, live."[55] What he means by this is the progressive extension of the need for legitimation that arose during the period of the French Revolution, not only in society, where everyone is subject to suspicion until proven otherwise, but also in philosophy, with Kant, when human reason itself was put on trial by undergoing rational inquiry. What else is theodicy other than a trial in which reason plays the roles of prosecutor, defense attorney, and judge all at once? The author of a theodicy, writes Kant, allows this trial to be brought before the tribunal of reason. He will defend the accused, as defense counsel, by a refutation of the charges *in the form of* the opponent's charges. During the trial he has no authority to dismiss them with an objection of incompetence on the part of the tribunal of human reason.[56]

The explanation for this tendency toward the juridicization of experience—recognizable in semantic terms in the very definition of the historical movement as a "trial" that must end in a "judgment"[57]—is to be found, says Marquard, in the progressive perspectival distance from evil that is established in the modern age, including physical, moral, and metaphysical evils. The more you loosen the grip of pain, once endured as obvious and inevitable, the more intolerable it becomes and, therefore, the greater the tendency to ask for an accounting from the alleged perpetrator: "the more negative things are abolished, the more vexatious—precisely as they diminish—the negative things that remain become."[58] This principle of the "increasing pervasiveness of the remains" is what draws theodicy and immunization together into a single node: in order to perform His immunitary role in the face of the community afflicted with evil, God must have previously been immunized from the suspicion of having made it possible in the first place. However, this route must not pass through the Gnostic solution of splitting the divinity into two—one good and one evil—because, as we have seen in Marcion, this would lead ultimately to the self-dissolution of the Christian body: if the finite were bad as such, it would be better to simply wait for its disappearance. The Christian body, as we have seen, is to be taken care of and kept alive, even without being able to definitively heal it, through the preventive neutralization of what threatens it.

But how? Sure enough, the answer to this question lies at the confluence of the two axes along which the immune paradigm flows: the biological and the juridical. This is exactly the answer that Augustine used as a solid *katechon* to block the possible Gnostic drift of Paul's discourse. Hans Blumenberg captures its existential roots in the ancient proximity of Augustinian theology to the Manichean heresy and, therefore, in the need to emancipate himself from it once and for all: "The inevitability of this train of thought in Augustine's actual situation lay in the fact that it made it possible for him to avoid the Gnostic dualism of good and evil world principles. To be sure, the converted Gnostic had to provide an equivalent for the cosmic principle of evil in the bosom of mankind itself."[59] He found it in the idea of original sin, interpreted on the one hand as a violation of a legal prohibition, and thus also necessitating reparation of a legal nature; and on the other, as a biological fault, thus transmittable hereditarily to all the descendants of the person who had originally committed the sin. In this way, "joining together in the concept of natural sin two heterogeneous notions, that of biological transmission by way of generation and that of an individual accusation of culpability,"[60] theodicy achieves its aim of exonerating God, but only provided it is handed over to a logic of remuneration, and therefore, to a logic of immunization, of its own salvific *munus*. The Christian community can be saved only by the sacrifice of an innocent that is equal to the guilt that has been attributed to it. The exoneration of God from the responsibility for evil takes place through a retributive compensation entailing its preventative enactment in the form of a rite of victimage: human life can be ensured only by the death of Christ. This is the legal, sacrificial version of the Pauline passage on the relationship between Adam and Christ *(Rom.* 5.12–17) that the Fathers used to oppose the Gnostics on the one hand and the Pelagians on the other. The desperate attempt of Paul to hold together the irreconcilable—love and law, gift and prohibition, faith and guilt—concludes in Augustine's work with a clear normative turn, where evil is taken as both *peccatum* and *poena (Contra Fortunatum)*: and, therefore, as a poison and a remedy, in the double meaning of *pharmakon*. All suffering, no matter how unfairly distributed, disproportionate, or incomprehensible, has the positive role of acting as a dialectical counterweight to original sin.

Marquard's thesis is that this first refutation of Gnosticism, made by Origen and Augustine through the attribution of evil to the free will of man, was not sufficient. In point of fact, it was in turn denied by the Lutheran theology of *servum arbitrium*, which restored to God the role of absolute subject of all reality, and therefore also of the evil contained in it. Modern theodicy—indeed, theodicy *tout court* as an integral structure of modernity—advances against this second offshoot, one that has not yet been completely neutralized and in some ways has even been enhanced. That we may conclude, as Marquard does, that "where there is theodicy, there is modernity and where there is modernity, there is theodicy"[61]—meaning that it will continue even beyond the crisis of the classic form given to it by Leibniz in accordance with new protective strategies—is subject to debate and even dissension. For example, Hans Blumenberg, as we know, rejected the argument that the idealistic philosophy of history would be a kind of secular theology. He placed the question of power rather than the question of guilt at the center of the modern process of self-legitimization. But the eminently juridical category of legitimacy that he uses, especially against Karl Löwith, attests more than he cares to admit to the crucial function performed by the theologically informed lexicon of immunization in the constitution of modernity.

The very conception of the Hegelian *Aufhebung*, for that matter, as the overcoming of evil by encompassing it, demonstrates the survival of the language of theodicy after it seemed to have been exhausted, signaled by Kant downgrading it to a transcendental illusion. Neither the attempt begun by Schelling to release God from the principle of non-contradiction and sufficient reason in order to rediscover His original relation with the void, nor the opposing one, initiated by Rousseau and continued by Fichte, to clear Him by handing over the entire responsibility for evil to man and to history, have been able to entirely escape the conceptual lexicon of theodicy. In fact, while Shelling puts forward the same model in an inverted form, trying to think of evil as the past that is never present to God, Rousseau exonerates God precisely through the emancipation of man from his transcendental constraint: "a sort of atheism *ad maiorem Dei gloriam* [to the greater glory of God] (a phenomenon to which, accordingly, the doctrine and later the myth of the 'end of God' also belong)."[62] The Nietzschean twilight of the gods once again speaks the language of theodicy, exactly at the moment it was meant to be outstripped: as Stendhal already noted ironically, what better excuse for God allowing evil in the world than His non-existence, inviting human beings to consequently become their own god?[63] This is the crucial transition from theodicy to anthropodicy whose echoes still reach us in a backward wave from the nineteenth-century philosophies of history: the immune function assigned until then to religion can now be assigned directly to man.

III

Compensatio

---

1. Immunitary anthropology

The category connecting theology and anthropology within the same immunitary lexicon is "compensation." The fact that this connection also takes the compensatory form of substituting the divine with the human is further confirmation of the central importance of the concept. Odo Marquard, who deserves credit for explicitly drawing attention to this point, argues that in order for anthropology to succeed theology in interpreting humankind to itself, the discipline had to inherit the compensatory function hitherto performed by the mythologeme of theodicy:

> Current anthropology denies man centrality as one who seeks refuge from his imperfections, and can only exist by means of compensations, as *homo compensator*. The modern and contemporary boom in philosophical anthropology takes place, representatively, under the sign of the idea of compensation, which is a theodicy motive in modern philosophy.[1]

As we saw in the previous chapter, if the ultimate justification of God for the presence of evil in the world is at one point found in the fact that He does not exist, this means human beings take personal responsibility for settling the score with the negative that marks their experience. This function of "getting even"—of bringing back into equilibrium the pans of the balance scale tipped to one side by the "weight" of a debt, a deficiency, or a lack—alludes, etymologically as well, to the paradigm of compensation. It signifies the reinstatement of a shattered order, the restitution of stolen property, reparation for damage suffered or caused. As Jean Svagelski has shown in a detailed, and now indispensable, reconstruction of the semantic category,[2] the idea of compensation, later transposed into fields ranging from cosmology to psychoanalysis, has a deep-seated economic and legal significance. Even leaving aside the connotation that its derivatives gradually assumed in the main modern languages—for example, the German term *Ausgleich*, used to signify reparative or commutative justice (*ausgleichende Gerechtigkeit*)—the Latin *compensatio* already hints at a legally defined remuneration that governs contractual relations between parties. More precisely, it refers to a legal practice of extinguishing obligations codified in the sixth century by the *Digest*: "*Compensatio est debiti et crediti inter se contributio* [Compensation is the mutual set-off of debts and credits]."[3] The legal and economic significance of the term remained absolutely stable from the *Istitutiones* of Gaius (4.66) to the formulation of the Napoleonic Civil Code; so much so that its theological adoption by the Fathers of the Church is visibly marked by these origins. Already nine centuries before the doctrine of reparative *satisfactio* formulated by Anselm (*Cur Deus homo?* 2.18), Tertullian interpreted the blood of Christ as an act of legal compensation for the lack of balance [*scompenso*] created by man's sin: *compensatione sanguinis sui* (*Apologeticum*, 50.15).

Now, because it will take center stage once again in philosophical anthropology, what needs to be noted in this semantic transfer between salvific economy and normative regulation is the negative character of the category. Compensation is never, properly speaking, an affirmative, positive, originary act; rather, it is derivative, caused by the need to negate something that in turn contains a negation. Rather than an action, compensation is a reaction, a backlash or counterforce, to a blow to be parried or a force to be neutralized in such a way as to restore the original equilibrium. It brings with it a gain, but never divorced from the loss that it is meant to reinstate: more than a win, it is a non-loss, the loss of a loss, the absence of an absence. Certainly, in relation to the decrease to which it responds, it bears a "plus" sign, but this actually comes from subtracting the "minus." It is the plus ensuing from the product of two minuses: a non-minus, or the disappearance of a minus. If, as Marquard defines it, "compensation means to remedy situations of lack through surrogate actions or acts of reparation,"[4] it implies, and reproduces, what it seeks to make up for. What else is a surrogate, or prosthesis, if not a device that substitutes a presence, thereby reaffirming its absence? Even in the strictly legal sense, in order for there to be forgiveness, or pardon, there must be some damage—the negative of a gift—to put right. Moreover, it must be done in a way that somehow brings it inside its confines, as is the case with all pardons or amnesties: they do not cancel out the crime, they simply release it from the punishment that it would entail, thereby reaffirming it. Or to switch to another field that brings us even closer to the semantics of immunity, dressings that cover and soothe a wound without making it go away, actually making it all the more evident, operate in a similar way:

> Compensating [*compenser*]—remarks Svagelski—is similar to dressing [*panser*] a wound. In order to be dressed, the wound is covered up and masked; it may remain under the dressing but that does not make it disappear. The dressing soothes the wound, eases the pain (after all, compensation has a consolatory function), aids in healing, but at the same time, it draws attention to the wound, giving it a different reality. On the other hand, all masks unmask. In other words, one thing that compensates for another alters it, and while seeking to hide it, actually puts it on display and places it in the realm of difference.[5]

Now this persistence of the negative in the form of its "cure" is the exact immunitary point of intersection between the paradigm of compensation and the approach to the study of humankind that over the past two centuries has come to be known as philosophical anthropology. In order for the discipline to acquire theoretical solidity, a double precondition had to be met: to begin with, the compensatory logic had to be transferred from a static equilibrium to a dynamic one; and second, the discipline had to meet up with the horizon of life. In reality these are not two different issues, since nothing partakes in a changeable equilibrium like organic life (the problem of its preservation): what needs to be preserved in life is not a given, but a process, a development, a growth. What needs to be stabilized is movement. Not by chance, when Pierre-Hyacinthe Azaïs—who wrote perhaps the most emblematic text on compensation, at the start of the nineteenth century[6]—argues that equality between action and reaction is not synchronic but diachronic, and thus measurable only in global terms, he illustrates the point with a biomedical example:

> when a major organ in the body is disrupted, life can only be preserved thanks to the effect of various compensations: healthy organs give part of their forces to the affected organ or take over functions it is unable to perform. . . . All diseases are decompensations. Excessive expansion, leading to acute diseases, must therefore be compensated for by means of sedatives, while excessive compression, causing chronic illnesses, requires stimulants.[7]

This is where the semantics of compensation slip into the more complex and meaningful lexicon of immunization. When he talks about autoregulation in the body through an exchange of functions between the healthy and diseased parts, it is no longer merely a matter of externally balancing a negative with a positive. It is rather a positivization of the negative. At stake is not a measurement, or a weighing, but an interweaving and overlapping between strength and weakness: a weakening of functional strength in order to strengthen a weakness, and vice versa. In this case the negative is not only equalized, but also exploited—made productive—for the purpose of its own neutralization. This is why, contrary to what Adorno[8] and Heidegger[9] thought in their opposition to it, twentieth-century anthropology is by no means the continuation (or attenuation) of humanism, but its reverse. What philosophical anthropology identifies with is not man duplicated on top of himself. Rather it is the fold that relates him to his otherness, to his absent center. This is what Michel Foucault grasped when he located the "place of the king" bestowed on man by modernity precisely in the open space of his unthinkability, "somewhat like the shadow cast by man as he emerges into knowledge; somewhat

like the blind spot from which it becomes possible to know him":[10]
it is that shadow, and that spot—the sharp profile of the negative—which no humanism was able to conceive, thus precluding
the possibility of conceiving the human at all. This was the step
forward (or sideways) taken by anthropology the moment it
sought the human not in what we are, but in what we are not; or
in any case, in an external "not," in a difference that carves out
the human with respect to what we are *not*: namely, animal or
god. But also, and above all, in an internal "not," in the "not"
that we *are*, which constitutes us as such, making us never able
to coincide with ourselves: the fracture, or fault, into which we
slide, like a ravine whose edges we cling to in vain. We do so in
vain, partly because the more anxious we are to arrive at ourselves, the more we are gripped and hollowed out by our own
distance from ourselves, by an emptiness that follows us and goes
before us until it ends up becoming one with our own movement.
Even more profoundly, it is precisely in that distance and in that
emptiness that anthropology identifies the refuge that can keep
us alive.

Beyond all the opposing and complementary critiques—of
idealism and empiricism, spiritualism and biologism—that philosophical anthropology has received over the years, its most pertinent interpretive key is actually to be found in this immunitary
dialectic: in embracing the negative as the only form that can save
humankind from its own negativity. This is true both in the epistemological sense that we cannot know ourselves directly, through
positive determinations, but only obliquely and by contrast; as
well as, to an even greater extent, in the biological sense—although
we should say bio-ontological—that human life can only last by
projecting itself outside itself, into something external that blocks
it and ultimately negates it. Without this externality that objecti-
fies life in ways that are perhaps different from its simple being,
from its immediate presence, life cannot survive itself. To survive
implies controlling the vital force, which inevitably winds up
reducing its intensity. The vital force does not spring freely from
the flow of life, or even from the spontaneous combination of its
elements, but rather, from its solidification in cages, which restrains
and curbs it to the point of driving it into the presence of its
opposite. The identification of man, in short, the preservation of

his identity, is one with his alienation. He is able to remain subject only if he is capable of objectifying himself in something other than himself: to submit himself to something that deprives him of his subjectivity or substitutes for it.

This premise is what both connects and distinguishes anthropology and theology. Like theology, anthropology also makes man's survival—no longer his immortality—conditional on a transcendence, on an externality, on an alterity; only it situates this inside life itself: it immanentizes and internalizes human survival in the figure of its negative. Of course, theology already views in the negative a constitutive element of human experience, as evil and sin. But the move that separates anthropology from its theological predecessor is the conversion of that negative into a positive: the affirmative negation of negativity. Luhmann is the thinker who, once again, most accurately captures this point:

> From then on, and certainly throughout the seventeenth century, nothingness was a modus operandi reserved exclusively to God. Only by passing . . . to the negativity of the subject or to the subjectivity of negation did the new anthropology explode the man/world connection of sins and privative corruption in order to establish a base, which, through the negation of its own negativity, allowed it to arrive once again at a positive cosmic connection, one which it in any case believed itself capable of achieving.[11]

The fact that in Luhmann's reconstruction Hobbes is cast as the precursor of this immunitary conversion throws light on the identity of the negative it restrains and at the same time reproduces: that is, order, in all its modern forms of discipline, norm, and institution. This ordering vector is what must channel life into forms that are compatible with its duration, since these forms do not arise from inside, but rather, are artificially superimposed, or even imposed, onto it: "Trust in order," concludes Luhmann, "becomes confidence in the fact that out of the negation of negativity there arises a new order."[12] Order, in short, is the origin, means, and outcome of the negative: not what takes it away, but what maintains it by productively converting its destructive power. The inherently nihilistic aspect of philosophical anthropology thus comes to light. As is typical of any form of compensation, the construction of the order it produces does not have the characteristics of a positive construction, but rather, those of the destruction of a destruction, the negation of a negative. But this is precisely where the possible counterfactual outcome of the strategy is revealed: wishing to negatively restore the negative of community, philosophical anthropology is likely to deliver it over to the nothingness from which it seeks to save it.

*

Since Hobbes is responsible for inaugurating modernity's most celebrated immune scenario, he can provide us with a preliminary clarification on what is meant, in this context at least, by nihilism.[13] As Heidegger has repeatedly explained, nihilism does not coincide with the revelation of the nothing that characterizes human experience, but rather with its concealment. Or better yet, it coincides with a substitutive repression that reproduces the nothingness in a more powerful form. Now this is precisely the position of Hobbes with respect to the *munus* of *communitas*, to that breach in individual subjectivity that constitutes the communal relation. He is not a nihilistic thinker because he "discovered" the essential void created by the withdrawal of the transcendental *veritas*, but because he "re-covered" it with another void intended to neutralize its dissolutive effects. This is the ultimate meaning of the passage from the state of nature to the civil state ensuing from the founding of the Leviathan: it is an annihilation of the nothing that the community naturally bears within itself, through the production of an artificial nothing capable of converting its destructive effects into ordering ones. The political order of sovereignty is thus made possible only by the drastic elimination of all social intercourse outside the strictly individual exchange between protection and obedience. Once the "*cum*" is taken to be constitutionally risky for self-preservation, it is drastically eliminated in favor of a political form that puts every individual in direct contact with the sovereign power that represents him or her. Now what is specifically immunitary about a process of this kind is not only the desocialization it presupposes, but especially its homeopathic mode of operation. Just as the fear caused by the Leviathan heals everyone from their mutual fear of the state of nature, similarly the equality of all the subjects before the king defuses the danger arising from their equal ability to kill or be killed prior to the establishment of civil order. The nothing that originally unites us can only be treated by using its own ingredients, but combined in a different way: to the point that the king does not put aside his natural right to exercise violence against those who seek to resist him, but he does lay his own sword over it, thereby deriving his power of life and death over his subjects from that natural right.

Since that time, the state institution has harbored this blind spot caused by the structural coincidence between what it seeks to neutralize and the effective instrument designated for this purpose, like an artificial void intended to fill a natural void, or, in other words, intended to empty it further. One of the reasons for the vertical crisis that has gripped the paradigm of sovereignty for so long is precisely the inability to stop this nihilistic dialectic, and even its tendency to reproduce it redoubled. Look at the way even our contemporary political sociology has tried to solve the "Hobbesian problem of order"—to use Talcott Parsons' celebrated phrase—while remaining inexorably within it. Of course, by rejecting the utilitarian model of maximizing the relationship between means and end, and thus replacing the atomistic-relational paradigm with a relational-functional one, Parsons shifts the axis of the terms away from classic individualism, toward the need for social integration. The term "social science" itself implies the collective framework of individual action. But this change in the anthropological presuppositions of Hobbesian immunization, instead of marking its passing, replicates it in a more powerful form, because it is true that individualism can no longer put itself forward as a complete alternative to the social bond;[14] rather, it makes up its content. As we know, thanks in part to the important studies on the subject by Matteo Bortolini,[15] the Parsonian theory of the "communitarian society" is the most obvious proof of this: the only value—even in the economic sense of the term—able to hold together a diversified society like ours is that associated with the sphere of the individual. It associates individuals through their functional separation. From this point of view, Parsons' "communitarian society" is the reverse of *communitas*, or, better yet, it is its double immunization: not only because it reiterates the regulative importance of the individual, but because it inscribes it within the very body of social integration. Unlike the first modern immunization, which eliminated the "*cum*" in favor of individual preservation, the one foreshadowed by current Parsonian political sociology functionalizes immunization to allow for its expanded reproduction. And so it immunizes it a second time: instead of limiting itself to simple nonrelation, it theorizes a relation of unrelated individuality.

2. The productivity of the negative

Nietzsche had a perfect grasp of the nihilistic endpoint where the category of compensation would lead once it was assigned to a preservative, immune-type function. It is paradoxical that philosophical anthropology recognized its immediate precursor in him without grasping the criticism *ante litteram* that his perspective constituted with respect to the compensatory outcomes that would later affect it. True, Nietzsche uses the same contrastive dialectic later used by the anthropological paradigm when interpreting reflective consciousness as "the result of a terrible 'must', which has ruled over the human being for a long time: as the most endangered animal, he needed help and protection . . . he first needed 'consciousness' i.e. even to 'know' what distressed him, to 'know' how he felt, to 'know' what he thought."[16] But he does so in a deconstructive tone that dryly reverses his intention: that doubling or rather that distance that life creates from itself to be able to protect itself from what threatens it, ends up condemning it to the same powerlessness it seeks to escape. It delivers life over to the same powers of annihilation from which, contradictorily, it seeks to defend itself. Contradictorily, because this defense of life makes use of an ideal of the ascetic type as an instrument, which simultaneously negates it; which negates it in order to affirm it, and affirms it only by negating it:

> the ascetic ideal springs from the protective instinct of a degenerating life which tries by all means to sustain itself and to fight for its existence; it indicates a partial physiological obstruction and exhaustion against which the deepest instincts of life, which have

remained intact, continually struggle with new expedients and devices. The ascetic ideal is such an expedient; the case is therefore the opposite of what those who reverence this ideal believe; life wrestles in it and through it with death and *against* death; the ascetic ideal is an artifice for the *preservation* of life.[17]

What Nietzsche sees with absolute clarity, in the logical difference between means and end, is the aporetic core of the immune strategy. To preserve itself, "the most imperiled, the most chronically and profoundly sick of all animals" (*GM*, 3.14)—human beings, that is—are forced to inhibit the vital forces that well up inside them, to suppress the impulses that naturally animate them, to open up a wound in the flesh of their own experience: "The No he says to life brings to light, as if by magic, an abundance of tender Yeses; even when he wounds himself, this master of destruction, of self-destruction—the very wound itself afterward compels him to live."[18] But Nietzsche's conclusion is implicit in his own assumptions: this homeopathic dialectic between preservation and destruction, between healing and wounding, is exactly what turns out to be calamitous. Even worse: it is counterproductive to the very need that engenders it; not because the "treatment" fails to "improve" the patient, but because the improvement that it brings about also strengthens the disease at the same time. The improvement is entirely contained within the treatment: "But when such a system is chiefly applied to the sick, distressed, and depressed, it invariably makes them *sicker* even if it does 'improve' them . . . one may without any exaggeration call it *the true calamity* in the history of European health."[19]

The fact that the origin of this particular history began with the forceful conviction of man's superiority over all other forms of life does not, for Nietzsche, take away the logical necessity for such an entropic drift. Once the compensatory model has been fixed to the assumption of an inverse proportion between natural power and the capacity of artificial mediation—or, in more general terms, between intensity and duration—the preservation of life is inevitably entrusted to the necessity of its reduction. The consequentiality of this passage is recognizable starting from the words that J. G. Herder places at the programmatic debut of modern philosophical anthropology:

The higher the degree of organization of a creature, the more varied and complex the relation between its organs—each one referring to its own world and environment—the weaker and more unsure its instinct and abilities, allowing the possibility for errors and obstacles in carrying out its activities. So, in the end, a creature capable of understanding must learn, it must train itself, because at this point nature and instinct teach it little, and it can achieve little by nature and instinct; but as compensation for this attenuation of instinct it acquires a much broader field of action and a greater possibility of ends and means.[20]

This passage reconstructs the pendulum motion of compensation in both its directions, ascending and descending: on one side there is the instinctual weakness of the human species leading to a superior learning capacity; on the other, this superiority bears the signs of the natural fragility out of which it emerges through struggle. Man's upright walking posture, and the greater adaptability to environmental conditions it provides, "has also exposed him to a greater number of diseases, compensated for by the greater refinement available to him for well-being and joy."[21] The human animal can live longer than all others *because*—not despite the fact—he is constitutionally sick. In order to "recharge" itself, life constantly needs what threatens it—a block, an obstacle, a bottleneck—because the constitution and the functioning of its immune system requires an "ill" to activate the alarm system.

When early nineteenth-century biology paved the way for a new wave of anthropology in the 1830s and 1840s, it remained tenaciously bound to the same assumption. The theory that the exclusion of organs benefitted the use of instruments put forward by the physician Paul Alsberg, the notion of morphological retardation contributed by the anatomist Lodewijk Bolk, and, lastly, the idea of early ontogenetic maturation developed by the zoologist Adolf Portmann—later variously picked up again by Helmuth Plessner and Arnold Gehlen—start from the same compensatory principle of functional correspondence between strength and weakness: not only is strength balanced by a weakness, but weakness acts as a spark in igniting and fueling strength. That is why when Max Scheler refuted Paul Alsberg and Alfred Adler's theory of "overcompensation" and the "negative" compensation of Schopenhauer and Freud as well—because in his view they diminished the autonomy of the spirit—he was only able to do so using a semantics that is every bit as compensatorily negative. In the same way, his challenge to Nietzsche's biologism fits almost verbatim into the polemical mold Nietzsche himself had reserved for the deadly therapy of the "ascetic ideal": "Compared to the animal that always says 'yes' to the actual reality—even when he abhors it and flees from it—man is 'he who can say no', he is the 'ascetic of life'."[22] Indeed, human life takes on meaning and importance only from that "no," from that last-gasp effort by which it casts itself out of itself: life negates itself so as to affirm itself. Not partially, as Max Scheler specifies, and not even on a temporary basis, but in all its depth and scope. Spirit, the element that elevates man over all other living things, is life negated to the limit of its intensity.

Here it is entirely clear how Scheler's criticism of the Nietzschean conception that views the human spirit not as an autonomous force, but as "a disease . . . a fundamental pathological tendency of universal life itself . . . a metaphysical parasite, which worms its way into life and the soul to destroy them,"[23] ends up unwittingly reproducing its movements, albeit from a symmetrically reversed position. In fact, the same spirit that Scheler hastens to defend is also defined by him as powerless with respect to the impulsive and instinctual sphere it is supposed to dominate. Not only that, it is forced to feed on the same vital power that it seeks to neutralize: if "what is inferior, is originally powerful," while "what is superior, is powerless"; if "any higher form of being is *relatively* powerless in comparison to a lower form, and cannot be realized through its own efforts, but through the forces of the lower form,"[24] this means that the spirit is invigorated precisely from the impulse that it must repress in order to affirm itself. The immunitary outcome, from the outset inherent to the compensatory mechanism, now comes into full view. What matters is not the spiritualist direction it is forced to take in Scheler's anthropology so much as the negative dialectic that objectively informs it. Spirit, the principle of health and safety, can exonerate itself from the material forces that bear down on it and oppress it only through a regular intake of the same forces:

> *Because of its nature and originarily, the spirit does not possess any of its own energy.* The most elevated form of the being "determines," so to speak, the *essence* and the essential reasons for the configuration of the world, but this form is *realized* thanks to a different principle, which, like the spiritual one, also belongs originarily to the primordial being: the principle that creates reality and determines the contingent images and which we shall call "*impulse.*"[25]

The sphere of freedom is destined to the same fate. In accordance with the spiritual autonomy that distinguishes it, it is defined in relation to the human capacity to break free from everything organic, to free ourselves from the ties with life and our immediate needs. Our openness to the world, then, stems from our independence from some predetermined environment like those that bind all other animals to a given context. Precisely because humans did not initially have *a* world, we can be open to *the* world: we are free to construct it for ourselves according to our preferences. Just a few years after Scheler's essay, Günter Anders pushed the terms of this compensatory equivalence between freedom and alienation even further: "Freedom of *praxis* expresses the fact that man knows to some extent how to compensate for his alienation from the world and his detachment: he creates relationships with the world which, without making him subject to things, puts them under his domination."[26] While animals, born in an environment familiar to them, are necessarily bound to it, man, being naturally excluded from a world that precedes him, can shape it into his own image and likeness. Since he does not spontaneously adhere to a reality that always precedes him, he can construct it in a form depending on his will. He is set free by the absence of an origin to which he must answer, because "he experiences himself as not-put-here-by himself, he senses . . . that he comes from something that is not him."[27] It is this autonomy from predetermined constraints that Anders seeks to highlight when he emphasizes that the essence of human beings lies in not having one, and that our nature is artificiality: man is the animal able to create the conditions of his life without receiving them from the outside. On these lines, it may well be said that the *a priori* of human beings consists in our being *a posteriori*, that we are *apriorily a posteriori*. Here, in this logical, chronological and ontological unevenness, lie the roots of human freedom. It is a freedom to "understand absence positively," and to "give a positive sense to Nothingness."[28]

But all this does not take away from, indeed implies, the fact that this same dialectic is equally readable in reverse. That is, not only is alienation from the world the condition of human freedom, but also, man's freedom is inhabited and sucked out by this alienation. It implies that this freedom is alien even to itself, to the point of losing itself as such, to the point of tipping over into its opposite. Thus, in freedom, the therapy coincides with the "pathology," as Anders titled his essay on "non-identification," embracing the nihilistic thesis by which, "even though man only reveals himself freely, through an act that freely emanates from him, he ends up discovering, precisely, that he is not free, that he is not determined by himself."[29] There are two reasons for this: first because this freedom is presupposed without man having chosen it, and therefore he is necessarily destined to it; but then, even more so, because this need is in the form of absolute contingency, of complete indeterminacy. In this paradox of a necessary contingency, or a contingent necessity, lies the "sham, the fatal gift of freedom."[30] Even the *a priori* assumption of the *a posteriori* which occurs in it—or from which it springs—lends itself to a symmetrically reversed interpretation of the one that emphasizes the aspect of opening to the future. It is true that the understanding of absence involves taking leave of the present for a future that remains to be determined. But this future, made such by its constitutively negative "not" being present, will always be so indeterminate that it escapes from human control; it will also reverse the time line, turning into an "already has been," according to the logical oxymoron of the "future perfect" which we saw previously at work in the deadly turn of the law. It transforms into a pure mental experience of surviving oneself, in which the freedom of the negative is made simultaneously into negation of freedom:

> But what man discovers in these acts of free transposition of himself is again something negative; he sees himself chased into the furthest past and already sees his—still future—death as passed like his birth. And all things are already seen as passed, and all things, like in *Ecclesiastes*, which by no coincidence expresses its nihilism in

the future perfect, are viewed as "vanity." Those who are yet to come will not be remembered by those who follow, because they will simply have been. And already the future becomes past.[31]

Once again, in this regard as well, the figure of nothing looms at the deepest heart of philosophical anthropology. Although it was created to immunize man from the lack that pursues him, it reproduces it, boosted, inside him.

3. The risk of community

This entropic outcome, still uncertain and contradictory in Scheler and Anders, comes directly into the open in the two authors who brought philosophical anthropology to its height of maturity, albeit along completely different routes. The first is Helmuth Plessner, who, with respect to his immediate predecessors, radicalized the anthropological project in terms of immunity. The fact that he was a student of the biologist Hans Driesch, and that he never abandoned his interest in physiology stemming from his early years as a medical student in Freiburg, is certainly pertinent to this development.[32] If Scheler was still trying to release the principle of the negative—the spirit—from the compensatory function of preserving life, while Anders, even though he adopted the semantics of compensation, interpreted it in terms of freedom, Plessner located the anthropological inquiry within the paradigmatic framework of the Hobbesian problem of order: "the urge to order" is "the latent attitude of all human life"[33] he declares while still under the influence of Driesch's *Ordnungslehre*. This is because only through order does human life draw the necessary resources for its problematic duration.

Not that Plessner indulges in a biologistic reduction of the idea of man. True, in agreement with Georg Misch's *Lebensphiloso-phie*, he certainly tends to locate the specific object of anthropological investigation in corporeality. He does not reject the organizational schema implicit to Scheler's perspective, but reincorporates the metaphysical gap that Scheler opened up between life and spirit into the same somatic sphere. In fact, for Plessner, not only is the body reducible to the quantitative, material dimension of the Cartesian *res extensa*, it is the field of tension within which it relates to its alterity: the body "is the form in which body and soul are closely intertwined with each other."[34] From this immanentist premise emerges an anthropology of the living, a genuine "biophilosophy" in which form and matter, inner and outer, subject and object, each occur as a mode of expression and deployment of the other. The body, in this sense, is no longer considered the shell or instrument of intellectual activity but rather its organic root, just as the intellect is then interpreted as the spiritual result of the bodily processes. This is what Plessner means by the "eccentric positionality" of human beings: unlike animals, whose needs are entirely met through their immediate relationship with their surrounding environment, according to the well-known idea put forward by Jacob von Uexkull, humans are always at a distance from themselves. Behind or ahead, to one side or the other, before or after where they are actually located, humans are out of their "inside" and inside their "outside," internal to their own exteriority and external to their own interiority. Hence the constant intertwining of identity and otherness that is knotted around the figure of the human being: we are neither entirely identical to ourselves nor completely other, just as we stand neither at the center nor to the side of our horizon of meaning, but precisely at the limit that simultaneously binds together and juxtaposes them. This liminality is identified by Plessner in the ontological gap between "being" and "having" a body. We do not possess the body that we are, and we will never really be able to be the body that we possess. This is true non-self-possession: "'I am, but I do not possess myself', this phrase characterizes the condition of human beings in their bodily existence," observes Plessner in *Conditio humana*.[35] On this line of thought, he can argue that "being human is to be other than oneself" because human beings are precisely those who do not coincide with what they are.[36] As if to say: alienation is the condition of identification and vice versa. Only in negative relation to the possibility of being an other is each person what he actually is, and what is properly human lies in not being an other. We inhabit our own distance, until we thoroughly coincide with it. It is the fissure that separates us from ourselves: the margin—the furrow and the threshold—in which the stranger is proper to itself and the proper is continually estranged from itself.

It is a perturbation, a laceration, a rift opened up and at work in the furrow of the same.

But this is the other side of the coin: the more Plessner emphasizes this difference, the deeper the wound is disclosed; the more he describes the subject as exposed to its own otherness, the more he is forced to weave a safety net capable of immunizing it. All the logic of his thought is governed by this need to build a compensatory artificial equilibrium able to balance the natural imbalance that places man beyond himself. He does so to the point of viewing the human being as a system of weights intended to equalize the burden that our eccentric nature places on us: "Human beings tend to escape from the unbearable eccentricity of their being, to compensate for the divided character of their life form and can only succeed with things heavy enough to balance the weight of their existence."[37] Only in this way can the creature who had been described by Herder as "handicapped by its superior forces" transform itself into a "fighter armed with its inferior forces," into a "Proteus of surrogates"[38] capable of productively evening out its initial lack. True, Plessner argues that "the idea of compensation, biologically related to the complex of human nature, does not include an explanation of the causes and conditions" that determine it;[39] that is, it does not suffice in itself to explain the dialectical reversal of weakness into strength without presupposing "specific points of support, needed to balance this new kind of organic system."[40] But in fact this specification roots the compensatory mechanism—otherwise reducible to a purely subjective dynamic—into a series of objective counterpoints, in a chain of normative constraints that stabilize its immune effect: "To be human means to be imprisoned by rules, to be engaged in repressing the instincts. Every convention, every custom, every law articulates, channels and suppresses the corresponding instinctual drives."[41]

This is the decisive step from anthropology to politics, or rather, the perspective point from which the original political shades of anthropology begin to come to the fore. To put it another way, this is the moment the topic of compensation acquires, or reveals, the functional traits of the immune apparatus, attested to not only by the protective, reassuring role that political forms assume against the natural risk that threatens human beings, but also by the explicitly communal way this risk is described. What politics must protect human life from is an excess of community. This is the basic thesis of the essay *Limits of Community* that Plessner wrote in 1924, immediately before the failed *putsch* of Munich and the attempted Communist uprising in Hamburg.[42] The pamphlet was designed by Plessner to be a defense of the Weimar regime against the left- and right-wing extremist groups who threatened its hold. But what is important to note, in accordance with its explicitly immunitary tone, is that the polemical objective used by the author is figured as a radical aspiration for community. This aspiration, interpreted by Plessner in conventionally organismic terms, is what tips the balance of social life toward forms of emotional overload that disrupt its normal functioning. Whence the need, once again, for a "restrainer," a control, an "order" that compensates for the fusional drift with a series of defensive strategies designed to reconstruct the limits and boundaries where flow and communication currently exist. Contrary to the closeness of the "common life," all these strategies go in the direction of distancing, of a functional separation, which primarily involves the reciprocal relationship between individuals, but then—even more thoroughly and in conjunction with the first— also the relationship each individual entertains with himself or herself. This aspect ushers in the return of the dialectic between proper and improper that we identified as the foundation of Plessnerian anthropology, but with a sharp immunitary inflection: human beings can protect their identity only by splitting themselves into the polarity between inner and outer, private and public, invisible and visible, and by arranging for each pole to safeguard the other. As the exteriority of public life is what cuts out the possibility of a private dimension from the other side of the mirror, so it is precisely the visibility of external attitudes that conceals the internal intention which moves them: to "make a person maximally visible and hidden at the same time."[43]

All the social functions Plessner analyzes—name, role, ceremony, prestige, diplomacy, tact—respond to this need for protection by splitting in two. In order for us to safeguard one part of us, we are forced to literally put the other "into play." Survival is not guaranteed in a direct, immediate fashion: it requires the presence of a mediation that cuts through subjectivity along lines of flight that are destined to never meet up, or to only intersect in the negative. In order for human beings to "realize themselves" in terms of appearance, they are forced to remain "unrealized" in terms of substance: "Everything psychological requires this detour in order to attain itself; what is psychological wins itself only when it loses itself."[44] Contrary to all negative theories of alienation, whether Augustinian-Lutheran or Hegelian-Marxist, Plessner argues in favor of its immunizing effects, as opposed to a direct organic relationship with others and with ourselves that will inevitably overturn into mutually destructive conflict. Social representation is what rules and regulates it. Plessner describes this in theatrical terms: impersonation, incorporation, disguise, in which each person becomes a double of himself or herself [*Doppelgänger*].[45] He takes his cue, to the letter, from the nihilistic-compensatory scenario sketched out by Nietzsche:

> As a means for the preserving of the individual, the intellect unfolds its principle powers in dissimulation, which is the means by which weaker, less robust individuals preserve themselves—since they have been denied the chance to wage the battle for existence with horns or with the sharp teeth of beasts of prey. This art of dissimulation reaches its peak in man. Deception, flattering, lying, deluding, talking behind the back, putting up a false front, living in borrowed splendor, wearing a mask, hiding behind convention, playing a role for others and for oneself—in short, a continuous fluttering around the solitary flame of vanity—is so much the rule and the law among men that there is almost nothing which is less comprehensible than how an honest and pure drive for truth could have arisen among them.[46]

The Hobbesian premise at the basis of this passage is only too evident: human society, whatever it may be, is unable to last unless it has an artificial order capable of neutralizing the potential violence that riddles it by nature. But this is its intrinsic immunitary valence: this order unavoidably bears inside it a fragment of the very violence it is meant to restrain. The negative cannot be eliminated; it can only be tamed into a form that makes its pathogenic consequences tolerable.

All the social rituals described by Plessner, no matter how toned down and urbanized in the semantics of civilization, at their core reveal this kernel of lesser violence that only by preserving itself as such can withstand the greater violence from which it nonetheless emanates and whose nature it shares. This holds equally true for the "role," which constitutes a sort of "mask," or better yet, "an armor that he can wear entering the battlefield of the public sphere."[47] Even more so, then, for prestige, for "which the struggle for a true face unrealizes and changes itself"[48] in a compensatory mode that makes us unassailable. And so it is, finally, for the art of "diplomacy," in which threat and cunning, trickery and persuasion, serve to "manipulate someone during negotiation until he is disarmed."[49] This is the only legitimate, necessary way to avoid "brute force":[50] by dressing it up in forms that range from polite manners to power; in fact, deriving subtle instruments from the former in order to more efficiently impose the latter. This soft transition, this taut cord between grace and domination, which alludes both to the Renaissance theme of "nonchalance [*sprezzatura*]" and the semantics of play, in all its variations, is what Plessner calls "tact," with symptomatic reference to the need for "social hygiene." Tact is the "art of not coming too close and of not being too open."[51] Not just a remoteness and not a pure closing either; rather, it is a relation at a distance and a controlled opening. From this point of view, Plessner cannot be characterized as a theoretician of solipsism or even of individualism, although he has been given this label. More accurately, he is a theoretician of the preventive immunization of all social forms, which are thereby desocialized at the level of the individual atoms that compose and simultaneously decompose it as such. He does not commit the mistake of abstracting individuals from the community, which he presupposes as their condition of existence, but according to a relation that unites them in separation and connects them in estrangement.

This overlap between unity and division has rightly led to his anthropology being defined as "a piece of political theology."[52] This is partly based on his celebrated relationship with Carl Schmitt, which earned him early recognition from the latter as "the first modern philosopher [who] dared to advance a political anthropology of a grand style."[53] But, more profoundly, it is due to the "katechonic" role assumed by the immunizing mechanisms of "social hygiene" against violence, which is both restrained and

incorporated by them, as Adorno had occasion to comment on
the category of tact: "The nominalism of tact aids the triumph of
that which is most general, the naked reach of administration,
even in the most intimate constellations."[54] Moreover, the direction of his anthropological project is laid open rather than contradicted at its rawest nerve when Plessner declares that without
"destruction, at least as a threat, there can be no politics at all,
just as rights do not exist without the destruction of freedom."[55]
While human beings are ordered to contain the nothing that
presses around them from all sides, they can only do so by means
of further, continuous destruction.

*

In his introduction to the Italian translation of the *Grenzen*,
Bruno Accarino explicitly disputes Plessner's immunitary interpretation. To be more precise, he challenges the antithesis to the term
communitas that could arise from Plessner's interpretation: "*Immunitas* is no longer the opposite of *communitas*, but one of its indispensable preconditions."[56] In my view, he is both right and wrong
at the same time. He is right specifically in asserting the dialectical
and aporetic character of the relationship between the categories
of "community" and "immunity," as indeed we have maintained
from the beginning. It is thus true that the community criticized
by Plessner based on fusion and authenticity is the maximum form
of immunization, to the extent that it rejects—or, conversely,
phagocytizes—any difference and alteration. As the largely fundamentalist and xenophobic currents of some neocommunitarian
groups demonstrate today, nothing has a stronger immunizing
effect than a community that completely "owns" itself, and which
is then not "common" with respect to what does not belong to it.
But this community of identity and belonging is precisely the opposite of the *communitas* from which *immunitas* derives its own
negative and privative significance. This is precisely the point that
Accarino apparently fails to see: in other words, *communitas* does
not presuppose *immunitas*, as he writes, but the other way around.
Of course, the assumption we are referring to here has nothing to
do with an earlier time, according to an interpretive stereotype that
Plessner rightly brands as romantically conservative. Rather, it has

to be understood in logical terms or, better yet, in ontological terms: starting from *immunitas* in order to define *communitas*, as Accarino does following Plessner and all post-Hobbesian anthropology, means to interpret relation, the "*cum*," through individualistic lenses that reverse the perspective or present it in a vocabulary that has already been philosophically immunized.

A similar comment can be made about Plessner's category of tact, certainly identified by Accarino with that of contact.[57] In reality, as can be inferred from his own studies,[58] the correspondence between these terms is anything but a foregone conclusion. It is true that the category of "tact," like that of "contingency," does not negate the relation with others. Indeed, it requires it; but it maintains it in a defensive form that preventively sterilizes it from its most dangerously contagious effects. This is why Plessner stresses its "hygienic" character, but also why it is inherent to the sphere of law and its delimitations: tact is first of all an apparatus or source of differentiation. It restores proper boundaries breached by indiscretion, indecency, excessive closeness, or even lack of distinction. Hence its kinship with correctness: *Richtigkeit*, in its turn, implies the idea of direction (*Richtung*) and law (*Recht*). And in fact touch was defined by Jhering as the faculty of grasping what is right, *das Richtige*, even beyond the abstractness of the rule.[59] But it is precisely this differentiating, delimiting trait that shifts tact into the area of immunization. The closeness that it connotes includes a certain distance, just as its action is negatively characterized by abstention from what could hurt or cause an injury. Through tact, perhaps, you touch without touching, or you do not touch the thing, or the person, that at the same time you touch. In this sense, tact is the reverse of contact, which is also well absorbed by the semantic chain of *tangere*: tact does not eliminate contact or even act specifically as its limitation; rather, tact is its negative: like a thin diaphragm that leaves the external surfaces that touch each other literally intact and, thus, unharmed by the contact which they nonetheless experience. Tact, as an eminently social category, calls for relationship with others; this relationship, however, does not favor association but maintains and increases the initial distance: "Situations of tact," says Plessner, "arise and are resolved between individuals based on an irrational and imperceptible intuition, and based on careful prior preservation of distance."[60] Under close conditions, the person with the most tact is the one who is able to firmly maintain his or her untouchability.

From this point of view, the consonance that has been suggested between Plessner and a thinker of contact like Maurice Merleau-Ponty seems somewhat extrinsic. They do not lack common references and themes, by any means; they also converge in the attention they direct to the sphere of the body and everything that touches it in any way. However, it is the semantic axis of touch that signals the most sensitive point of divergence between the two, one which we might summarize as follows. While in Plessner—and generally in German philosophical anthropology—"touchability" is tactically contained within a threshold beyond which it cannot go without generating negative consequences, in Merleau-Ponty it takes on meaning starting exactly from that limit-point: "To touch and touch oneself (to touch oneself—the toucher—the touched). They do not coincide in the body: the toucher is never exactly the touched. This does not mean that they coincide 'in the spirit' or at the level of 'consciousness'. For the juncture to be realized, something different from the body is needed: it is realized in the *'untouchable'*."[61] The untouchable, then, is not what delimits the touchable from the external; but rather the touchable itself, in the difference that removes it from an absolute coincidence with itself. What is at stake here is not, as in Plessner, the need, or opportunity, to protect the subjects of contact from an emotionally unsustainable relationship, but on the contrary, the impossibility of conceiving the subjects, and the objects, outside of the relationship that constitutes them as such. This is why they cannot *touch each other the whole way through*: because there is neither the "toucher" nor the "touched," but only the touch in which they reciprocally carve each other out. And indeed neither is there "touching" in itself, understood substantively, as something absolute from what or who experiences it from time to time. From this point of view, rather than what resists touching, the untouchable is touchability as such. But this, of course, takes us out of Plessner's conceptual vocabulary, out of anthropology altogether, towards the same horizon of meaning that Merleau-Ponty described in the still enigmatic terms of an "ontology of the flesh."

4. The power of the void

The thinker who brings this nihilistic transition to its final comple-
tion is Arnold Gehlen.[62] In his work, nineteenth-century philosophical anthropology seems to close down on itself in terms of
a very conservative stabilization. All the hesitations, antinomies,
and openings that continued to be expressed in the views of Scheler,
Anders, and Plessner are stitched together by Gehlen into a functional grasp that leads the anthropological paradigm to fully coincide with its bare immunitary effectiveness. Not that he lacked an
interest in the ontological question of relationship, especially in
the early stages of his career, given that in his postdoctoral dis-
sertation of 1931 on *Real and Unreal Spirit* he wrote that "the
only adequate object of man is the *other*."[63] But this interest was
pursued in a way, preventively neutralized, that led him early on
to turn this communal inclination into an explicit and pressing
need for preservation: "Life, to be completely itself, must seek out
the negative in order to preserve itself from it."[64] Already in this
early work, the "negative," declared to be necessary for survival,
takes over the primacy awarded to relationship with the other. Or
to put it more accurately, it reveals the instrumental importance
Gehlen reserved to the theme of alterity. Because unlike Scheler,
who with respect to the constitution of the individual posits the
sphere of common experience in relational forms of sympathy and
love,[65] and Plessner, who was always oriented toward the political
dimension of intersubjectivity, for Gehlen, the "other"—rather
than an *alter ego*, another subject—is primarily and essentially a
"*non-I [Nicht-Ich]*": the "non" that allows the ego to identify
itself as that which is, precisely, other than its own other: "Beset
by the enigma of his own existence and his own nature, man must
define himself by referring to a *non-I*, to something different from
the human."[66] Even when that non-I has the "human" appearances
of a "you," it is always and only in relation to the self-construction
of the "I": it is the objective medium through which the subject
is preserved by means of its own alienation into a formal device
which both substitutes and protects its natural essence.

The historical and philosophical origins of this theory—
probably Fichtian—matter little here compared to its functional
use in explicitly compensatory terms:

man, placed like an animal in the face of his raw nature, with his
innate *physis* and his lack of instincts would be unable to live in
all situations. These are however offset by the capacity, allowing
him to respond to even the most urgent need, to change this raw
nature, and indeed any kind of nature, in any way this can be done,
in order to allow it to become usable to him for life.[67]

What is reflected here, in its definitive formulation, is the classic
anthropological theory of the dialectical inversion between the
organic retardation and effective power—thought, action, language—of the human species: precisely because it is structurally
affected by primitivism, retarded development, and lack of organic
specialization, the least fit of natural beings is endowed with the
most adaptive versatility. As Gehlen worked out from Herder's
theory of the *Mängelwesen* and from Nietzsche's *Unfertigkeit*, as
well as, especially, the new bio-ethology of Bolk and Portmann,
Buytendijk and Schindewolf, Storch and Lorenz, when it comes
to human beings, there is no direct passage between life and survival. When he writes that man "does not live, but rather leads a
life"[68] what he is saying is that survival is not a spontaneous
reward of life, but on the contrary, something that requires life to
be managed in a controlled, limited, restrained form that somehow
inhibits and contradicts it. In short, contrary to the linear, progressive model of evolution as it is traditionally conceived, the ontog-
eny of man is seen to occur through a series of organic blocks and
functional leaps in which any progress only compensates for a
regression that balances and simultaneously allows for it to occur,
according to a bivalent feedback mechanism marked by the need
for renunciation and self-constriction.

This negative characterization combines Gehlen's perspective
with Freudian theories as well as those of Norbert Elias on the
civilizing process as a repressive channeling of natural impulses.
It provides further clarification about the peculiar nature of the
Gehlenian immune paradigm. It does not proceed through a simple
defensive closure, but also, and above all, through the principle
of "exoneration" [*Entlastung*], programmatically defined by the
author as "the key to understanding the structural law governing
the development of all human skills."[69] If we go back for a moment
to the etymological meaning of the term *ex-onerare*—understood

as the procedure of relieving and removing the common *onus* that binds members of the community to the obligation, or to the law (in both cases *munus*), of a mutual commitment—it perfectly captures the specific variation as well as the semantic intensification that Gehlen gives the category of immunization. In his conceptual lexicon, immunization not only involves the retranslation of a negative—the *ex* of *ex-onerare* or the *ent* of *Entlastung*—into affirmative potential, but also the negative capacity of this affirmation. To orient ourselves in this game of facing mirrors we must review all the junctures in the logical route that Gehlen takes in constructing it: the primary task of exoneration is to fill man's biological void with some replacement that can compensate for or even overturn its naturally negative effects into a condition of easier survival. This is accomplished through a process of selection and distancing [*Distanzierung*] from the unruly profusion of stimuli that regularly strike us, through a delay in responding to them which performs the function of preserving life for a longer duration. Hence the formation of a "hiatus" between the needs and requirements that subordinate our behavior to an anticipatory practice whose aim is not only to cope with the present emergency, but also to anticipatorily satisfy our unquenchable "future hunger."[70] But precisely in this future-oriented action is revealed the doubly negative meaning of immunization thus arrived at: as we know by now, it proceeds homeopathically through controlled reproduction of what it seeks to neutralize. What else is the "hiatus," the space-time delay Gehlen refers to, if not a similar, even deeper, artificially produced void, than what it is meant to therapeutically fill? On the other hand, the maintenance of the onus that is reversed—and thus made productive—is implicit in the privative concept of exoneration. *Entlastung* is the action on himself by which "man transforms his fundamental handicaps into opportunities for survival."[71] As we were saying: it is the way he *transforms*—inverts and converts—rather than abolishes the impulses that negatively constitute him and which he can only reproduce. He is separated from himself and turned against himself, since "this can only happen if one part of the impulses are used to inhibit the others."[72]

So far, however, Gehlen has done nothing but translate the usual contrastive dialectic of the immune paradigm into anthropological terms. He takes an extra step in a direction that seems to double the negativity count, however: he not only defines the biological process by which the human organism is immunized against the risks implicit to its deficient nature, he also defines a cage of a juridical type to immunitarily protect this immunization, like an external prosthesis added to the body to mechanically ensure its physiological development. This is the function that Gehlen assigns to the institution he begins to explicitly theorize about in the 1950s, with a self-critical eye to his own earlier theories as well. As long as immunization remains at an individual level, and is not incorporated into a wider social mechanism, it remains exposed to the risk of rapid dissolution. Now what is immediately clear is that this position of Gehlen—developed in its mature form mostly in response to Maurice Hauriou's *theorie de l'institution*[73]—does not put into question the essentially individualistic assumption that he links, as we have already seen, to the principle of exoneration. But he subjects it to a movement that preserves it only through its opposite, according to the dialectical process we have become familiar with: in order for individuals to exonerate themselves in a lasting way, they must first do so in relation to themselves. They must exonerate themselves from their own individual subjectivity. Individual exoneration is always also exoneration *from* the individual. Only by delegating the burden of decisions that human beings are continually urged to make in response to environmental stimuli to an objective system of control and reproduction can the individual free up energy for higher skills (to use the standard terms Luhmann drew from Gehlen's theories as inspiration for his own perspective). This means that freedom expands in proportion to the growth of an institutional apparatus—and of behavioral norms, certainties, automatic mechanisms—which replace individuals as subjects of free choice and indicate not only what they *must* do, but also what they must *not* do: "The principles consist mainly in what we are *not* to do."[74] They free us from excessive freedom of action. Freedom, in short, springs from the same necessity that holds it in check, and which only in this fashion makes it compensatorily possible.

Gehlen's entire discourse is inclined toward this heteronomous tendency. This is confirmed by its horizon of political theology, in which he sees the genesis of the process of institutionalization in a secularized form that both surpasses and maintains it: "Institutions were in every sense, originally transcendences of this world."[75] This is the set of rites, rituals, and religious practices to which human beings assigned the role of compensating for the pain and injuries arising from events they experienced in their lives that were not otherwise controllable. This is the classic reflective mechanism of totemism, which in its archetypal form inaugurates the negative dialectic of incorporation of the other later adopted affirmatively—that is, in a *doubly negative* mode—by philosophical anthropology: "Identifying himself with a non-I [*Nicht-Ich*], the individual comes by way of contrast to a sense of self which he can hold firm in the more or less permanent *representation* [*Darstellung*] of another being."[76] What the juridical, political institution inherited from its ritual predecessor is exactly this kind of negative self-identification, which individuals accomplish by recognizing themselves in the common otherness of that which represents them, not because it corresponds to them, but because it stands literally "in their place" by exonerating them from the weight of an otherwise unbearable subjectivity. Just as the eyes of ritual imitation converge on the same empty spot that eludes the gaze the moment it is brought into view, so the institution associates those who recognize themselves in it through the sharing of the same alienation. Human beings are united in institutions by their alienation; they are immunized against what they have in common. Gehlen perfectly expresses this compensatory node, aimed at the preservation of life, which makes immunization our only common behavior, and the common the very object of immunization: "we see no other task for a human community, for a people, other than to preserve its own existence."[77]

The intrinsically aporetic character of this type of conclusion is all the more evident as Gehlen strives to neutralize it by the strict geometry of his own reasoning processes. This contradiction is confirmed by the final direction his later works seem to take, no longer oriented exclusively to the diagnosis and treatment of our time but also to its prognosis, now crystallized in the appearance of an eternal present. This is what Gehlen means by the term *posthistoire*, alluding to a sort of definitive stabilization of the processes of compensation that characterize late-modernist societies. The complete institutionalization of life in forms of conservative reproduction seem to create a perfect balance between environment and system, instincts and norms, onus and exoneration. And yet in achieving that equilibrium, Gehlen recognizes a number of countereffects destined to shake its very foundations. This is what he calls processes of "primitivization" or "reinstinctivization," meaning a kind of artificial return to nature caused by the excess of subjectivity freed up by technological progress. No longer subject to compulsory manual labor and its powerful inhibitory restraints, human beings are increasingly exposed to an abnormal growth of their psyche, their inner world, while the reality principle is proportionally stunted in its growth. Subjected to the erosive forces of this subjective hypertrophy, institutions are first weakened and then overwhelmed by a flood of demands with which they are unable to cope. No longer objectively mediated by the established order, the more all spheres of life appear protected by an artifice that by now is a new nature, the more they risk exploding. Gehlen juxtaposes this subjective drift on the one hand with an attitude of asceticism toward individual consumption, and on the other with a reinforcement of institutional barriers. But if the first request is simply ineffectual, the second is actually self-contradictory since, as we have seen, the multiplication of institutions is what produces their entropy. Nothing is more institutional today than the crisis of institutions, which Gehlen not unsurprisingly defines as those "great fatalities that preserve while devouring,"[78] in the sense that it is the irresistible tendency toward overdetermination that counterfactually gives rise to renewed indeterminacy, just as the reinforcement of norms creates increasing abnormality.

What is described here, in all its destructive and self-destructive power, is an immune mechanism that has gotten out of hand because of the continuous strengthening of its core. Because the onus is a product of our own creation, as the exoneration is generalized, it creates yet another, heavier burden: "If man overly exonerates himself from the seriousness of reality, from necessity, from the 'negative' as Hegel called it, then all this unfurls with no further restraints."[79] What threatens to catastrophically break down is precisely the immune apparatus that turns the negative into a positive, since at this point it identifies with the negative precisely in order to absorb it dialectically: like a machine that has to produce more and more order, it loses contact with the disorder that establishes its confines and provides its material, eventually becoming prey to it; or like a homeopathic treatment that has grown beyond the organism's threshold of tolerance, thus winding up destroying it. Once again, in battling against itself in the attempt to immunize itself from its own effect, immunity slips into the vortex of infinite duplication.

*

As we know, Gehlen's theory has received countless objections from contemporary critics—but directed primarily at his conservative conclusions rather than at the philosophical premises on which it rests. One exception to this ideological bent is the essay by Heinrich Popitz, *Der Aufbruch zur artifiziellen Gesellschaft*.[80] What Popitz criticizes at its roots is neither the overall tone nor the institutionalistic point of arrival of Gehlen's philosophical anthropology, but rather, the compensatory paradigm that animated it from the outset. After having traced its matrix back to Plato's *Protagoras*—and more precisely in the balanced distribution of strengths and weaknesses bestowed on living beings first by Epimetheus and then by Prometheus (*Protagoras*, 320d–322d)—Popitz identifies the effect of this compensatory mechanism in the dialectical relationship established by Gehlen between organic deficiency and survival of the human animal. The overcoming of this natural deficiency, accomplished by technical artifice, by substituting or relieving bodily organs, is what immunizes the human species from environmental hazards that it would otherwise be unable to withstand. Popitz's critique focuses on the negative character—and indeed doubly negative, the negation of a negation—of the relation that is thus established between technical invention and the organic apparatus: contrary to Gehlen's view, "technique does not compensate for organic deficiency but instead exploits a specific organic capacity."[81] The role of artifice is not to substitute or exonerate, but rather to reinforce the effort already implicit in man's organic makeup. The relationship between natural organs and artificial objects is not one of negation but rather enhancement: there is no solution of continuity between them, only mutual reinforcement. The surest evidence of this functional contiguity is provided by the human hand—certainly enhanced by the use of tools, but in a manner that is determined originally by the hand itself. At this point Popitz dwells on the countless physiological capacities of the hand with respect to a series of actions that involve the entire range of human experience: it can feel, hold, mold, hit, throw, but also caress, finger, extend, give. In a word, it enables that opening to the world that Gehlen had attributed to technical action: "The fact that man could leave the habitat where he was born is the work of his hands not his feet. The *power of transformation* of the hands is at the same time the *force of opening to the world*."[82]

Is this line of reasoning convincing? Yes and no, I would say. Yes, to the extent that he unhesitatingly identifies the point that holds philosophical anthropology blocked in an immunitary orbit, and which actually makes immunization its guiding principle. No, because it seeks to combat it on the same anthropological horizon— adding a more humanistic emphasis that is missing in Gehlen's lexicon. The first sign of this is the emphasis given to the discussion on the hand, immediately confirmed by the allusion to Aristotle's classic formulation that serves as a normative reference: "The point," as Popitz sums up Aristotle's perspective (*De partibus animalium*, IV), "is that man has the best organs because he is the rational animal. In fact, nature assigns every instrument to the being who can make the best use of it."[83] There is no need to emphasize the apologetic, and even rhetorical, character of the connection that a long tradition has established between the "thinking" character of the hand and the destiny of "master of the universe" assigned to its only bearer. Suffice to note, we owe the statement that man has no hands, even if the hand constitutes his essential character, precisely to the harshest critic of humanistic metaphysics.[84] The basic problem, of course, lies in the definition of this essence in relation to what has been defined as technique. What is the relationship between the two? And are they really two distinct "things"? Anthropology has always responded affirmatively to this second question—otherwise, if there was no "human nature" as such, what meaning could we give to a "human science"? But in this way, technique—whether its contribution to the human endowment of organs is viewed positively or negatively—necessarily takes a secondary, supplementary character.

From this point of view, while Popitz reverses Gehlen's perspective, he still remains within the same conceptual lexicon: even though technical action enhances rather than replaces the organ, it is nonetheless an external postposition to it. Unless we recognize—as Bernard Stiegler suggests[85]—the essence of human nature precisely in the expropriating character of technique. If this were the case, obviously, if man's *physis* was one with his *logos*, then the question of the relationship between man and technology would not even be posed to begin with. The question to be posed instead would be about man's originary techno-logicality. But at this point, the language of anthropology—or paleontology—would slide directly into the language of ontology, and the problem of *immunitas* would be no different from that of *communitas*.

IV

Biopolitics

1. Incorporations

It is all too evident that politics enters fully into the immune paradigm the moment life becomes the immediate content of its action. When this occurs, all formal mediation disappears: the object of politics is no longer a "life form," its own specific way of being, but rather, life itself—all life and only life, in its mere biological reality. Whether an individual life or the life of the species is involved, life itself is what politics is called upon to make safe, precisely by immunizing it from the dangers of extinction threatening it. When "biopolitics" is talked about as a form of politics in which the existence and very possibility of the living being is at stake, this radical reduction in meaning is what points to the original, most general sense of the term. And yet, this approach only brings into view one facet of the matter, its most obvious. To infuse it with greater significance, it needs to be examined from another angle as well, focusing not just on the object of biopolitics, but also on the way that object is grasped: to be able to save life from its tendency toward self-dissolution, politics has to lead life back to the realm of the body. What appeared to be a relation between two terms, politics and life, must instead be interpreted as a more complex game that includes a third term upon which it depends: the bodily dimension is where life lends itself to being preserved as such by political immunization.

After all, in order to be conceived in the first place, life needs some type of organic representation binding it to reality, or at least the potential of a bodily structure. When looked at from the point of view of its protection from a danger that imperils it, whether endogenous or exogenous, the need for life to be included within the confines of the body is all the more pressing. Bodily confines are exactly what act as lines of defense against whatever threatens to take life away from itself, expel it to its outside, or reverse it into its opposite. It is in the body and only in the body that life can remain what it is and even grow, be strengthened, and reproduce. Of course, this works equally both ways: if the body is the privileged locus for the unfolding of life, it is also the place where the presence of death is most noticeable; and even before that, the effects of illness, aging, and deterioration. But this constitutive binarism—life and death, growth and decay—is precisely what makes the body the liminal zone where the immunitary intention of politics is carried out: namely, to delay the passage from life to death as long as possible, to drive death to the farthest point from the presentness of life. The body is both the instrument and terrain of this battle. As long as it holds out, there will be no death. When death arrives on the scene, the body is what vanishes: not only its physiological activity, but also, shortly thereafter, its very material substance, doomed to rapid decomposition. The fact is, death and the body do not go together for very long. Their encounter is only momentary: once dead, the body does not endure. To be a body, it must keep itself alive. It is the frontline, both symbolic and material, in life's battle against death.

This explains why it has been by far the most influential metaphor used in political discourse to represent life in society. Even a rough outline of the complex history of the analogy between the body natural and the body politic (touched on in the second chapter) is out of the question in this context. However, we may recall that for centuries it was the most common figural *topos* through which political authorities and men of letters represented the constitution and functioning of the body political. Each part was compared to an organ of the human body, with all the normative consequences that a correspondence of this sort naturally gave rise to, both in terms of the ensuing hierarchy that was established between the king/head and subjects/limbs, and between the different estates and orders of the kingdom. This point, which has received a great deal of scholarly attention, is not my focus here. My interest lies instead in the immunitary character that the metaphor of the body politic lends to the modern political lexicon as a whole. True, this would seem to be belied by the chronological limit that has been set to its development around the mid-seventeenth century, beyond which it seems to fade out in favor of the mechanistic and individualistic paradigm established by Hobbes.[1] But even apart from the essential lack of distinction between organicism and mechanism that persisted at least until the eighteenth century—to which we owe the extensive contamination between body and machine culminating in Hobbes's reference to "the artificial animal"[2]—it is clear that the metaphor did not disappear at all, but simply adapted to the changed historical and conceptual context.

Indeed, it can be argued that the gradual predominance of mechanistic metaphysics and the individualistic model was precisely what signaled a growth in the immune-oriented significance of the State-body analogy. The key to this step lay in the increasing complexity of the relation between life and body politic. The naturalness of the relation began to fade when the body politic was subjected to increasingly violent environmental pressures: uprisings, wars, revolutions. But this intractability was exactly what made the relationship between life and body politic even more necessary: precisely because the life of the body politic was constitutively fragile, it needed to be preventively protected from what threatened it. Nobody grasped the mortal precariousness of the body politic better than Hobbes, who no longer ascribed it to the natural decay of all forms of government envisaged by the traditional Polybian model, but rather to the destructive powers [*potenze*] latent in its organism.[3] But this fact—that death was not natural so much as induced, and as such, avoidable or at least deferrable—was precisely what made an immune strategy of containment indispensable for Hobbes:

> Though nothing can be immortal which mortals make; yet, if men
> had the use of reason they pretend to, their Commonwealths might

be secured, at least, from perishing by internal diseases. For by the nature of their institution, they are designed to live as long as mankind, or as the laws of nature, or as justice itself, which gives them life. Therefore when they come to be dissolved, not by external violence, but intestine disorder, the fault is not in men as they are the *matter*, but as they are the *makers* and orderers of them.[4]

If the causes that expose the body politic to the catastrophic possibility of its dissolution are attributable to human error rather than being natural, they can be tackled through a type of order that takes the impending risks into account beforehand. Following this line of reasoning, the machine lexicon is adopted by Hobbes not to oppose the body lexicon, but to supplement it. The machine metaphor is meant to strengthen the precarious connection between life and body, like a sort of metal skeleton designed to keep the body alive beyond its natural capacity. This does not mean eliminating the possibility of death: on the contrary, death is meant to be kept in mind at all times to avoid being taken by surprise. Nor does it mean indefinitely postponing the death of each of the individuals who together make up the body of the State, depicted in the famous frontispiece of the first edition of *Leviathan*. The idea rather is to establish a functional relationship between the inevitable deaths of the individuals and the duration of the artificial body of the State, ensured by the ununinterrupted continuity of sovereign power: "Of all these forms of government, the matter being mortal, so that not only monarchs, but also whole assemblies die, it is necessary for the conservation of the peace of men that as there was order taken for an artificial man, so there be order also taken for an artificial eternity of life."[5] That this life is artificial—like the "great Leviathan" in which it inheres—is the most unmistakeable sign that a body has been immunized rather than replaced: not only does it survive the death of its members, it even periodically derives its reproductive energy from them, like an organism first nourished with the life of all the parts that compose it and then additionally with their death. Or like a body capable of incorporating its own discorporation, exactly like what happens to the organismic metaphor with respect to its own artificial counterpart. The body-machine, the machine-body, is a body that can no longer be undone, because it is already undone and rebuilt, as if embalmed, in its bodily armor. As a body that is permanently such as it is—because it has no gaps, no openings, no wounds—it is entirely coincident with itself and therefore everlasting: all body, one body, forever body. And because it is accustomed to living with the death that lives inside it, this is a body that does not die—at least until death is roused one day with so many lethal effects that it explodes into a thousand pieces.

The fact that contractualist language far from dismisses the metaphor of the body politic, moreover, can be illustrated even more effectively in Rousseau, who, after having declared it to be "inaccurate" in the *Discourse on Political Economy*,[6] in the *Social Contract* then goes on to reinstate it in all its salvific powers:

> "Each of us puts his person and all his power in common under the supreme direction of the general will, and, in our corporate capacity, we receive each member as an indivisible part of the whole." At once, in place of the individual personality of each contracting party, this act of association creates a moral and collective body, composed of as many members as the assembly contains votes, and receiving from this act its unity, its common identity, its life and its will.[7]

What we have here is a double incorporation, a reciprocal cross-incorporation, between the body of each individual and the collective body, derived from the incorporation of each individual body into a common body. But for this to happen, each individual body must have incorporated each of its parts, beforehand, as a member of a single body. The middle term in this passage from body to body or doubling of the body lies of course in the concept of "general will," which founds and at the same time deconstructs the individualistic logic of the contract when it assumes incorporation as a premise that should be its outcome and yet is instead its precondition. This is because, unlike the Hobbesian model, the immune mechanism of this body politic has no need of artificial support; it is, so to speak, inside the same corporeal (meaning, intrinsically unitary) constitution of the body: "As soon as this multitude is so united in one body, it is impossible to offend against one of the members without attacking the body, and still more to offend against the body without the members resenting it."[8] From this point of view, the ancient hierarchy between the different parts of the body, and between the corresponding organs of the State, ceases to be meaningful, because what makes it so is the correspondence between the subject and object of the sovereign function inherent to a body without a head, or to a head extending over the entire surface of the body.

This reinstatement of the head within the body politic is the strategic move that allowed the ancient metaphor to survive and even regenerate itself from its apparent demise, during and after the revolution, when the royal beheading should have done away with its semantic force forever. The reason it did not is because, even before falling, the head had been dissolved as such and incorporated into the collective body of the nation. By then, through the representation of the National Assembly, it had become the new subject of the analogy, now transposed from the ancient king's body to that of the citizens united together in a single population. When Emmanuel Joseph Sieyès's texts are read from this perspective, not only is it clear that the metaphor of the body stubbornly remains the centerpiece of his argument, it actually acts as the rhetorical and figurative go-between through which the revolutionary rupture, far from putting the life of the nation into danger, is actually portrayed as necessary to it. If revolution is viewed as the nation's only possible salvation, the reason is because it does not split the body into parts, but rather regroups it, contrary to the divisive threat represented by the ancient privileges. This body—in seeking to be such: namely, the principle and safeguard of the nation's life—can only be one. Hence, it cannot host any other privileged body inside itself, as is stated in no uncertain terms at the end of "What is the Third Estate?"

> In the end it is not worth asking what kind of place there should be for the privileged classes in the social order. It is like asking what kind of place a malignant tumor should have in the body of someone who is ill, as it devours and ruins his health. It is essential to restore every organ to health and activity so that any malign combination able to vitiate the most essential principles of life can no longer occur.[9]

What most stands out in this passage is not only the thorough overlapping between the political lexicon and the medical lexicon, once again connoted by the metaphor of the body, but also the immunitary consequence that directly follows from it: in order for the body to heal permanently, the power of the illness afflicting it must be leveraged, and, precisely for this reason, drastically eliminated. Only if it is assumed in all its negativity can it be fought through and through. On these lines Sieyès can claim that healing takes place through an excess of disease, and that only when the disease is taken to its extreme pathogenic consequences does regeneration become possible: because in reality it is essential to the process. The concept of "regeneration" is said to have taken on a specifically political meaning in addition to its medical and religious ones only after its negative antonym, the concept of "degeneration," had been firmly established.[10] But what we have here is not a simple chronological antecedence: as is implicit in the turn taken by the immune metaphor of the body politic, there can be no regeneration that does not begin from, and within, a prior degeneration. After all, what would health be without the nuisance of illness?

*

How can we explain this irresistible tendency of political philosophy (and political practice) to incorporate social plurality? What is the source of this veritable repetition compulsion that drives it to continuously incorporate what so doggedly resists it? Jacob Rogozinski traces its origin back to the dialectical backlash engendered through opposition from the phantasmic methods adopted by this resistance; whence the oscillating movement between a drive toward incorporation and a symmetrically opposed drive toward "discorporation."[11] To understand this explanation, we have to go back to the phenomenological horizon that constitutes its premise and conceptual framework: to be specific, to the theme of *carne* (flesh), specifically in the version provided by Husserl and later by Merleau-Ponty. For both, albeit stressing different aspects, the semantics of the flesh (German *Leib*, French *chair*) do not coincide with those of the body (German *Körper*, French *corps*) to which it is nevertheless linked by a close relation of

implication. Whether involving a singular experience or potentially plural one—such as what Merleau-Ponty referred to with
the terms "flesh of the world" or "flesh of history"—the process
of mutual incorporation of two members of the same body or
between several different bodies can never be fully achieved
because it is interrupted by an original difference which the author
calls "carnal difference" [*difference charnelle*]. This impossibility
of essential co-belonging, or simultaneous co-givenness, which
suspends the chiasm between the hand that touches and the hand
that is touched, has the effect of undoing any possible identification between flesh and body. There is something about the
flesh, like a hiatus or an original break, that resists incorporation,
reversing it into the opposing movement of disincorporation. But,
as we were saying, this stubborn resistance of the flesh to being
made body cannot come about without aporetic consequences. It
generates a series of phantasmic figures of laceration and disloca-
tion that return to the flesh, threatening to drive it back into a
place of absence resembling a true disembodiment: as if the crisis
of the chiasm—affecting the body proper or the body of others—
gives rise to a non-flesh within the flesh, an abject object, destined
to suck it into a deadly maelstrom or prompt it to self-expulsion.
It is at this point that the phantasm of necrotic decomposition—
ensuing from the imaginary intensification of the distance toward
the body—by contrast produces a new and stronger process
of incorporation. This prohibits the obsessive fantasies of strip-
ping the flesh, recomposing the scattered fragments into a
new identificatory synthesis, until it, too, is dismantled in its turn
and its demand for fusion is negated by the irreducible carnal
difference.

The most important instances of political self-interpretation in
the modern era can be traced back to this reading grid. From this
point of view, despite their liberating capacity, the return to the
organismic metaphor of Rousseau and Marxist opposition to the
alienation of the social body created by capital actually represent
a counter-reaction to the modern processes of individualistic disincorporation. This does not mean that political thought oriented
to the celebration of the individual is able to represent instances
of the flesh free from totalizing hypostases. Indeed, the self-cen-
tering concept of the individual is itself born from a corporeal

hypostasis that overlaps onto the pluralistic character of carnal existence. Moreover, it is precisely the incapacity of the concept of the individual to grasp the unquenchable need for social bonding that produces the totalitarian reaction, in which the will to incorporation and the phantasm of stripped flesh are redoubled in the most catastrophically destructive way. The collapse of totalitarian regimes, however, brings this seemingly inexhaustible dialectic of discorporation and re-incorporation to a point of no return beyond which a new horizon of meaning opens up. What finally comes into view is the possibility of bringing to the surface that "primal flesh" no philosophy has yet been able to name, except by negatively deducing it from the element that negated it. When this happens, out of the final dismemberment of the body politic and its organismic metaphors, instead of the neurotic obsession for new incorporations there will emerge the silhouette of a "flesh that rebels against the One, always already divided, polarized into the Two of the chiasm, but such as to ignore all hierarchies, all irreversible separations between one part that controls and the other that obeys."[12]

Although this perspective is highly intriguing, the conclusion leaves some question marks. Without going into the more technical issue—which, I believe, remains to be resolved—regarding the political-historical translatability of transcendental categories (at least as far as Husserl is concerned, but also in part for Merleau-Ponty), I have some reservations about the interpretation of "primordial flesh." How are we to understand "primordial"? As an original background, covered and disfigured by the dynamics we have described, and which can therefore only come into view when it has been exhausted? Or as something that same dynamic brings inside as its own antinomic opposite? Are we to understand it as an ontological alternative that opposes the hegemony of the body from the outside—or the void inside which inhabits it and exposes it to its otherness? More pointedly: is there another flesh beyond the body, or is this not the locus of its constitutive non-belonging—the differential limit that separates it from itself by opening it up to its outside? I think that Rogozinski vacillates between these two hermeneutic possibilities without opting for one or the other; I think that this indecision should be attributed to the utopian and even slightly eschatological tone that transpires

from the sentence quoted above. There is no doubt that the category of "body" no longer responds to questions posed by a world
with no internal borders; and therefore it should be deconstructed
through a different lexicon, one in which "flesh" is the most
meaningful term.[3] This must be done without losing sight of their
connection, however, and also acknowledging the fact that we are
talking about *the same thing*. Flesh is nothing but the unitary
weave of the difference between bodies. It is the non-belonging,
or rather the intra-belonging, that allows what is different to not
hermetically seal itself up within itself, but rather, to remain in
contact with its outside. What we are talking about is not just an
externalization of the body, but also the internal cleavage that
prevents its absolute immanence. To fully grasp the meaning of
the flesh requires that we be capable of simultaneously conceiving
the outside and the inside of the body: one in the other and one
for the other. It is the internal threshold that everts the inverted;
and which therefore makes the individual body no longer such.
No longer exclusively proper (which, in the end, makes the translation of *Leib* as "the body proper" untenable),[14] it is at the same
time "improper," as Didier Franck also words it: "The flesh as
originally proper and the origin of the proper is originally improper
and the origin of the improper."[15] But if the flesh is the expropriation of the proper, then it is also what makes the proper common.
This is why both Husserl and Heidegger, in a different way, associate it from the outset with the semantics of givenness: "*Bodily
presence is a superlative mode of the self-givenness of an entity
[Leibhaftigkeit ist ein ausgezeichneter Modus der Selbstgegeben-
heit eines Seienden]*" (italics in original).[16] The originary relationship between the figure of the flesh and that of the *munus* suddenly
leaps out at us. The flesh is neither another body nor the body's
other: it is simply the way of being in common of that which seeks
to be immune.

2. The *pharmakon*

If the organological metaphor is at the heart of political treatises,
at the heart of the metaphor lies disease. True, the point of intersection between political knowledge and medical knowledge is the

common problem of preserving the body. But this preservation takes on a central role precisely from the perspective opened up by disease. Of course, logically speaking, the physiological, or morphological, determination of the body precedes its pathology. But, in point of fact, its physiology and morphology derive their meaning from the layout of the pathological condition: what is healthy is only defined through contrast by the "decision" about what is diseased—the origin, development, and outcome of the illness. If, for example, the ultimate evil is identified in the threat of insurrections and rioting, the health of the State will be viewed as residing in an order guaranteed by the control of the head over the other parts of the body. If, on the contrary, what we fear instead is the tyranny of a despotic ruler, the salvation of the body politic will be located in a balanced equilibrium between its different members.

So far, however, we have remained with the traditional sources that seem to resurface essentially unchanged throughout the centuries, from classical and Christian antiquity to the Renaissance and Modernity, along a line that arrives at the organismic sociology of Auguste Comte, Herbert Spencer, and Emile Durkheim. In reality, if we follow this approach we end up losing sight of those very steps, or epistemological leaps, that imbue the metaphor with a specifically immune tonality. It is undeniable that even the simple figurative superimposition of the biomedical on top of the legal-political language in the representation of the body implicitly points to the question of its immunity. But for it to acquire a more specific connotation, the advent of two changes in the metaphor of the body were required, initially regarding the location of the disease and, subsequently, its relation to health. As for the first question, the two causes of decay and subsequent collapse of the body politic were traditionally attributed first to natural aging—in accord with the ancient Polybian principle that all living entities necessarily decline—and second, to a violent shock due to a civil war or coup d'état. In both cases, therefore, disease was endogenous, generated from within the body politic, and could be addressed by treatment methods aimed at gently restoring the shattered equilibrium, or surgically, by cutting out the diseased part.[17] It is precisely this topological order that gradually, but more and more clearly, came to show cracks at the beginning of the modern period, in association with intensified interstate conflict and the transformation of medical knowledge. There remains, of course, the classic pairing of disease with discord, with all its retinue of signs, symptoms, and remedies, but whose center of gravity faced outward more than inward. The pathogenic matrix of the disease that attacked the body politic—whether a foreign invasion or civil war—lay outside the body, and the pathogen was transmitted through the infiltration of a contagious element that was not engendered by the body.

It may be useful to recall that, in conjunction with the increasingly catastrophic spread of major epidemics—especially syphilis and the plague—between 1536 and 1546, Girolamo Fracastoro published his two treatises *Syphilis sive Morbus Gallicus* and *De Contagione et Contagiosis Morbis*. For the first time, the traditional Galenic humoral theory was flanked and then opposed by the theory that disease is communicated through contamination caused by the body's intake of tiny infectious agents *(semina)* of an exogenous nature, and therefore by means of a mechanism structurally different from the endogenous processes involved with the putrefaction of bodies. During this same phase—of course, without any direct connection, but within a common horizon of meaning—in political treatises as well attention shifted from the overall state of health of the body politic, to preventive prophylactic measures to keep it safe from the infiltration of allogenous elements. Hence the need, increasingly emphasized, for immunitary barriers, protection and apparatuses aimed at reducing, if not eliminating, the porosity of external borders to contaminating toxic germs. How much actual or threatened invasions contributed to this obsession with self-protection, such as the Spanish one in England, or even contact with unfamiliar cultures and ethnicities such as the Native American, not to mention the growing Jewish immigration to Western Europe, is not difficult to imagine: the greater the vulnerability of the body politic must have appeared, the more urgent the need became to hermetically seal the orifices that had opened up in its frontiers. The images of besieged cities, fortified castles, and territories surrounded by potential invaders that filled the pages of English, French, and Italian political treatises between the sixteenth and seventeenth centuries offer tangible evidence of this point.

But even more important than the external origin of the pathogenic germ—in keeping with the immunitary character of the
bodily metaphor—is the dialectical function assumed by the
disease in relation to the therapy intended to treat it. While an
entirely negative portrayal of illness, understood as the absolute
opposite of health, predominated until a given time, at a certain
stage—pinpointed to the second half of the sixteenth century—an
appreciable change occurred in the semantics. Of course, illness
continued to be mentioned as the cause that weakens the body
politic to the point of endangering its life. But this did not exhaust
its function, which gradually even assumed a positive value. To
begin with, disease is seen as strengthening or even creating the
diseased organism's self-defense through opposition. From this
point of view, we should not underestimate the indirect influence
of Machiavelli's conception of the political productivity of social
conflicts.[18] But political treatises from the sixteenth and seventeenth centuries draw another, more sinister teaching from Machiavelli as well, according to which political power can use insurrections and tumults to legitimize and strengthen its repressive
apparatus, or even use its art to create them, by infiltrating potentially subversive groups with government agents, for example.
Nothing reinforces the host body politic better than an ill that has
been dominated and turned against itself.[19]

But this is only one axis of the immune character assumed by
the metaphor, which is doubled when the dialectic function—
neither purely negative nor purely positive, but rather one in the
other and one arising from the other—transmigrates from the
political sphere of conflict into the same interpretation of disease
and its treatment. To fully elucidate this latest twist, Jonathan
Harris brings up the figure of Paracelsus and the epistemic break
that he makes with the Galenic medical paradigm (leaving aside
his unresolved relation with the tradition of medieval magic and
alchemy).[20] While Fracastoro still places his theory of infectious
semina within the framework of the classical conception of the
humors, Lucretian atomism, and the Hippocratic miasma theory,
Paracelsus, on the other hand, without breaking with the Neopla-
tonic assumption of the microcosm-macrocosm analogy, introduces a new perspective based on chemical principles. As we were
saying, this is not only because it situates the origin of disease

outside the body—transmitted contagiously into the openings of the body through the penetration of mineral or gaseous elements—but because he interprets it explicitly in ontological terms: disease is no longer the simple effect of a disruption to the overall balance of the body, but a separate entity located in a determined part of the body. What resulted from this new localistic approach to diagnosis—the overall condition of the body is not what causes the disease, but rather, the converse—was also a drastic transformation of the treatment. For traditional medicine to heal the body's imbalance from the lack or excess of one of the four humors of the body meant to add or subtract what was missing or in excess, in accord with a compensatory type of logic. Paracelsus initiated an approach that was diametrically opposed: what heals is not the allopathic principle of the contrary, but rather the homeopathic principle of the similar.[21] Contrary to the Galenic assumption that "*contraria a contrariis curantur*," that heat cures cold and vice versa, he asserted the isopathic rule that "like cures like":

> You should be able to recognize diseases according to their anatomy, for it is in its anatomy that the remedy is identical with the agent that caused the disease. Hence a scorpion cures scorpion poisoning, because it has the same anatomy; [thus to the anatomy of the outer man corresponds that of the inner man, the one thing always corresponds to the other.] Arsenic cures arsenic poisoning, the heart the heart, the lungs the lungs, the spleen the spleen; not ox spleen, nor is the brain of a pig any good for the brain of man, but that which corresponds to the brain in the outside world can cure the human brain.[22]

Even in the highly imaginative lexicon of astral correspondences, we come closer the heart of the matter: if the cure against a poison is poison, then disease and health no longer lie along the axis of a frontal opposition, but in a dialectical relationship that naturally makes one the opposite of the other, but also and above all, the instrument of the other. Along these lines, Paracelsus can say that "every single thing is double. Where there is disease, there is medicine, where there is medicine, there is sickness,"[23] since "at any one time, a medicine is often a poison and often a drug for a disease."[24] The way to remedy a disease is by administering it in forms and doses capable of bringing about permanent immunization. Of course, Paracelsus does not express himself in these terms, but the entire tenor of his iatrochemical medicine goes exactly in this direction.

True, the philosophical principle that associates a disease with its remedy has a long history rooted in the classical world, continued through Montaigne, Shakespeare, and Rousseau, by which providence has placed "salutary simples beside noxious plants, and [made] poisonous animals contain their own antidote."[25] But up until a certain moment it remained essentially a literary motif: the fire extinguished by another fire (Tertullian, *De pudicitia*, 1.16), the wound healed by the same hand that inflicted it (Ovid, *Remedia amoris*, 43–48), the spear that heals the gash it opened up (Macedonius, *Greek Anthology*, 5.225). In Paracelsus's etiology it becomes not only a hermeneutical principle, but also a principle of active intervention in the face of disease: what Paracelsus advanced, far ahead of the microbiological theories of the nineteenth century, is none other than therapeutic inoculation using a portion of the same poison from which one seeks to be protected. This is exactly the same prescription that the political treatises of the Tudor and Stuart period absorbed and translated through a bodily metaphor now very distant from its canonical formulation, one that was capable of giving expression to a profound change in the discursive order.

If read in chronological order, the most important political texts of the period constructed around the State-body analogy—*A Mervailous Combat of Contrareties* (1588) by William Averell, *A Comparative Discourse of the Bodies Naturall and Politique* (1606) by Edward Forset, and *The Whore of Babylon* (1606) by Thomas Dekker—provide a sort of diagram of the era's growing immunitary bent. Beyond their marked ideological differences, what unifies these texts is the proto-functional principle that all parts of the body, including toxic germs that come to infect it from the outside, when looked at a little farther away, ultimately contribute to the body's health and safety. Unlike the old concept of the body as a structure differentiated according to a clear hierarchy between its members—still active in the *Dialogue Between Reginald Pole and Thomas Lupset* (1535) by Thomas Starkey, for example—what we have now is its representation as an integrated system of functions, in which even the potentially destructive elements can be used productively to strengthen the whole of which they are a part. For this reason, enemy infiltrators—Catholic or Jewish—are depicted as purgative medicines designed to promote healthy expulsion, or even as a poison necessary for the preventive vaccination of the body. Just as governments often make legitimate use of agents provocateurs or encourage sedition to ferret out potential conspirators, disease can also produce good and therefore be artificially reproduced for this purpose, at least if there is someone who is able "to make even poysons medicinable" as Forset expresses it.[26] The result is a true dialectical exchange between a good that comes from an evil and an evil that is transformed into good, in a sort of progressive indistinctiveness comparable to the structurally double-edged character of the Platonic *pharmakon* (but also of the Latin *medicamentum* or High-German and Anglo-Saxon *Gift*).

As Derrida has argued in a form that reinstates the logic and semantics of the immune lexicon, the *pharmakon* is what is opposed to its other not by excluding it, but, on the contrary, by incorporating and vicariously substituting it.[27] The other resists the *pharmakon* by imitating it, and confronts it by obeying it, like the ancient *katechon* in the face of anomy. The *pharmakon* is both the evil and what opposes it by bowing to its logic. It is itself to the extent it is other, and it is other to the extent it is itself; the point at which one passes away into two while remaining one; the one-two that is neither one nor two, yet both, overlapping across their line of opposition. This difference remains ungraspable by any identity, including the contradictory one of the *coincidentia oppositorum*. Disease and antidote, poison and cure, potion and counter-potion: the *pharmakon* is not a substance but rather a non-substance, a non-identity, a non-essence. But above all, it is something that relates to life from the ground of its reverse. More than affirming life, it negates its negation, and in the process ends up doubling it: "*Morte mortuos liberavit*" (*De doctrina christiana*, 1.14.13), wrote Augustine in an expression that contained the nucleus of the modern *pharmacy*. The secret movement of the *pharmakon* is thus revealed: it is a gentle power that draws death into contact with life and exposes life to the test of death.

3. *Zellenstaat*

Before we can make out this dialectic at the nerve center of contemporary biopolitics, we need to focus our attention on one further metamorphosis of the organismic metaphor. We have discussed the semantic turn it took during the eighteenth century at the same time the concepts of machine and body, which had remained closely linked until then, became autonomous. As a result of this divergence, and fostered by the new Romantic climate, an opposite reaction arose starting from the early nineteenth century. It was precisely at this point that the legal and political treatises began once again to speak the language of the body, regardless of their different ideological bents, from conservative to radical, and even revolutionary. This occurred in England and France, but especially in Germany, where the works of Karl Salomo Zachariä, Johann Caspar Bluntschli, and Lorenz Stein are the best known of many that reworked the theme of the *Staatsorganismus*. Once again, the categories used by political theory to think about the form of the State organism and its internal organization were borrowed from the life sciences, especially from medicine. Just as the philosophies of the time tended to absorb images and conceptual terms from the embryological conceptions of preformism and epigenesis, similarly, administrative and economic doctrines came to represent themselves modeled on the physiological systems of the circulation of the blood. It was a seamless transfer from the natural sciences to what were known as the sciences of the spirit, a process that continued throughout the course of the century and beyond, shaping a plethora of important works including those by Friedrich Trendelenburg, Herbert Spencer, Wilhelm Dilthey, Friedrich Nietzsche, Max Scheler, and Georg Simmel.[28]

But what is even more relevant to our discussion is the opposite transfer that took place over the same years: not the influence of biological and natural sciences on sociopolitical thought that we have examined until now, but the reverse tendency: to import suggestions from the legal and political lexicon into the analytical framework of biomedical knowledge. This always took place within the confines of the State-body analogy, but along a line that went from the State to the body instead of from the body to the

State. An example of this striking reversal between the sender and the recipient of the metaphor is already detectable in the Malthusian theory of population. This interpreted the natural sciences question of the species in sociopolitical terms, based on a process partly taken from Darwin through the theory of natural selection, which was obviously influenced in its turn by the Hobbesian *bellum omnium contra omnes*. Something similar can be said about how Adam Smith's concept of the division of labor was transposed from the field of zoology, conceived by Henri Milne-Edwards to explain the functional differences of animal organs.

However, the most emblematic case—because of the breadth and accuracy of the terms of comparison in this exchange of parts in the metaphoric process—can be found in the work of the great pathologist Rudolf Virchow in Berlin, best known as the greatest proponent of cell theory in the field of medicine. It was Virchow who was responsible for this linguistic and conceptual turn, allowing the simile between the State and body to be moved onto a whole new terrain. He did this by shifting the comparison from the parts of the body (the orders or classes of the absolutist State) or its totality (the people-nation of the later phase), to the individual elements composing it. As we know, the central premise of *Cellulartheorie*, which grew out of the work of Theodor Schwann in the late 1840s, is the thesis that the body is not an indivisible whole, but rather a set composed of elementary particles defined as cells. In them is contained the main driving force of life, namely, the function of nutrition and growth. This means that a body is not based on a single life force *(Lebenskraft)* aimed at specific ends, but on a multiplicity of discrete entities that interact with each other and mutually influence each other. Schwann built on the work of Matthias Jacob Schleiden by extending to animals the cellular structure that Schleiden had identified in plants,[29] but neither made use of the analogy between the body natural and the body politic. In both their works, it is true, cells are modeled as "individuals," each endowed with an independent vital principle. And it is also true that some steps in Schwann employ expressions with possible political origins, such as the "autocracy of the organism" *(Autokratie des Organismus)*.[30] But by no means is this accompanied by explicit use of the organismic metaphor. This was used at the end of the eighteenth century by Johann Christian Reil, from a perspective that highlighted the mutual autonomy of the individual parts of the body potentially affected by disease, but on a lexical horizon related to the concept of fiber rather than to that of the cell. François-Vincent Raspail also used a number of similarities when defining primary nuclei in plant and animal bodies, but he did not go so far as to represent them in terms of political assemblies.

The first to do so was undoubtedly Virchow. How much weight should be given to his intense participation in the Prussian democratic movement—which took him from the barricades of 1848 to a firm decision to oppose Bismarck during the years of constitutional conflict [*Verfassungskonflikt*]—is difficult to establish. Probably, as Renato Mazzolini observes in a wide-ranging, well-documented essay on the subject,[31] there was a sort of dialectical circuit between political position and scientific research which projected conceptual references from one sphere onto the other and vice versa. Georges Canguilhem, when discussing Ernst Haeckel, Virchow's student who radicalized the metaphorical device, goes so far as to argue that "a biological theory holds sway over a political philosophy. Who could tell whether one is a republican because one is a partisan of cell theory, or rather a partisan of cell theory because one is a republican?"[32] The fact remains that when the decisive moment came for Virchow to present his cell theory to the general public, he did not hesitate to use an analogy with social institutions:

> The characteristics and unity of life cannot be limited to any one particular spot in a highly developed organism (for example, to the brain of man), but are to be found only in the definite, constantly recurring structure, which every individual element displays. Hence it follows that the structural composition of a body of considerable size, a so-called individual, always represents a kind of social arrangement of parts, an arrangement of a social kind, in which a number of individual existences are mutually dependent, but in such a way, that every element has its own special action, and, even though it derive its stimulus to activity from other parts, yet alone effect the actual performance of its duties.[33]

This famous passage from *Cellularpathologie* seems to tie together all the different threads we have laid out thus far. First, it reproduces all the figurative traits of the body politic metaphor, and second, it reverses the meaning by removing it from the conservative semantics of the *Staatsorganismus*, sending it into an ideological orbit that turns in the opposite direction. But even more remarkable is the fact that this changeover of the metaphor is accomplished through the same analytical tools that led to its development during its classical phase. When Virchow argues against the perspective that assigns the brain the primary role as source and distributor of life over all other parts of the body, he is picking up again and embracing the "localist" and "territorial" position of Paracelsus versus the "generalist" approach of Galenic medicine. While an abyss certainly divides the scientific methodology of the Berlin physician from the magical-alchemical language of his distant predecessor, it is not so wide that Virchow feels no compunction about repeatedly referring to the doctrines of Paracelsus, or to those of his successor van Helmont, as well as to others coming later who argued for the autonomy of individual existences.[34] Virchow's two-pronged attack against hemopathology, which attributed diseases to a defect in the blood circulation as a whole, and against neuropathology, which attributed them to a disorder in the entire nervous system, should be interpreted in the same vein. The opposing thesis that he advances against both is that the cells are not just a substrate of the blood and nerves, but its constitutive components endowed with a specific identity. It is true that blood and nerves are the parts of the body most likely to affect the others, but this is not in the form of a hegemony of the center over the periphery; rather, it is a mutual dependence. Not only does each stimulus generate a local response that affects the body in its turn, the more its individual components behave independently with respect to each other, the more effectively the body is regulated. In short, there are no parts of the body in which life is concentrated more than any other because life, as such, resides in each individual cell.

This is simultaneously a point of continuity and rupture with the entire biopolitical horizon: life—its preservation and development—remains connected to the figure of the body, but multiplied by the number of elementary entities that compose it. It is as if a body contained infinite lives within it, or as if life distributed itself into each of the individual particles that "make" the body. If we absolutist & hierarchical = Heart & Brain.

recall the absolutist and hierarchical connotations that the primacy of the heart and brain gave to the organismic metaphor, the significance that Virchow's cellular theory has for the political paradigm from which he drew his inspiration is obvious:

> A historian is inclined to forget, secluded in his room, the living individuals that make up a State or a people. He speaks about the life of peoples, about the character of nations, as if a unitary power animated and pervaded every individual people, every individual nation, and he is easily persuaded to place the total action of the nation as a whole into the broader context of the history of mankind, without regard to the individual actions which make up that action. Yet every action consists in its instances, and the life of a people is nothing more than the sum of the lives of its individual citizens.[35]

divided & distributed

Virchow's *Zellenstaat* differs from Bismarckian theories of *Staatsorganismus* with respect to where life is situated: neither in the unitary power of the body nor in the point of command that unifies it, but rather, divided and distributed among the individual elements that form it. These do not constitute an organic whole, but a structured assembly, a complex of independent, intertwined relations that recall a "unity based on community and not a despotic or oligarchic unity as the humoral and solidist schools would have it,"[36] or even a "federal arrangement of the body" since "unity, not federation, is an axiom."[37]

This is an extremely important step for the establishment of the biopolitical language. It goes so far as to assume an explicitly communitarian connotation. This is because, in Virchow's formulation, the metaphor of the body politic seems to refer to a societal institution, or even to a community open to the constitutive difference of its members, rather than to a fully-fledged State. When Virchow argues against scientists who model their theories on a "monarchical principle of the body" or on the "aristocracy" and "hierarchy" of the blood and the nervous system, opposing them to a conception of the body whose members are "dependent on each other and connected by the solidarity of their mutual need,"[38] what he ultimately does is dismantle the very principle of sovereignty which the organismic metaphor had always employed as its vehicle. The body is neither an absolutist kingdom nor a nation unified by its general will, but rather a community constituted by the equal difference of all of its members. A few years after the publication of Virchow's *Cellularpathologie*, Claude Bernard, the greatest French physiologist of the century, again using the metaphor of the political city to describe the structure of the living body, remarks about its inhabitants that "everyone has their own craft, work, attitude and talent through which they participate in the social life and on which they depend. The builder, the baker, the butcher, the industrialist and the artisan provide different products that are more varied, numerous and diversified the higher the degree of development attained by the society we are describing."[39] What emerges is a veritable deconstruction of the idea of the individual, understood etymologically as that which cannot be further divided. Nothing like the individual—a subject that would soon be taken up and radicalized by Nietzsche—is divided into a thousand fragments united solely by their difference: the "I" of the philosopher, says Virchow, is just a consequence of the "we" of the biologist.[40] Rather than being a part of the community, the individual is an infinitely plural community.

*

Once the originality of Virchow's perspective in the history of the organic metaphor is recognized, we must be cautious about extending its scope beyond the specific context of the late nineteenth century. I am not referring only to the next stage—during which the exhaustion, or the radical transformation, of cell theory would undermine the very possibility of using the analogy—but also to the previous stage, when the terms of the comparison between State and biological organism are arranged in a semantic constellation that is difficult to reduce to Virchow's conceptual apparatus. This applies particularly to the controversy he engaged in against a model of the body internally unified by the circulation of the blood and nerve ramifications. If this organic body appeared to Virchow as metaphorically proximate to a monarchical and conservative conception—versus the republican, democratic one he supported—this latter model was exactly the kind of organic body that had been associated with the monarchical conception in revolutionary France. Antoine de Baecque reconstructs the phenomenology of this conception in a frame of reference in which the metapolitical associations established by Virchow turn out to be diametrically reversed. While these associations juxtapose a localist taxonomy against the principle of corporeal unification—which Virchow identified with that of authority and hierarchy—the authors of the revolution sought precisely in the unity of the body politic, represented by the third estate, the point of rupture with the traditional theory of anatomical distinction between classes, organs, and functions of the monarchy. No matter which organ is given the power to command the other parts of the body—the brain, heart, or stomach—what is asserted in all the treatises with monarchical and aristocratic roots is actually the non-equivalence of each individual in relation to the governance of the all. It is precisely to counter this—its anti-egalitarian political consequences—that the democratic pamphleteers opposed the image of one big body replenished by the blood and nerves of all the citizens reunited into one.[41]

But even more interesting for our investigation into biopolitics is the homology created between this polemical front and the controversy that during the same decades divided the exponents of the two great French medical schools: the classical clinical tradition that went from Valsalva to Morgagni passing through Bonet, and the new anatomical pathology that culminated in the teaching of Xavier Bichat. A comparison of *De causis et sedibus morborum* by Morgagni (1760) with the *Traite des membranes* by Bichat, published at a distance of forty years, provides the clearest evidence of this. While the first—in line with the regional and localist conception just described—located the origin and cause of disease in a specific area of the body, the second situated them in a wider, more complex scenario, defined by the vital relationship that connects the various body parts to the inseparable unity of a single organism. In this case, in accordance with the Jacobin unification of the body politic, the different organs are nothing but functional tributary tools of the general system of tissues that compose them. As Foucault points out, providing the most vivid representation of the epistemological contrast between the two schools,[42] the principle of diversification in organs that dominated the anatomy of Morgagni was replaced by Bichat with an isomorphic criterion of tissues based on "the same in parts distinct in their external conformation, their vital properties, and their functions."[43] Starting from this premise, the physician Cabanis, a leading exponent of the revolutionary front, was able to conclude almost in *ante litteram* opposition to the autonomist and federalistic theses later advanced by Virchow that "whole, perfect little lives exist only in the totality of one single life accompanied by all the great organs."[44]

Of course, Foucault himself points out that Bichat, Pinel, and Corvisart do not exclude the nosological division made by the great anatomists of the past from the new clinical knowledge. Rather, they incorporate this division into a spatial and temporal sequence that acknowledges the entire development of the disease. This is exactly when the decisive difference arose that made it impossible for the two perspectives to be assimilated: to reinstate the life course of the disease, it was necessary to expose the body that contained it to a gaze informed by the knowledge of death. While in eighteenth-century medicine death was nothing but the end of life and of the disease that interrupted it, for the medicine beginning in the following century, death took on an independent status that detached it from the preceding pathological stages. By being removed from its indistinguishability with illness in this way, death could now shed a light on disease that made it possible to a provide a detailed reconstruction of all its different stages, including the last one, which may—although not necessarily—have caused it. Death thus became an essential structure of medical perception: just as pathology illuminated physiology through contrast, beginning with Bichat, death became the starting point from which medical knowledge was able to grasp the truth of life.

4. The governance of life

It was Foucault who connected the crisis in sovereignty to the birth of biopolitics in the same epochal transition: while sovereignty was still exercised through the right to put to death, the focus of biopolitics was centered on the care of life. Foucault also cautioned, however, against an overly mechanical interpretation of this opposition: in neither case are life and death placed in an alternation that entirely excludes one another. Certainly this is not the case in the classic framework of sovereign power, in which the right to put subjects to death was limited to defending the State and the person of the king, and hence directed toward the need to keep the body politic alive. But nor is it the case in the context of modern biopower, which was established for the purpose of developing life, certainly, but in a form that did not lose all contact with the presence of death. One could say that if the ancient sovereign right looked at life from the perspective of distributing death, the new biopolitical order subordinated even death to the demands of reproducing life. This stubborn persistence of death within a politics of life was confirmed early on by the singular fact that the greatest international effort made toward setting up a health organization—the Beveridge Plan—took place in 1942, in the midst of a war destined to kill fifty million people, almost as if the right to health could temporarily substitute for the right to life, or even be deduced from its opposite. But so far death still remained outside the life-producing mechanism, like a non-metabolized residue or one term in a dialectical opposition. What takes on even greater importance, though, is the way death enters into the enclosure that seemed to exclude it. This is where Foucault seeks to discover the black box of biopolitics: in the liminal space where death is not solely the archaic figure against which life defines itself, nor the tragic price that life must pay in order to expand, but rather one of its inner folds, a mode or tonality of its own preservation.

This is the mechanism that we have thus far traced back to the logic of immunity. To recognize its most typical movements at work in biopolitical practices, we must go back to the particular place where it operates—at the juncture between the spheres of the individual and the species. When Foucault identifies the object of biopower as the population, he does not refer to individual holders of certain rights, nor to their confluence in a people defined as the collective subject of a nation, but rather to the living being in the *specificity* of its constitution."[45] In other words, he is referring to the only element that groups all individuals into the same species: the fact that they each have a body. Biopolitics addresses itself to this body—an individual one because it belongs to each person, and at the same time a general one because it relates to an entire genus—with the aim of protecting it, strengthening it, and reproducing it, in line with an objective that goes beyond the old disciplinary apparatus because it concerns the very existence of the State in its economic, legal, and political "interest." This explains Foucault's comment about the Prussian health system: "the workers' body was not what interested this public health administration, but rather the body of the individuals themselves who, by reuniting, constituted the State."[46] As we noted in the metaphorical device used by Virchow, just as individuals are an integral part of the State, in the same way, the State does not exist outside the body of the individuals who compose it. These bodies—each and every one—have to be cared for, stimulated, and multiplied as the absolute good from which the State derives its legitimacy. From this point of view, rather than viewing the shift from the sovereign to the biopolitical as a further development of the organismic metaphor, it actually signals the effective realization of the body-politic metaphor in the material body of the individuals who constitute a population. It is as if the metaphor of the body finally took on its own body: "The social 'body' ceased to be a simple juridico-political metaphor (like the one in the *Leviathan*) and became a biological reality and a field for medical intervention."[47] While the bodies of the subjects inscribed in the great body of *Leviathan* were necessary for its life, to the point that one could sacrifice one's own life to it, following the sovereign logic of an appropriative and subtractive power, these bodies are now one with the larger body, in the sense that the power of the State coincides literally with the survival of the individuals who bear it in their bodies.

This explains the growing political importance that medical knowledge assumed starting from the middle of the eighteenth century: when the body of citizens became the real as well as metaphoric place where the exercise of power was concentrated, the issue of public health—understood in its widest and most general sense as the "welfare" of the nation—clearly became the pivot around which the entire economic, administrative, and political affairs of the state revolved. This perspective brings into view another difference between biopolitical governance versus the traditional procedures of sovereign rule.[48] These, too, were set up and arranged to defend the State from both internal and external threats to its survival, of course, but in a form that was only indirectly related to the actual life of individual citizens, in a way that was institutionally mediated. On the contrary, what characterizes the horizon of biopower is rather the way the whole sphere of politics, law, and economics becomes a function of the qualitative welfare and quantitative increase of the population, considered purely in its biological aspect: life becomes government business, in all senses of the word, just as government becomes first and foremost the governance of life. This is when the institution of health care began to undergo progressive expansion into spheres that had previously fallen strictly under political and administrative competence. Foucault describes these using the term "nosopolitics": meaning not so much mandatory State intervention in the domain of medical knowledge as the emergence of health care and related practices on the scene of every public sector. The resulting limitless process of medicalization thus extended well beyond the health sector in a growing interplay between the biological, legal, and political. It is well represented by the semantic passage from the sovereign language of the law to the biopolitical language of norms: while law still subjected life to an order that presupposed it, norms are based on an absolute implication between biology and right. By establishing the boundaries of medical competency, normativity allows the physician to define the threshold of criminal liability for illegal behavior through the distinction between criminality and abnormality. Moreover, current law-making on matters of life and death—such as artificial insemination, eugenics, and euthanasia—demonstrates that the sphere of the living being has been effectively superimposed onto that of the political, as summed up by Foucault in a justly famous observation: "For millennia, man remained what he was for Aristotle: a living animal with the additional capacity for a political existence; modern man is an animal whose politics place his existence as a living being into question."[49]

But what does it mean to say that politics is enclosed within the boundaries of life? That life is the primary object—and purpose—of politics? What is the horizon of meaning that is given to biopolitics as a result of this co-belonging? In my view, the answer to this question should not be sought in the folds of a sovereign power that includes life by excluding it. Rather, what I believe it should point to is an epochal conjuncture out of which the category of sovereignty makes room for, or at least intersects with, that of immunization. This is the general procedure through which the intersection between politics and life is realized. The purpose of biopolitics is not to distinguish life along a line that sacrifices one part of it to the violent domination of the other—although that possibility can never be completely ruled out—but on the contrary, to save it, protect it, develop it as a whole. But the point we have focused on from the outset is that this objective involves the use of an instrument that is bound to it through the negative, as if the very doubling that life experiences of itself through the political imperative that "makes it live" contained something that internally contradicted it. A look at the process of generalized, undefined medicalization described by Foucault over the last two centuries provides a powerful confirmation of this notion.[50] He describes it as taking place through three different parallel scansions that he traces back to the medicine of the German State, the medicine of urban France, and English occupational medicine. Without reconstructing the entire dynamic, the element that unifies them is the leading role given to the fight against the risk of infection in each of these experiments. Connected with this prophylactic need is the importance granted to public hygiene as a prerequisite of sanitary practice, but also the function of social control that was associated with it from the outset.

The first step is to isolate places where infectious germs may develop more easily due to the storage of bodies, whether dead or alive: ports, prisons, factories, hospitals, cemeteries. But the entire territory is gradually divided into strictly separate zones based on the need for both medical and social surveillance. The original model from medieval times is that of quarantine, separated in its turn into the two pathogenic archetypes of leprosy and the plague: while the first led to the expulsion of the sick outside the city walls, the second provided for their placement into individual settings that would allow them to be numbered, registered, and assiduously controlled. Overlapping onto this more archaic model, over time there arose another variation coming from the worlds of the military and schools, also tending toward spatial division, first by conglomerates or classes and then by individual places. What is formed at the confluence of both these dispositifs is a kind of *quadrillage*, or pigeonholing, that placed individuals in an extensive system of institutional segments—family, school, army, factory, hospital—prohibiting, or at least controlling, circulation in the name of public safety. All the urbanization that developed in Europe starting in the middle of the eighteenth century took on the appearance of a dense network of fences between places, zones, and territories protected by boundaries established according to political and administrative rules that went well beyond sanitary needs. The impression we get is actually of a continuous passage—and mutual reinforcement—between sanitary measures, such as compulsory vaccination, and inclusionary/exclusionary ones of a socioeconomic nature. For example, the separation between rich neighborhoods and poor neighborhoods that was carried out in many nineteenth-century English cities was the direct consequence of the cholera epidemic of 1832, just as the formation of large urban safety systems was parallel to the discovery of antibiotics against endemic and epidemic infectious diseases.

The immune framework which contains this general process of superimposition between therapeutic practice and political order is all too obvious: to become the object of political "care," life had to be separated off and closed up inside progressively desocialized spaces that were meant to immunize it against anything arising from community. This first form of coercion against any external excess of the life force was flanked by another that penetrated to its interior as well. Foucault draws attention to it primarily in a text written in 1976 on the potentially lethal nature of medicine: "It was not necessary to wait for Illich or the disciples of anti-medicine to know that one of the capabilities of medicine is killing. Medicine kills, it has always killed, and it has always been aware of this."[51] What Foucault is trying to draw our attention to here is how the premise he began with has been transformed from being attributable to the ignorance of medicine to the skill of medicine. As in Paracelsus's poisonous pharmacopia, the potential danger of treatment arises not from lack of medical knowledge, but from its progress:

> what one might call positive iatrogenicity, rather than iatrogenicity: the harmful effects of medication due not to errors of diagnosis or the accidental ingestion of those substances, but to the action of

medical practice itself, in so far as it has a rational basis. At present, the instruments that doctors and medicine in general have at their disposal cause certain effects, precisely because of their efficacy. Some of these effects are purely harmful and others are unable to be controlled, which leads the human species into a perilous area of history, into a field of probabilites and risks, the magnitude of which cannot be precisely measured.[52]

The methods causing these adverse effects in the history of medicine are various. One of the main culprits is immunotherapy, which in acting to defend the body ends up weakening it, thereby lowering its sensitivity threshold to aggressors. As in all areas of contemporary social systems, neurotically haunted by a continuously growing need for security, this means that the risk from which the protection is meant to defend is actually created by the protection itself.[53] The risk, in short, requires protection to the same degree that the protection creates the risk. "Bacterial and viral protection, which represent both a risk and a protection for the organism, with which it has functioned until then, undergoes a change as a result of the therapeutic intervention, thus becoming exposed to attacks against which the organism had previously been protected."[54] This potential outcome, inscribed at the heart of modern biopolitics, becomes less and less hypothetical when physicians and biologists "are no longer working at the level of the individual and his descendants, but are beginning to work at the level of life itself and its fundamental events."[55] This is obviously a limit-point beyond which the entire horizon of biopower is likely to come into deadly conflict with itself. This does not mean that we can go back, by re-establishing the old figures of sovereign power, for instance. Any form of politics not directed toward life as such, which does not regard citizens from the point of view of their living bodies, is inconceivable today. But this can happen in mutually opposing forms that bring into play the very meaning of biopolitics: either the self-destructive revolt of immunity against itself or an opening to its converse, community.

*

For Foucault, as we have noted, the biopolitical horizon is defined by the passage from the sovereign order of the law to the disciplinary order of the norm. But what exactly is a norm? And how does it statutorily differ from the law? The answers Foucault provides in historical terms would seem to leave this question unanswered from a strictly conceptual point of view. Beginning with his *Maladie mentale et personnalite*[56] a system of norms is defined as a set of social, institutional, and linguistic rules that structure human life according to given orders of control and power.[57] In this sense, even if it is different from the law in terms of its effect—repressive but also productive—a norm reiterates the way law relates to its object, which remains by way of a presupposed anticipation. Although based on different objectives, both in the case of the law and the norm, the subjects are preconstituted by something that both exceeds them and precedes them. Or, as we have seen, it exceeds them in the form of precedence: life is already included in its normative decision, just as in the sovereign model life was already prejudged by the efficacy of the legal system. It is this structural homology that maintains the disciplinary norm in the immunitary circle of the law. What unites them, though in inverted form, is the negative connection that both establish between the singularity of the living being and the preservation of life: the conditions of preservation, or reproduction, of life are located outside and before the living being's natural line of development.

To force this interpretive grid into a different conception of the norm, we must look to the work of Georges Canguilhem. Without tracing out the entire course of his reflection on the normal and the pathological, the point we need to focus on, because it gives an indication of the extent to which it differs from Foucault's lexicon,[58] is precisely his attempt to remove the norm from the transcendental presupposition of the law. Rather than presupposed, and therefore outside the sphere of deployment of the living being, the biological norm is intrinsic and immanent. It is not prescribed, as is the law, but inscribed in the matter through which it exerts itself: "an organism's norm of life is furnished by the organism itself, contained in its existence . . . the norm of a human organism coincides with the organism itself."[59] What Canguilhem accomplishes—in the double wake of René Leriche and Kurt Goldstein's physiological research and the psychiatric experiments by Daniel Lagache, Charles Blondel and Eugène Minkowski—is a true reversal of the relations between precedence and succession: while the law is what establishes the threshold of the infraction by sanctioning it, the infraction is what determines the need as well as the possibility of the norm. Thus if the illegal is preceded by the legal both on the historical and logical planes, "the abnormal, while logically second, is existentially first."[60] Not only that but, in addition to preexisting and then resisting the normativization that invests it, the abnormal somehow gets inside it, to the point of changing it. This dynamic issues not only from the individual and differentiating character of the norm (not its general and homologizing aspect), but also, more deeply, from its tendency toward permanent self-deconstruction. Since every norm can only establish itself through the infraction of, or deviation from, the one that precedes it, it follows that the organism that is most "normal" is able to break and change its own norms more often. The norm for an organism, in short, is the ability to change its own norms. This means first that biological normality coincides with normativity, or the power to create new norms; and second, that normativity, far from being reducible to a form of preventive or even subsequent normalization, is a measure of the vital force of existence.

Without now probing more generally into Canguilhem's vitalism, let us go directly to where we want to arrive: unlike the law, the norm he refers to is not situated in the boundary of separation between the living being and life, but at their point of tangency. This conceptual difference is what removes it from the immune paradigm: as Walter Benjamin said, the preservation of life is not based on the sacrifice of the living. It no longer constitutes the original motive of living things. If anything, preservation is the residual commitment life assumes when it has already lost some of its vitality. As Kurt Goldstein already noted, the survival instinct is not a general law of life, but that of a life that has retracted into disease.[61] By contrast, the healthy organism is measured by its capacity and willingness to experience the unexpected, with all the risks this entails, including the extreme risk of a catastrophic reaction. One might say that for the organism, disease represents the risk of not being able to take risks: not a lack, but an excess of preservation. This is where the main axis of Canguilhem's perspective joins up. To say that the pathological is not just a quantitative change in physiology is to assert that disease, like health, has it own norm, but a norm that lacks the ability to modify itself, to produce new norms. It is a non-normative norm. To return to how it differs from sovereign law, "bare life" is not the object or effect of the norm, but the place of its invariance. It is not the sphere of anomy or anomaly; nor is it the contrary of *nomos* or *omalos*. Rather, it is the entropic contrary of anormativity.

V

The implant

1. Biophilosophies of immunity

To grasp the dual potential that biopolitics holds for destruction or affirmation, we have to go back to its founding relationship with the immune system, which constitutes both its transcendental condition and functional model. Donna Haraway does precisely this in an essay whose title ("The Biopolitics of Postmodern Bodies: Determinations of Self in Immune System Discourse") already makes explicit the connection still implicit in Foucault between the governance of life and the immune paradigm:

> The chief object of my attention will be the potent and polymorphous object of belief, knowledge, and practice called the immune system. My thesis is that the immune system is an elaborate icon for principal systems of symbolic and material "difference" in late capitalism. Pre-eminently a twentieth-century object, the immune system is a map drawn to guide recognition and misrecognition of self and other in the dialectics of western biopolitics.[1]

The fact that Haraway, a former student of Georges Canguilhem and an influential feminist thinker, is specialized in technobiology, cell biology, and cell development goes some way in explaining both the relationship and the distance she maintains

vis-à-vis Foucauldian discourse. From Foucault she takes the centrality of the body as a specific object of biopower, but from a
perspective she calls "material semiotic"—which tends to deconstruct the unitary character he still attributed to it. While Foucault
thought in terms of normalization and medicalization, Haraway
approaches the body from the standpoint of its dismantling and
multiplication, engendered by the dramatic increase in new bionic,
electronic, and information technologies. This amounts to a real
paradigm shift in interpretation. If in the 1930s the discursive
regime on the body attained its ultimate ideological solidity in the
concept of "race," and around the 1970s it was reconceived by
Foucault in terms of "population," today it must be looked at
from the standpoint of its technical transformation.

This does not mean that Haraway loses sight of the biopolitical
horizon—namely, the actual relations of power into which the
management of the living being is inscribed and which tends to
change continuously—but she pushes this horizon to its extreme
limit and, in a sense, even beyond itself into this new strategic field,
both symbolic and real, in which the connection between politics
and life is radically redefined by the unstoppable proliferation of
technology. Of course, to some degree Foucault also took these
developments into account, as is clear not only from his repeated
discussion on various governmental techniques, but also from the
hermeneutic path he started on in the final phase of his work,
focusing on "technologies of the self." And yet this very focus
exposes the still analogical (thus external) understanding that he
had of the relationship between technique and body: as if the body,
although historically determined, ontologically preceded the technical practice destined to transform it. Following these lines of
reasoning, Haraway is in the position to point out that Foucauldian biopolitics tend to interpret the constitutive, degenerative, and
healing processes of the living being according to a temporal protocol of an evolutionary type still dependent on the humanist tradition.[2] As exposed as it is to the practices of control and reproduction that shape and stimulate it, the body of Foucauldian analysis
remains defined, in short, by the same space-time boundaries that
marked the path from the Greco-Christian civilization to the
modern. This missing step is what Haraway refers to when she
observes that Foucault "names a form of power at its moment of

implosion":[3] the relation between politics and life passes today
through a biotechnical filter that disassembles both terms before
reassembling them into a material and figural combination that the
Foucauldian conceptual apparatus is incapable of grasping.[4] Precisely because he is able to describe the genealogical mechanisms
of modern society so thoroughly and extensively, he runs the risk
of remaining hermeneutically imprisoned in its dynamics, and thus
losing or not fully grasping the limit point at which modernity
comes face to face with its outside: the moment, that is, when the
differential margins that for centuries separated and juxtaposed
the domains of the real and the imaginary, the natural and the
artificial, the organic and the inorganic, finally explode or implode.
When Haraway writes that the human body is no longer a biological given, but a complex field inscribed by sociocultural codes
represented by the hybrid figure of the cyborg, equally divided
between organism and machine, what she is referring to is a
process of technicization of life that is unassimilable into the sociocultural or even ontological framework of the modern period.
Understanding it means bringing into focus the apparent change
in direction of technological development, which no longer goes
from inside to outside, but from outside to inside. While up to a
certain point human beings projected themselves into the world,
and then also into the universe, now it is the world, in all its components—natural and artificial, material and electronic, chemical
and telematic—which penetrates us in a form that eliminates the
separation between inside and outside, front and back, surface and
depth: no longer content merely to besiege us from the outside,
technique has now taken up residence in our very limbs.

Of course, the current process of artificialization—or denatu-
ralization—of the body was preceded by countless premonitions,
forewarnings, and previsions that, starting from the seventeenth
century, took form as the complementary figures of the mechanical
body and the living machine. But what has long been no more
than a fruitful metaphor, or an auxiliary support confined to the
inventions of robotics, is now becoming realized in the human
body itself, which is open to processes of modification, implants,
and explants that only a short time ago would have been absolutely unimaginable, even by the great tradition of philosophical
anthropology. The insight philosophical anthropology offers into

humankind's store of technical knowledge, as a compensation for lack of organic specialization or as an exoneration from an excess of drives, brought to its height of analytical power by Gehlen, is not to be confused with the actual replacement of organs using technological grafts. This is not a symbolic surrogate or even a functional extension of a natural limb, but rather, the real presence in the body of something that is not body. Of course, the most advanced thinking on human nature had already made it clear that our technical character is originary rather than contingent: not only our erect posture or prehensile grip but language itself, qua expression, is already supplement, externality, prosthesis. But language is a natural prosthesis, not an artificial one like a cardiac pacemaker, a silicon microchip implanted under the skin, or a telecamera inserted near the brain. What we are talking about here is not just the overturning of the relations of mastery between subject and instrument dreaded by a long anti-technological tradition, or even the conception of technology as a physical extension of our bodies that makes the wheel the continuation of the foot and the book the continuation of the eye, a conception clearly still based on a taxonomic distinction between the body and its external projections. Rather, this is an interaction between species, or even between the organic world and the artificial world, implying a veritable interruption of biological evolution by natural selection and its inscription into a different system of meaning.

Even leaving aside the prognosis on the outcome of this process—seemingly suspended between the possibility of unprecedented development in the quality of human life and the risk of its colonization by powers external to it[5]—what we are certainly facing is a radical restructuring of what until now we have called "body." Without going so far as to predict our disembodiment into autonomous forms of artificial intelligence, or our digital translation into the hardware of cybernetic systems—which the epistemologists, philosophers and artists of cyberculture have no hesitation in doing[6]—there is no doubt that the body is experiencing a state of profound alteration, down to its essential fabric. This body demands to be thought of as a text written in code whose genomic key must be found, or as the terminal of a planetary-wide computer network, or as an object that is modifiable through plastic surgery, and even before that, by genetic engineering. In all cases it enters into a direct, or actually symbiotic, rela-tionship with what is other than itself: in the specific and literal sense that it carries its other within itself. It bears within itself another body—one of its parts—or an other-than-body: a thing, device, or machine. This is exactly what a prosthesis is: an outside brought inside; or an inside that sticks out, no longer kept inside the limits that traditional subjective identity made to coincide with the skin. On these lines, the subject is no longer an originary given but a functional construct, the result of a mixture with something that is not subject, or which is subject to a different ontological status than the one classically conceived for subjectivity: some-thing that is both less than a human subject—because it has no life—and more, because when it replaces a diseased organ it allows the human subject to continue living. It is something non-living that serves to preserve life. We might say that this need for self-preservation is at the root of all contemporary forms of body modification: the body suspends itself—it interrupts and doubles itself—with the aim of extending its duration. It exposes itself to what lies outside it in order to save what it still bears inside. It enters into a problematic relationship with the other in order to protect itself from itself, from its natural tendency to be consumed. On these lines, from this perspective, once again the figure of the immune system rises out of the heart of biopolitics. Situated at the crucial point in which the body encounters what is other than itself, it constitutes the hub that connects various interrelated enti-ties, species, and genera such as the individual and the collective, male and female, human and machine. Precisely because of this power to combine, the immune apparatus has become the point of tangency—of connection and tension—between all contempo-rary languages:

> That is, the immune system is a plan for meaningful action to construct and maintain the boundaries for what may count as self and other in the crucial realms of the normal and the pathological. The immune system is an historically specific terrain, where global and local politics; Nobel prize-winning research; heteroglossic cul-tural productions, from popular dietary practices, feminist science fiction, religious imagery, and children's games, to photographic techniques and military strategic theory; clinical medical practice;

venture capital investment strategies, world-changing developments in business and technology; and the deepest personal and
collective experiences of embodiment, vulnerability, power, and
morality, interact with an intensity matched perhaps only in the
biopolitics of sex and reproduction.[7]

Taking this semantic crossroads as our point of departure, the
immune system is revealed as the nerve center through which
the political governance of life runs. The immune system pushes
the governance of life beyond the biopolitical paradigm or gives
another meaning to the paradigm of biopolitics, one that is different from its usual formulation. What drops away is precisely
the presumption of a direct and immediate relationship between
politics and life. In reality, they are increasingly related through
the great figurative device that medical science has developed
around the body's need for self-protection. From this, from this
concentration of real and metaphoric functions, a semantic wave
destined to wash over the entire gamut of social languages is set
in motion. No wonder: if the semiotic axis around which every
social institution is constituted lies in the boundary between self
and other—between us and them—what constitutes both its interpretative key and effective outcome better than the principle of
immunity?

*

The philosopher who has thought most deeply about the relationship between the body and the technical supplement is undoubtedly Jean-Luc Nancy. From his point of view, even to talk about
a "relationship" between the two terms is misleading. What we
should be talking about is the supplemental, or technical, character of the body itself; but at the same time, the mode of *technē*,
which is fractal, local, and precise. Contrary to an interpretive
school that tends to see *technē* as a large homologating apparatus,
as opposed to existence as such,[8] for Nancy the two coincide.
When restored to its original status, *technē* is nothing but the gap
separating existence from itself—the point, more precisely, where
its withdrawal from immanence intersects with its withdrawal
from transcendence. The existent does not coincide fully with

itself; neither does it imply any transcendental basis: this is the condition of *techné*. *Techné* is the non-essential, non-teleological, non-presupposed mode of that which exists: not that which alters—rapes or saves—nature, but the fact *that there is no nature*. For this reason, *techné* is always about bodies, about all bodies and each body: about "each body" in the sense that *techné* is the place of the body's opening to what is not itself; and about "all bodies" because this place is precisely the broken contour through which each body comes into contact with the other. The instant transcendence and immanence withdraw together in the diversion of any pre-established meaning, *techné* (or the technicity of existence) comes to coincide with the partitioning of bodies, with their being always *partes extra partes*, with their constant "hand-to-hand" [*corpo a corpo*]: there is no body that is not "*a corpo*." Never before have we had such an accurate perception of this community of bodies—the endless contagion that combines, over-laps, soaks, coagulates, blends, and clones them. Its openings in the flesh and transfusions of blood are identical to those in meaning: every definition of the healthy and the sick, the normal and the pathological, immunity and community, vacillates. In the flow of magnetic resonance imaging and the radiation of X-rays, reflected in ultrasound scans and the infiltration of implants, all bodies are "sliding, opened, spread out, grafted, exchanged. Neither a healthy *state* nor a sick *stasis*: a coming-and-going, a jumpy or smooth palpitation of skins side to side, wounds, synthetic enzymes, synthetic images."[9]

Nancy's attitude in describing this phenomenology—or rather ontology—of the mechanized body is far from reactionary. The fact that the body is originally technical means that these ongoing processes do nothing but lay bare the mode that is proper—and therefore, necessarily improper—to our corporeality. Not only is it not possible or desirable to go "back," there is nothing lying behind what we are today. This is not to imply any shades of euphoria, however, whether speaking in general or specific terms: neither for all bodies—hungry, raped, ravaged by being amassed in ever more distant corners of the world—nor for each individual body. As we know, Nancy has directly experienced bodily partition in the invasive form of a heart transplant. The account he gives of it in "The Intruder" probably constitutes the most radical and at the same time the most sobering state of awareness regarding the meaning of the technicity of one's body: its inability to be in any way exclusively proper to itself; the inextricable mixture of potentiality and finiteness, strength and suffering, acceptance and struggle that characterizes it. What penetrates the body of the person who receives a transplant, even before the tubes, pliers and probes traverse it, is not even simply its outside. It is the acute point of intersection between several forms of estrangement that oppose and impose upon each other, each challenged, replicated, and, finally, overwhelmed by the other. The first is the estrangement of our immune system from the transplanted organ. The second, with an equal force of collision, is the estrangement of the immune system of the transplanted organ that strikes against our own. The shared line between the recipient body and the donor heart coincides with the frontline in the clash between these two opposing immune systems: one committed with all its power to rejecting the other while simultaneously not allowing itself to be rejected. For this reason, the resistance on the part of the person receiving the transplant must be redoubled: against the protection system of the other and his or her own; against the maelstrom of estrangement and the impossible demand for appropriation. For this reason, even to distinguish between "self" and "non-self" is no longer admissible, since it is not simply the improper that is the intruder, but the proper as well, inasmuch as it is estranged: "Thus, then, in all these accumulated and opposing ways, my self becomes my intruder."[10]

When cancer arrives as a side effect—if one can call it that—of cyclosporine and its immune-suppressive action, the need for further intrusion is created by the combined effect of the estrangement caused by chemotherapy and the morphine designed to alleviate these sufferings in exchange for others. But what leads to even more estrangement—because it is overly proper, more proper than the proper—is the sort of "self-transplant" of one's own white blood cells, which are collected, frozen, and reinjected into the body after yet another massive suppression of the immune defenses, with all its ensuing consequences. The most extreme of these is the absolute inability to recognize one's own identity; it is pulverized into an infinite number of waves refracted farther and farther away in an alternation and overlapping of pain, failures, and powerlessness. Referring to oneself at this point is more than difficult, it is literally impossible, since there is no longer a self with which the new self—its deconstruction and reconstruction— can identify. Rather than a first person, that self has now become a third person: not a "he or she," but the non-person who bears both its reality and shadow. Places, perceptions, and times are splayed, so that what heals also makes ill, and what rejuvenates also ages: how old are you if your heart is twenty years younger than the rest of your body? And what is the identity of a man with a woman's heart or a woman with a child's heart? Without being able to call the body that belongs to me "mine" and without "belonging" to my body anymore, I am deprived of what has always been thought of as the truth of the subject. And at the same time I grasp that the subject has a truth other than its own: "its infinite exposition. The intruder exposes me to excess. It extrudes me, exports me, expropriates me. I am the illness and the medicine, I am the cancerous cell and the grafted organ, I am these immuno-depressive agents and their palliatives, I am these ends of steel wire that brace my sternum and this injection site permanently sewn under my clavicle, altogether as if, already and besides, I were these screws in my thigh and this plate inside my groin."[11] Here, lit up like a flash, is the "terrible and disturbing" quality [*deinos*] that Sophocles glimpsed in the technical foundation of human nature.

2. War games

But in what sense does immunity constitute the strategic focus of contemporary societies? What kind of relationship connects it with the biopolitical dynamics of our time? And more to the point, how does it contribute to guiding them? Donna Haraway mobilizes her most convincing arguments in discussing precisely this set of issues: if the biomedical paradigm is not merely conditioned by our perception of the world but actually influences it to an ever-greater extent; if, precisely because the biomedical paradigm directly affects our fundamental distinction between life and death, it is a powerful generator of meaning for our individual and collective existence; and if, finally, the immune system is now the cutting edge in this performative dynamic, then a decisive game is played in defining it, not only on the ground of biology but also specifically on the ground of politics. Anyone who has a basic familiarity with the history of immunology[12] also knows very well that few objects have undergone such a practically continuous—and still ongoing—series of analytical and interpretive redefinitions of its structure, and even its significance, as the immune system. In spite of this, the most prevalent representation in everyday parlance but also in the scientific community is based on the body's defense against foreign elements that threaten its physiological and functional integrity. This is how the great immunologist Sir Frank Macferlane Burnet expresses it in a book programmatically entitled *The Integrity of the Body:* "The production of antibodies or any other immunological reaction by an organism is carried out against foreign materials, that is, against anything that is not part of that organism."[13] But the rhetorically decisive step that has generated the most widely held stereotypes in defining the immune system is the transposition of the defense function into aggressively military terms. The immune mechanism takes on the character of an out-and-out war: the stakes are the control and ultimately the survival of the body in the face of foreign invaders who seek first to occupy it and then to destroy it. From this point of view, all the tropes in the seventeenth-century treatises on the body politic cataloged in the previous chapter—from the obsessive attention to the boundaries of identity, to the phobic fear of infection from potential infiltrates, to the continuous erection of new defensive barriers—are now reinforced and given authority by a very different scientific endorsement.

The fact that the influential metaphors of immunological discourse re-echo the armamentarium of the clashes against "invading hordes of hostile microbes and the protection of the sanctity of the body" has historically been attributed by one of the leading specialists on the topic to the circumstances out of which the discipline grew: the fight against major infectious diseases at the beginning of the twentieth century. Only partly ironically, he notes that "the term itself goes to show that this process was seen as a battle between two opposing forces, one good and one very bad. Since history is written by the victors, we shall see how well the good fare."[14] Moreover, it would be hard to miss a subtly apologetic effect in this phylogenetic reconstruction that, beyond descriptive, also acts as a normative premise in the whole immunological story. As explained in most textbooks, the immune system, which did not arise at the same time as the origins of life (it actually dates back to a relatively late stage of its evolution), has developed in parallel with the more complex species on the zoological scale rather than with other more primitive ones.[15] This means that this system, whose function is to carry out the fight for survival, is the result of a previous selection, itself determined by the predominance of stronger life forms over other weaker ones. But the most obvious commonplace regarding this evolutionary dynamic is its interpretation in terms of a battle between civilizations: between the principle of order and the principle of chaos, identified in their turn as the defense of the integrity of the individual on the one side, and the entropic powers aimed at its dissolution on the other.

> Every living thing is an example of the *vis naturae*'s effort to counter the tendency of matter toward disorder. . . . From this perspective, the immune system takes on the significance of a system working to counter entropy, maintaining the integrity of the individual against the tendency toward destructuration performed by other organisms whose very existence and that of their species is based on colonization and their highly frequent reproduction. The failure of the immune system functions following the death of the individual causes putrefaction, which, when viewed as uncontested colonization by other individuals and as destructuration, satisfies the tendency of matter toward disorder.[16]

This line of discrimination between the identity of the individual and the threatening magma that presses in on its outer boundaries is the fundamental distinction around which the most widely accepted immunological theory has constructed its story, and thus its meaning. Jan Klein's manual *Immunology: The Science of Self/ Non-Self Discrimination* is exemplary in this regard: it begins with a section entitled "Four Threats to Individuality," immediately followed by a description of the defense of individuality against the risk of "fusion" with heterogeneous entities.[17] The best defense obviously lies in an attack on the "non-self"; indeed, the "self" can only recognize itself in relation to and *in opposition to* the "non-self," based on a polemogenous definition of identity that conversely gives rise to an increasingly virulent representation of its enemies: "repelling invaders" as Marion Kendall calls them in a book punctuated by section headings such as "The Fight Begins," "General Defence Policy and the Enemy," "Subversive Agents," and so forth.[18] A well-known article by Peter Jaret in *National Geographic* describes the immune mechanism in terms of Star Wars, in which a cancer victim bombards the cancerogenous cells in a "T-Killer cell" videogame.[19] Without necessarily identifying the ideological source of this allophobic vocabulary, as others have suggested, in the discourse of the Cold War and, prior to that, in the racist literature of the colonial period,[20] what is particularly striking is the intensification and even escalation it undergoes not only in popular science texts but in scientific research papers as well.[21]

Susan Sontag argues that modern medical thinking began when the metaphors of war that had always been used in the history of medicine became specific: that is to say, instead of referring to disease as such, they became directed toward the microorganisms declared to be the carriers of each particular disease.[22] But today this process has been raised to a whole new level of intensity. This is especially true when what are involved are the activities of the immune system—its mechanisms, victories, and failures—as demonstrated most sensationally in the case of AIDS. Paula Treichler has justly spoken of an "epidemic of signification,"[23] alluding to the uncontrollable semantic current that submerges a medical problem the moment it meets up with certain biopolitical onsets. Reading together John Dwyer's *The Body at War*[24] and, for the illustrations, Lennart Nilsson's *The Body Victorious*[25] provides extraordinary evidence of this observation. All the phases of the immune battle between "self" and "non-self" are reconstructed with such a wealth of details one begins to wonder if these are medical accounts explained using military images, or military strategy books illustrated by medical metaphors.[26] The narrative sequence leads in a crescendo of dramatic intensity from the detection of the enemy, the activation of the defense lines, the launch of the counterattack, the physical elimination of the captured opponents, to the clearing away of casualties from the field. The first operation—the search for infiltrators—is made difficult by their ability to blend into the body environment and even to camouflage themselves as its guards: "One refined method employed by many bacteria and all viruses is to hide inside the body's own cells. They disguise themselves, as it were, in a uniform which the immune system has not learned to recognize."[27] Under these conditions, continues Dwyer with an unexpectedly ethnic-racial stab, "it may be equally difficult for our immune system to discover a foreign entity as it would be for a Caucasian to identify a Chinese intruder at a crowded ceremony in Tiananmen Square in Beijing."[28] To trace the cunning saboteurs hiding in the tissue, all that remains is to set up a surveillance mechanism through a "closed circuit television system that can pick up the suspect and secure his face with a close-up picture on half the monitor screen" while an inspector reviews all the profiles of the legitimate personnel, projected on the other half of the video screen. In this way "the instructions to the security men in this essential 'first line of defence' will be created, who can thus be sure that this person is really an intruder and thus justify the severity of the response that they must put into action."[29]

Yet even the closed-circuit systems can fail, or be bypassed by professional saboteurs. It is then necessary to resort to a more personalized surveillance system using automatic indexing—a sort of identity card—provided by the special mark imprinted on the cells of all living beings: "A cell whose identification is faulty is immediately destroyed by the armed force which is constantly on patrol. . . . The human body's police corps is programmed to distinguish between bona fide residents and illegal aliens—an ability fundamental to the body's power of self-defence."[30] At this point, alerted by the "inspectors" through their "receiver sets," the actual soldiers intervene, deployed based on a differentiated strategy setting out strictly defined tasks: bands of attackers, containment units, corpse removal specialists:

> A response group will include commandos who will lead a unit of variously armed individuals into the war zone, inciting them to attack. Some of these tactical units will be more engaged in the work of disarming and immobilizing than direct killing. The group's modus operandi is so well-organized that some men are specifically assigned to the cleanup, removing the corpses and other remains

from the battlefield, which took place outside the installation, so
that peace may reign again.[31]

The kinds of armed forces the immune system has at its disposal
are described in detail by Nilsson: "highly mobile regiments, shock
troops, snipers, and tanks." If these are not enough, "we have
soldier cells which, on contact with the enemy, at once start producing homing missiles whose accuracy is overwhelming. Our
defence system also boasts ammunition which pierces and bursts
bacteria, reconnaissance squads, an intelligence service, and a
defence staff unit which determines the location and strength of
troops to be deployed."[32] This is the formidable army of granulocytes and macrophages; unfortunately, precisely because of their
heavy weaponry, they can be bypassed and infected with viruses
and bacteria. In this event, faced with a particularly tough infection, when a million brave granulocytes fall in the fight against
the invaders, the task of the macrophages—the larger-sized phago-
cytes—becomes to ingest them in a sort of spectacular "small-scale
cannibalism."[33] It is then that the defense staff unit launches the
storm troops onto the field—the lymphocytes—which are not
"feeding cells. They kill their opponents differently: by using
homing projectiles (antibodies), and with some form of poisoning
(killer cells)."[34] Now all resources are deployed: from traditional
"tanks" to "chemical mines," and "biological dynamite." The
bacteria that are captured by the antibodies are taken before
the "execution patrol. Now complement factor 1 can bind to the
bacterium surface, followed by factor 2, and so on. When
the ninth factor joins, the process is complete. The complement
factors have perforated the surface, injecting a fluid inside it that
causes it to explode."[35] The outcome of the battle appears to be
a foregone conclusion:

> If the bacteria break through and manage to spread, they meet the
> migrant macrophages in the tissues. If they nonetheless intrude
> farther, they are usually absorbed by the lymph and taken to the
> lymph nodes. These are the fortresses of the immune system,
> manned by macrophages and lymphocytes. Now the specific defence
> forces are in position: antibodies and killer cells throng the blood
> and deliver the coup de grace to all microorganisms they find.[36]

The description of the immune war could very well come to a close at this point. The invaders have been vanquished: they have been disarmed, killed, or forced to commit suicide, following a self-suppressive procedure technically defined as "apoptosis": "No one is pardoned, no prisoners are taken—although fragments of the invader bacteria, viruses, rickettsias, parasites and fungi are transported to the lymph nodes to provide rapid training for those that can be considered the true police corps of the defence system, the so-called 'killer' cells."[37] With the corpses of the enemies removed or reused for exercises, the battlefield has now been cleared. The body has regained its integrity: once immunized, it can no longer be attacked by the enemy.

3. The defeated

But is this really how things stand? Can the body's victory over its enemies ever be so complete and final? It would appear that a mythical streak ends up concealing the problematic and counter-factual elements in these sorts of reconstructions of the immune process: first, as regards the very concept of the "self," modeled as a spatial entity protected by strict genetic boundaries and practically identified with the struggle for their defense; and second, most significantly, in the salvific effect attributed to this defense, immediately converted into an offensive machine no enemy can withstand. What is drastically omitted from this total mobilization is the essential relationship the body has with its vulnerability, whose ontological counterpart is the inevitably finite nature of human existence. Contrary to what these war games suggest, there no such thing as an apparatus or device that can ever, even potentially, grant us some form of immortality; even more, the simple presumption of an eventuality of this sort only brings us back brusquely to the reality of our insuperable condition. This also, and especially, applies to the immune system. It is a far-from-perfect device, and its victories are far from definitive. This is not only based on the obvious consideration that just one defeat is enough to cancel out all the previous successes, but also because its very functioning is inherently full of what, in philosophical terms, are called structural aporias: as we know by now, the immune process entails the presence of a negative driving force (the antigen) which it must not simply eliminate, but rather, recognize, incorporate, and, in this fashion alone, neutralize.

Of course, this inherence of the negative in the mechanism of its therapeutic control can take on different and even mutually opposing modes, alternating between a condition of lack to one of excess, but which can also be combined with each other in a perverse superimposition. Let us start from the first one, that is, from the pathological phenomenology commonly referred to as "immune deficiency." It is well known that it may present in different degrees of severity, ranging from hypogammaglobulinemia, a relatively moderate deficiency that can be controlled through antibiotic treatment, to full-blown agammaglobulinemia, a condition that makes life untenable: in other words, the absolute inability to produce defensive antibodies. In either case, it involves a congenital or acquired deficiency of T cells (thymus-dependent) and B cells (derived from bone marrow). Although it is not entirely clear at which stage of lymphocyte differentiation the block occurs, the fact is that immunodeficiency diseases expose the body to such a traumatic series of infections that it cannot last long. The most relevant aspect with regard to the biological aporia we mentioned earlier is that some of these viruses—the sadly notorious HIV, for example—not only evade the immune system, they exploit its own resources to harm it. This means that the vehicle used to proliferate and spread out through the affected organism is often the immune system's own defenses. The apparent paradox stems from the fact that CD4 T cells, where the virus prefers to reside, are more "hospitable" to it when they are activated, in other words, when the immune system is alerted, than when they are in a resting state. In addition, the cytokines produced by T cells when they recognize viral antigens can lead to replication of the virus in the CD4 T lymphocytes, providing yet more evidence of that perverse short circuit linking the activation of the defenses with the strengthening of what it seeks to defend itself from.

These observations alone are enough to put in question the picture sketched out earlier of the superior strategic intelligence of the immune system. The harsh combat image characterized by violence, deviousness, surprise, and deception can be substantiated, but its outcome is hardly the foregone conclusion depicted in such triumphal tones. When the battle is viewed from the other side of the mirror—that is, from the standpoint of the absolute fragility of the body—the defenders are now the ones who risk retreat and defeat. The pathological picture of HIV most notably presents a battle whose outcome remains uncertain for a protracted period of time: the stages of the disease pass through frequent pauses and even regressions thanks to continuous counterattacks from the immune system. But most of the time the immune system is destined to the irreversible defeat that comes in the form of AIDS. The technical cause of this failure lies in the gradual elimination of the T helper cells needed to activate the T killer cells, specialized at mounting a head-on collision with the virus. In fact, according to the perverse logic just described, the cells that fight the HIV infection also damage the helper lymphocytes they require to act effectively. Once again, the story can be told as a military drama, but with an ending that is the exact opposite of the victorious one narrated by Dwyer and Nilsson. This, too, is a war with no holds barred. And in this case, too, it ends with the capitulation of one of the two armies. What changes is which party comes out of the battle as the defeated. Initially, the situation seems perfectly balanced: "Each member of the HIV army is a generalist," write Martin Nowak and Andrew McMichael, "able to attack any enemy cell it encounters. But each member of the immune army is a specialist, able to recognize an HIV soldier only if the soldier is waving a flag of a precise color."[38] This proves to be the decisive element. The HIV soldiers need only change their "flag" to throw the opposing camp into complete bewilderment:

> Now suppose that the HIV army consisted of three groups, each carrying a different flag and that, in response, the immune specialists also divided into three groups, each recognizing a separate flag. Under these conditions, the immune army would be at a serious disadvantage. Any given immune specialist would recognize and attack only one out of every three enemy soldiers it encountered—the one carrying the right flag. The HIV soldiers, meanwhile, would continue to pick off every specialist they met and would ultimately win the war.[39]

The reason we are talking about a war lost by the immune system, and not simply a battle, is due to the physically and symbolically devastating character of the immune system's defeat. The reason AIDS quickly took on the disfigured face of the second-millennium plague—not so much as a serious illness, but as evil itself manifested in the individual and collective body—is because of its frontal attack on the salvific myth of the immune system. In crushing the immune system's defenses, it penetrates the boundaries of the self and causes it to implode: "AIDS is not simply a physical malady; it is also an artifact of social and sexual transgression, violated taboo, fractured identity."[40] What is affected by AIDS is not only a health protocol but an entire ontological scheme: the identity of the individual as the form and content of its subjectivity. True, cancer also eats away at it, just as vascular diseases shake its foundations. But AIDS ravages its subjectivity because the disease destroys the very idea of an identity-making border: the difference between self and other, internal and external, inside and outside. Naturally, it comes from the outside: from another individual, group, or country.[41] In some ways, it is actually the "outside" itself, in its most uncontrollable and threatening guise. But then, once it takes up residence inside the body, it turns into another "inside." Indeed, its specificity could be said to lie precisely in the way it turns the inside out, the way it makes the inside an outside: "The body's own cells *become* the invader."[42] From this standpoint, as its arch enemy, AIDS is the exact opposite of the immune system: not the internalization of the outside, but the externalization of the inside. It is the inside projected outside itself.[43]

Yet if the diseases from acquired immune deficiency most baldly reveal the fragility, weakness, and congenital insufficiency of the immune system, it is the autoimmune diseases which express, by their very name, its most acute contradiction: rather than a failure, a block, or a flaw in the immune apparatus, they represent its reversal against itself. Of course, autoimmune pathology is also not limited to a single cause, degree of severity, or manifestation. Even the category of autoimmune diseases—of which systemic lupus erythematosus, chronic active hepatitis, insulin-dependent diabetes, and multiple sclerosis are only the most well known—varies according to the criteria used to define it. And this does not include the vast adjacent area of allergies and mixed conditions in which immunodeficiency syndromes may present characteristics similar to autoimmune diseases (possibly the case for AIDS itself, in Montagnier's opinion). What is certain is that in all these cases an "overactive defense" of the body in seeking to strike at the enemy also causes harm to itself. Dwyer attributes this perverse effect to an overzealous immune army that, in the heat of the attack, uses weapons of war that are sometimes disproportionate to the actual size of the opponent: "As you can imagine, the commandos can let themselves be carried away by their success in battle and use a missile where a hand grenade would have been more than adequate."[44] A whole series of manuals describing this phenomenon makes constant reference to the imprecision of conventional weapons that, once fired, are unable to target the enemy with enough accuracy to avoid causing damage to the surrounding environment. To stay with the military metaphor, if you drop a bomb with a hugely destructive potential from an aircraft at a high altitude, it is difficult to limit the damage to specific targets, hence the possibility of striking allies along with enemies.[45]

Yet this way of looking at it—overactive defense, lack of precision, target error—does not take the most destabilizing element of the autoimmune response into account. And that is the self-reactive turn it takes, evoking the self-dissolution of a civil war rather than an erroneous or disproportionate conflict, as Gus Nossal rightly remarks in commenting on Paul Ehrlich's famous Latin expression.[46]

Paul Ehrlich coined the phrase "horror autotoxicus," which describes vividly his picture of the horror and chaos which could result if the lymphocytes started to mount an immune attack against autologous constituents. This would represent a form of civil warfare—white cells against red, lymphocytes against liver and kidney—leading to anarchy and to grave disease. In fact, a limited form of such civil warfare is not uncommon and the diseases in which it occurs are called autoimmune diseases.[47]

Why so much horror? Why this allusion to chaos and anarchy, with a dramatic intensity that seems to even go beyond being defeated on the battlefield by the virus? The answer lies precisely in the absence of an external enemy, in its purely reflexive nature. This is not about losing a war against an unstoppable opponent, or even, strictly speaking, about a real war—a *polemos* between two opposing forces battling each other for dominance; rather, this is a *stasis*: a force that turns against its own essence, causing the destruction of everything that surrounds it and, ultimately, itself: "Autoimmune diseases are for the body what civil wars are to society."[48] There is no passage from outside to inside in them: the inside fights against itself until it self-destructs. So instead of the victory of one of the two camps over the other—good over evil or evil over good—the result is pure anarchy. The concept of "autoantibody"—whether or not caused by the presence of a corresponding "autoantigen"—is an even more semantically charged expression: an *anti* which goes against what it belongs to; an *autos* which coincides with what fights it in a relentless proliferation of internal conflict, resulting in an antibody, an autoantibody, an antiautoantibody, and so on.

But the most antinomic aspect of this process lies not so much in its pathological character as it does, paradoxically, in its *non*-pathological or *normally* pathological character. By that I mean it does nothing more than express the logic of the immune system in its pure state, so to speak. If the immune system works by opposing *everything* that it recognizes, this means that it has to attack even the "self" whose recognition is the precondition of all other recognition: how could the immune system recognize the other without first knowing the self? "The situation appears paradoxical," admits Golub. "On the one hand we have seen that recognition of self is necessary, but on the other, we know that this reaction against the self may be suicidal."[49] This paradox, well known to students of immunology, is reflected in the observation that what needs explaining is not the fact that in some cases the immune system attacks its own parts, but the fact that this normally does not happen. This non-aggression is well known as being due to the phenomenon called "autotolerance," or tolerance of self. What we want to draw attention to is how this leads to the reversal of a common perception: it is not autoimmunity, with all its lethal consequences, including death, that requires explanation, but rather its absence. When it is stated that "autoimmunity can be viewed as a breakdown of the tolerant state to autologous constituents,"[50] it is to be understood that autoimmunity is what would occur under *any* circumstance in the event the tolerance mechanism fails to block it. Here we arrive at the key point of the argument: the destructive rebellion against the self is not a temporary dysfunction, but the natural impulse of every immune system. In countering all that it "sees," it is naturally led to *first* attack its own self. As for this aporetic consequence fully revealed by the figure of autoimmunity, we might ask, was it not already implicit in the principle of homeopathic correspondence between treatment and poison? If the immune dialectic always implies the incorporation of a negative, this is both confirmed and radicalized by the functioning of autoimmunity: the dissolution of the negative from any positive role and its destructive doubling up on itself, or in other words, the destruction, through self-destruction, of the entire body it is intended to defend.

4. Common immunity

But is this destructive—and self-destructive—reading of the immune system the only possible interpretation? Or is there another standpoint from which a radically different interpretive perspective is opened up? In short, if a philosophical question is at stake in addition to the biological one, as Burnet maintains,[51] can we imagine a philosophy of immunity that, without denying its inherent contradiction, even deepening it further, reverses the semantics in the direction of community? Haraway has already responded affirmatively to this question by seeking "to imagine the immune system differently from the Cold War rhetoric that has always represented it as a battlefield. Rather than as a discourse of invaders, why not think of it as a discourse of shared specificities in a semipermeable self able to interact with others (human and non-human, internal and external)?"[52] In the same vein, Polly Matzinger has formulated an immune theory that, instead of being identified with a strenuous defense of the self against any exogenous invader, is likened to a sophisticated alarm system set off by a series of "positive and negative communications from an extended network of other bodily tissues."[53] Following this line of thought, Anne Marie Molin[54] argues that in the theoretical elaboration of immunology, the vocabulary of recognition begins to take over from the lexicon of war in a new interpretive framework that takes into account not only contemporary episte-mology, but also some segments of the philosophical tradition, especially with regard to Leibniz's metaphysics.[55]

But the person who developed this thesis to its full maturity—tracing its genealogy in a line that builds on the insights of the Russian zoopathologist Ilya Mechnikov—was Alfred Tauber.[56] Arguing that maintaining organic integrity is only a secondary, derivative function of the immune system, while its main function is to define the identity of the subject, he interprets it as the ever-changing product of a dynamic, competitive interaction with the environment rather than a definitive and inalterable given. From this perspective, far from being a unit closed within blocked, impassable borders, the body is posited as an ecosystem that has evolved over time into what the author unhesitatingly describes as a "social community."[57] At the heart of this historical, process-based conception of identity as a system open to the challenges of the outside world, and indeed ultimately formed by them, lies the complex function of immune tolerance. For the sake of brevity, we must leave aside the stages of its discovery, starting from the experiment by Ray Owen on dizygotic cattle twins (which were able to tolerate a tissue graft from their twin because of their shared circulatory system *in utero*), in order to get immediately to the definition that interests us: tolerance is a specific suppression of the immune response induced by previous exposure to an antigen. But how should this lack of response be interpreted? As a kind of "lapse," a failed intervention on the part of the immune system; or, conversely, as the active effect of its self-restraint? Should it be interpreted as a lack of recognition, or as a kind of recognition that is so sophisticated that it prevents a negative response to antigenic components belonging to the same organ-ism? The answers to this crucial question—how to characterize tolerance but immunity as well—have been ambiguous. Burnet himself has fluctuated between a passive, negative conception of tolerance as an inadequate training of the immune system and another, positive view that traces it to an active learning skill acquired during the embryonic stage. Eventually the pendulum has come to rest on what is known as the clonal selection theory, according to which the elimination of autoreactive clones protects the body from the terrible potential of self-dissolution caused by an attack from its own defenses.

Even in this account a blind spot remains surrounding the real protagonist of the operation. When Burnet says that lymphocytes entering into early contact with the antigen are unable to proliferate, or when Nossal attributes the effect of tolerance to a sort of clonal abortion due to disruption of cell differentiation, are we meant to understand a real exclusion of the cells or the production of signals that inhibit the response to the antigen? Are we to understand an anergy—an inactivity—on the part of the self-reactive lymphocytes, or their elimination by other lymphocytes, accordingly dubbed "suppressors"? In short, what ultimately is at issue is the relationship between immunity and tolerance: is this a free zone opened up by the silence of the immune response, or rather one of its "negative" products? Peter Medawar had pointed to the latter possibility when he demonstrated that tolerance can be induced artificially: after inoculating a fetal mouse belonging to one genetically uniform strain by injecting it with cells from another, the first mouse subsequently becomes tolerant to cells belonging to the donor mouse strain. What we know from this is not only that an organism can learn to recognize originally foreign components as its own if it is trained early on, but also that it is the immune system that mediates this process of recognition. When Medawar describes tolerance as a very special situation, because the immunosuppressive agent is the antigen itself, although its use in adults should be supported by that of the immunosuppressive agents,[58] he is inscribing it, albeit with unique, self-limiting characteristics, within the very immune apparatus. And in fact tolerance can be induced, depending on the case and at different doses, by administering either antigens or antibodies. This means that tolerance is not a non-immunity, a kind of virtuous immunodeficiency; if anything, it is a reverse immunity: that which reverses the effects within the same lexicon. But if so, if tolerance is a product of the immune system itself, it means that, far from having a single-response repertoire, that of rejecting other-than-self, it includes the other within itself, not only as its driving force but also as one of its effects.

It appears that Alfred Tauber reached the same conclusion, starting from a different discursive context traceable back to the network theory of Niels Jerne, especially in the version formulated by the so-called School of Paris (ANT: *Autonomous Network Theory*). Again, without being able to go into too much detail, this is a cognitive perspective according to which the system also includes what is external to it, in the sense that its functioning is self-reflexive. This means that when the traditional opposition between antigens and antibodies is dropped, now replaced by the terms "epitopes" and "paratopes," each reticular element alternately, or even simultaneously, performs both roles, since each one recognizes and is recognized at the same time: "If we accept these statements," writes Jerne, "we may conclude that, formally, the immune system is a complex, enormous network of paratopes that recognizes groups of idiotopes, and idiotopes that are recognized by groups of paratopes."[59] But if this is true, any distinction between self and non-self, proper and improper, inside and outside vanish. How could the system expel something out of itself if the "outside" dimension itself is nothing but the reflection produced by an internal movement? Of course all this is not without its problems: "The reader with a mystical bent," writes Golub in an intentionally provocative tone, "might think that this situation is similar to what happens when, looking in the mirror, he sees the entire world in the reflected image."[60] The risk inherent to this perspective is indeed that all reality will come to be included in the standpoint of the self, which is exactly what authors like Varela and Coutinho seem to ascribe to when they state that "there exist only the self and its slight variations."[61] But, without underestimating the possible mentalistic derivations of this statement, the most striking aspect about it is its necessarily reversible nature: if all forms of alterity refer back to the self, this also means that the self is always and constitutively altered; indeed, that the self coincides with its alteration. It equally implies that if the subject is potentially everything—because it is absolutely indeterminate and indeterminable—it is also nothing. Moreover, a constitutively ambivalent outcome, located at the point of indistinguishability between the reinforcement and deconstruction of the subject, is somehow implicit in network theory: the moment it rejects the traditional view that the immune system only recognizes the other because if it recognized the self it would destroy it, the entire focal point is on the self. But in doing so, it ends up making the self indistinguishable from the other it seeks to differentiate itself from: "The immune system," writes Tauber, in fact "not only must work to identify itself in opposition to the other, it must also constantly define the self based on itself. On this kind of basis, immunity is a *process* that always involves an open system of self-definition that consistently produces self and other."[62]

At this point the whole immune dynamic takes on a shape that cannot be assimilated into the current interpretation: rather than acting as a barrier for selecting and excluding elements from the outside world, it acts as a sounding board for the presence of the world inside the self. The self is no longer a genetic constant or a preestablished repertoire, but rather a construct determined by a set of dynamic factors, compatible groupings, fortuitous encounters; nor is it a subject or an object, but rather, a principle of action, "a verb without a subject, or perhaps a predicate," as Tauber expresses it.[63] This signals the return of the idea—developed in different ways by Virchow and Nietzsche—of the body as a place of confrontation and competition between diverse, potentially conflicting cellular segments.[64] It is never original, complete, intact, "made" once and for all; rather, it constantly makes itself from one minute to the next, depending on the situation and encounters that determine its development. Its boundaries do not lock it up inside a closed world; on the contrary, they create its margin, a delicate and problematic one to be sure, but still permeable in its relationship with that which, while still located outside it, from the beginning traverses and alters it. We could say that, contrary to all the military interpretations, the immune system is itself the instrument of this alteration—even if, or precisely because, it seems to resist the alterations: every time it goes into action, the body is modified with respect to how it was before.

Perhaps the most extraordinary example of this dialectic— partly due to its symbolically germinal character—is pregnancy. How does it manage to happen? How can the fetus, encoded as "other" based on all normal immunological criteria, be tolerated by the maternal antibodies? What is the protective mechanism which, except in rare cases, allows or encourages its development as an exception to the natural principle of allograft rejection? As for all tolerance phenomena, the answer to this question firstly involves the blind spots of the immune system: namely, a kind of block that inhibits the normal expression of histocompatibility antigens in the cytotrophoblasts of the mother. Women develop certain types of antibodies permitting the embryo to survive by hiding the signals it secretes indicating that it is foreign. This answer does not give sufficient heed, however, to a far more complex dynamic, one that can be seen as a case of immunitary silence only from a superficial point of view. Far from being inactive, the immunity mechanism is working on a double front, because if on the one hand it is directed toward controlling the fetus, on the other hand it is also controlling itself. In short, by immunizing the other, it is also immunizing itself. It immunizes itself from an excess of immunization. The fact that the entire operation is performed as part of the immune function activities—and not as a failure to act—is proved by the fact that the antibodies are still what block or "fool" the self-defense system of the mother. But even more significant is the fact that their production—necessary to prevent the fetus from being recognized as foreign and, therefore, rejected—depends on a certain degree of genetic foreignness of the father: if too similar to the mother, the antibodies will not be generated, resulting in miscarriage. The antinomic picture this creates is clear: only if the paternal sperm is foreign enough to produce the blocking antibodies will the mother be able to tolerate the foreignness of the fetus—by ignoring it; so much so that to avoid miscarriages, the woman's body is inoculated with the father's antigens. This means that what allows the child to be preserved by the mother is not their "resemblance" but rather their diversity transmitted hereditarily from the father. Only as a stranger can the child become "proper."[65] In fact, contrary to the myth of symbiotic unity between the mother and the child she bears inside her, the mother is engaged in a furious battle with the fetus, with the externalization it introduces inside her:

> We always have before us the picture of a happy mother with a Mona Lisa smile, gazing at her protruding abdomen, with hands resting lightly on that "tumor" that she obviously deeply desires. Deep down, however, her body is doing its best to reject this foreign parasite. The fury of that attack, which nonetheless allows the fetus to survive, is inexplicable. How can a continuous immunological

reaction against a developing fetus end up protecting it, rather than destroying it?[66]

This is the ultimate—and prime—issue around which the entire immune paradigm wraps itself until reaching the point where it becomes indistinguishable from its opposite, "community": the force of the immune attack is precisely what keeps alive that which it should normally destroy. The mother is pitted against the child and the child against the mother, and yet what results from this conflict is the spark of life. Contrary to the metaphor of a fight to the death, what takes place in the mother's womb is a fight "to life," proving that difference and conflict are not necessarily destructive. Indeed, just as the attack of the mother protects the child, the child's attack can also save the mother from her self-injurious tendencies—which explains why autoimmune diseases undergo regression during pregnancy. This is the outcome of the dialectic that develops in the immune system between antibody cells and self-regulatory cells: in their mutual opposition, they promote each other's growth. Like a tug of war, the equilibrium of the whole is determined not by subtraction, but by the sum of the forces that oppose each other. In the same way, self-regulation is determined by the force of the immune response. A perspective is thus opened up within the immunitary logic that overturns its prevailing interpretation. From this perspective, nothing remains of the incompatibility between self and other. The other is the form the self takes where inside intersects with outside, the proper with the common, immunity with community.

*

The problem raised by immunology regarding the ability to know the other through the definition of self—or to know the self through the delimitation of the other—is such a classic one that it was already framed in its fundamental terms by Plato. The issue is certainly related to the aporia raised by Socrates in the *Meno* (80e): that in order to start to know something, you already have to know it in some way; otherwise you would not know what you were looking for, or even if there were something to look for in the first place. If the other (the stranger, the alien) really is such—not only different, but totally unknown—how can it come to be known, and how can the need to know it arise in the first place? This question has been raised once again in contemporary philosophical discussion by Bernhard Waldenfels: how is it possible to have an experience—not to mention a science—of the stranger or the alien (the German *Fremde*) starting from one's own perspective, that of the "proper"?[67] His basic thesis is that as long as the two terms remain completely unrelated—closed off in their absoluteness—this is in no way achievable. But this is the case even if they overlap to the point of losing their originary difference and hence their very identity. The inaccessible, in order to achieve its status, may not be either totally inaccessible or directly accessible—otherwise it would negate its own status. The only way to overcome this logical obstacle would seem to be to aim—as Husserl suggested—for a "verifiable accessibility of what is originally not accessible."[68] This hardly solves the problem, though. Where does the point of transition between what is originally not accessible and the accessible lie? Waldenfels locates it in a modification of subjective experience capable of making absence present: "What is not accessible becomes accessible in the experience of the strange, just as the past becomes accessible in memory and in nothing else."[69] This reference to remembering is precisely what brings even phenomenological estrangement into the sphere of the Platonic assumption that ultimately you may only know that which is, albeit in an altered form, already known. In this way the experience of the stranger is already anticipated— and thus neutralized—in that of the proper.

It could be said that the entire Western tradition has remained held in this antinomic turn: the strange is conceivable only in terms of its preventive dissolution. Not even the attempt carried out by the most radical ethnology to shift the point of observation from the self to the other has managed to escape it. On the contrary, it winds up contrastively confirming it, since the self-estrangement of the stranger—its absolute "property" of strangeness—is nothing but the reverse mirror image of the appropriation of the proper. The terms of the aporia are the same as those laid down by Socrates: either the stranger is truly strange—and therefore not accessible—or it is not, and therefore, it is proper from the outset. Is it not odd that even though the science of immunology shifts the question onto its most originary plane, meaning into the bio-logical sphere (or perhaps, precisely because it does so), it is still gripped in the same vise? I am thinking particularly about the theory that the immune system expels everything that is marked as non-self by the major histocompatibility complex (MHC). Now the analogy, actually the homology, with the Platonic model is based on the fact that, just like in the myth of anamnesis, the MHC also only recognizes as its own the elements it has already met during the stages of embryogenesis. More than a few of the terms commonly used in immunology—"training," "apprentice-ship," "competence," "memory"—reveal this ancestry in the lexicon as well. Moreover, Niels Jerne—to whom we owe the most systematic formulation of the theory of clonal selection—unhesi-tatingly illustrated its functioning precisely by referring to the *Meno*:[70] the ability of antibody synthesis is not learned from the outside, but is inherent from its origins, exactly in the way the ideal forms in the Platonic theory are prerational, inherent to soul. Not only that, but just like in the classical distinction between icons and simulacra—in other words, between copies that directly imitate the ideas and copies that imitate the copies—the histocom-patibility of antigens is measured by the degree of their "likeness" to the original parts of the body. It would seem that from this point of view as well we have to admit that there is no experience of the stranger that is not presupposed by that of the proper: the stranger is acceptable, and accepted, only if it is already part of the proper.

As we have said, however, this is not the only possible conclu-sion; this was the major route that immunological science took in its historic development, but it does bear the figure of its opposite impressed upon itself. Starting from Jerne again, the originator of the theory of clonal selection but also of the previously described network theory, Adrian Mackenzie has argued convincingly that if you look at the immune system function in the light of network theory, it not only escapes the Platonic assumption, it actually provides for its radical deconstruction.[71] Indeed, once a criterion of complete reversibility between antibody binding sites and anti-genic determinants has been established, any prior discrimination between "copies" and "originals" drops away. Since every antigen can interact with any antibody, and indeed since the antibody itself becomes an antigen when looked at from another point of view, the primacy of like over unlike becomes meaningless, just as the separation between inside and outside no longer makes sense. Not because—as is sometimes stated in an exaggeratedly mentalistic key—the outside does not exist, but because the outside is related to the inside in a form that is already determined by their preliminary encounter. If the external antigen is "seen" from the inside as an antibody, just as, from another perspective, the antibody assumes the function of the antigen, what occurs in this fashion, rather than a confrontation between two different positions, is a comparison; or better, a continuous exchange, between an internalized outside and an externalized inside. In this way, far from being the result of an exclusion—or even a selection—of the differences, it becomes their own product. The equilibrium of the immune system is not the result of defensive mobilization against something other than self, but the joining line, or the point of convergence, between two divergent series. It is not governed by the primacy of the same over the like and the like over the different, but by the continuously changing principle of their relationship. In this sense, nothing is more inherently dedicated to communication than the immune system. Its quality is not measured by its ability to provide protection from a foreign agent, but from the complexity of the response that it provokes: each differential element absorbed from the outside does nothing but expand and enrich the range of its internal potential. Beyond the various theoretical, anthropological, or literary formulations, this is perhaps the only—certainly the first—experience of the stranger in relation to but also in the very constitution of the proper. At its foundation there does not lie the remembrance of an uncontaminated genetic principle, but the experience of its own original alteration. Before any other transformation, each body is already exposed to the need for its own exposure. This is the condition common to all that is immune: the endless perception of its own finitude.

*

What is the "immunological self"? The problematic nature of this question lies in its formulation even more than in its answer. Is the immune system "something"? And, more specifically, can it be defined, as is commonly done in the scientific literature, using the term "self"? To what extent, in other words, can it be designated using a personal reflexive pronoun? As is well known, especially over recent years, the immune system has been depicted as a corporeal nucleus, a mental construct, a semiotic system, not to mention the political and military representation we have dwelled on most extensively. Quite apart from any judgment as to how pertinent these metaphorical transpositions may finally be to a biological phenomenon, our preliminary question concerns the term that all of them use to name it: *self, selbst, soi, se.* Is it legitimate—or simply plausible—to denote the biological immune system using the positive form of a personal subject? Or should a negative form be used instead? Considering the basic aporia that defines its functioning, the answer seems obligatory. If, as is generally believed, the fundamental task of the immune system is to reject what is other than self, we must necessarily exclude the possibility that it can be aimed directly at itself. From an immunological standpoint, the "self" is defined only negatively, based on what it is not. This is the paradoxical conclusion, but one that is irrefutable, at least starting from the assumptions of the interpretive approach that passes from Ehrlich to the theory of clonal selection: as is implicit in the evocative concept of *horror auto-toxicus,* if the self recognized itself in an immune form, it would annihilate itself. The only way to survive is to be unaware of oneself. The object of the immune function, in short, is never the self (except, of course, in the catastrophic case of autoimmune diseases) but rather everything that is not self. The "self" can only be immunologically expressed in the negative. Then why use the very grammatical term that it can logically never identify with in order to represent it?

Yet the grammarians tell us that this is not exactly how things stand, that they are far more complicated. This is not because the immunitary logic can escape the aporia that defines it but because, albeit in a different sphere, the grammatical aspect both reproduces and illuminates it. Claude Debru has spoken about a true "grammatical paradox" in this regard, about a "series of enigmas" that are generated around the third person reflexive pronoun.[72] To begin with, they concern its complex relationship with the noun: when the definite article "the" is put in front of the pronoun "self"—as the language of bioimmunology does—it tends to be nominalized. In other words, it shifts from a purely grammatical function to a conceptual term designating a reality that is external to the instance of discourse. The result is that in this case we are faced with a pronoun that is no longer only a pronoun and a noun that maintains its pronominal character, as is the reflexive. Of course, the grammarians teach that a distinction still exists: while nouns refer to an indeterminate type of entities, since pronouns do not really have any reality outside the linguistic event, they refer to entities of a personal nature, most clearly apparent in the form of personal pronouns. And yet, this point is precisely what gives rise to a further asymmetry. As Benveniste especially has stressed, while the first and second person pronouns have no existence except in the act of being uttered, the third person has the distinction of referring to a non-discursive reality. This explains why many languages have no pronouns or verbal endings for the third person. This is particularly important in Arabic, in which the third person specifically designates "he who is absent." It is true that Indo-European languages have a third-person verbal form, but this can be used even when the person is not designated or as an impersonal form. The conclusion Benveniste draws from this is disconcerting: "The 'third person' is not a 'person'; it is really the verbal form whose function is to express the 'non-person'."[73] Rather than toning down this definition, it needs to be examined in all its significance. It does not allude to a kind of depersonalization of what would remain a person, but specifically to a non-person: "There is no apheresis of the person; it is exactly the non-person."[74]

This gives us a glimpse of a first correspondence with the negative identity of the immunological self. As this may not coincide with itself—it can be defined only by what it is not—so the pronoun that represents it is a non-personal person, characterized by the status of non-person. If we shift our attention from the pronoun, as such, to its reflexive character,[75] the similarities are even more exact. Once again following Benveniste—in the wake of the essential studies by Antoine Meillet[76]—we learn that the Latin pronoun *se*, like its modern derivatives, carries inside an ancient Indo-European root destined to assume even greater importance when, as in our case, it is nominalized.[77] This is the term *swe* from which the Latin *suus* and *soror* derive, and the Greek *ethos* and *etes* (relative, ally). Benveniste concludes from this that it descends from two different semantic lines, the first referring to the individual self, and the second to a wider circle of relatives or some kind of community. The "property" the theme *swe* refers to is, in short, shared by multiple individuals within the same group. This consequently explains both *idios* (belonging only to itself) and *hetaîros* (belonging to a larger whole): something that is proper, but only to the extent it is common to those who are thus characterized. It is a cross between the singularity of *idiotes* and the plurality of *sodalis*, but also between the reflective *se* of "itself" (*se stesso*) and the disjunctive *se-* of *sed*. Enriched by these references, we can now return to the immunological self. Even on the simple level of conceptual resonances between heterogeneous semantic contexts, what results is a breathtaking correspondence. If we cross the original dual nature of the root *swe* with the non-personality of the third person pronoun, the resulting effect casts new light even on the "ontological" negativity of the immunological self. More than a simple logic of negation, it seems to refer to a contradiction by which identity is simultaneously affirmed and altered at the same time: it is established in the form of its own alteration. Like the pronoun that names it and the root from which the pronoun descends, the immunological self would thus be that which is more individual and that which is more shared. By overlaying these two divergent meanings onto one figure, what we get is the unique profile of a shared individuality or a sharing of individuality. It is perhaps in this chiasm that the enigma of immunity still lies preserved.

Notes

Introduction

1   See J. Korpela, "Das Medizinalpersonal im antiken Rom. Eine Sozialgeschichtliche Untersuchung," in *Annales Academiae Scientiarum Fennicae, Humanae Litterae* 45 (1987), pp. 35 ff.

2   J. Scarborough, *Roman Medicine*, Thames & Hudson, London 1969, p. 113.

3   See in general, K. H. Below, "Der Arzt im römischen Recht," in *Münchener Beiträge zur Papyrusforschung und antiken Rechtsgeschichte* 37 (1953), pp. 22 ff.

4   See J. André, *Être medecin à Rome*, Payot & Rivages, Paris 1995, pp. 140–43.

5   G. W. Bowersock, *Greek Sophists in the Roman Empire*, The Clarendon Press, Oxford 1969, p. 31.

6   See V. Nutton, "Two Notes on Immunities: Digest 27, 1, 6, 10 and 11," in *From Democedes to Harvey*, Variorum Reprints, London 1988, p. 62.

7   M. Vegetti and P. Manuli, "La medicina e l'igiene," in *Storia di Roma*, Einaudi, Turin 1989, vol. 6, p. 395.

8   Ibid., pp. 396–97.

I Appropriation

1   See Roberto Esposito, *Communitas: The Origin and Destiny of Community*, trans. Timothy C. Campbell, Stanford University Press, Stanford, Calif. 2010.

2 Simone Weil, *Need for Roots*, Routledge, London and New York 1996, p. 3.

3 "Human Personality," in *Simone Weil: An Anthology*, ed. Sian Miles, Grove Press, New York 1986, p. 64.

4 Weil, *Need for Roots*, p. 4.

5 Ibid., p. 64.

6 The genealogy of the *proprium* traced out by P. Barcellona in *L'individualismo proprietario*, Boringhieri, Turin 1987, is still useful in this regard.

7 Friedrich Nietzsche, *Genealogy of morals*, Dover Publications, Mineola, N.Y. 2003, p. 45; in German: *Zur Genealogie der Moral*, in *Sämtliche Werke*, De Gruyter, Berlin 1967 ff., vol. 6, p. 2.

8 Weil, "Human Personality," p. 61. For this interpretation of Weil, see my *Categorie dell'impolitico*, il Mulino, Bologna 1988, pp. 189–244.

9 Ibid., p. 62.

10 Weil, *Need for Roots*, p. 275.

11 Martin Heidegger, *Parmenides*, in *Gesamtausgabe*, Klostermann, Frankfurt am Main 1982, vol. 64, pp. 58–59.

12 Rudolf von Jhering, *Geist des römischen Rechts auf den verschiedenen Stufen seiner Entwicklung*, Scientia, Aalen 1993 (Leipzig 1866), vol. 1, p. 109. See also the introduction by F. Fusillo to the Italian translation of *Das Schuldmoment in römischen Privatrecht* (1867), *Il momento della colpa nel diritto privato romano*, Jovene, Naples 1990, pp. xxiii ff.

13 Ibid., pp. 112–13.

14 Walter Benjamin, "Critique of Violence," in *Reflections*, Harcourt Brace Jovanovich, New York 1978, p. 287.

15 See also E. Castrucci, *La forma e la decisione*, Giuffré, Milan 1985, pp. 67–89.

16 Benjamin, "Critique of Violence", p. 281.

17 See F. Garritano, *Aporie comunitarie*, Jaca Book, Milan 1999, p. 26.

18 I am referring to Giorgio Agamben, *Homo sacer*, Einaudi, Turin 1995, pp. 36 ff.

19 Carl Schmitt, *Political Theology: Four Chapters on the Concept of Sovereignty*, trans. George Schwab, MIT Press, Cambridge, Mass.-London 1985, p. 5.

20 "Fate and Character," in *Reflections*, Harcourt Brace Jovanovich, New York 1978, p. 204.

21 For more on "this" Kafka, see the intense pages written by M. Cacciari in *Icone della legge*, Adelphi, Milan 1985, pp. 56–137, as well

as, more in general, on the theological character of law, also by Cacciari, "Diritto e Giustizia," in *Il Centauro*, 1981, n. 2, pp. 58–81. On the relationship between Benjamin, Kafka, and Schmitt, see F. Desideri, *La porta della giustizia*, Pendragon, Bologna 1995, pp. 23 ff.

22   Benjamin, "Critique of Violence," p. 286.
23   Ibid., p. 295.
24   Ibid., p. 296.
25   I am referring especially to Jacques Derrida, *Force de loi*, Galilée, Paris 1994.
26   Thomas Berns, *Violence de la loi à la Renaissance*, Kimé, Paris 2000.
27   Jacques Derrida, *Otobiographies. L'enseignement de Nietzsche et la politique du nom propre*, Galilée, Paris 1984.
28   Benjamin, "Fate and Character," p. 203.
29   René Girard, *Violence and the Sacred*, Continuum, London-New York 2005, p. 153–54, 157.
30   Ibid., p. 31.
31   Simon Weil, *The Notebooks of Simone Weil*, vol. 1; Routledge, New York 2004, p. 497; in French: *Cahiers*, vol. 3, Plon, Paris 1974. See also p. 266. On the relationship between Girard and Weil, see W. Tommasi, *Simone Weil*, Liguori, Naples 1997, pp. 95–117.
32   Girard, *Violence and the Sacred*, p. 35.
33   Ibid., p. 18.
34   Ibid., p. 305.
35   Ibid., p. 305.
36   Ibid., p. 8.
37   Ibid., p. 258–59.
38   Ibid., p. 37.
39   Ibid., p. 33.
40   Ibid., p. 22.
41   See in this regard L. Alfieri, "Dal conflitto dei doppi alla trascendenza giudiziaria: Il problema giuridico e politico in René Girard," in *L'immaginario e il potere*, ed. G. Chiodi, Giappichelli, Turin 1992, but also, more generally, R. Escobar, *Metamorfosi della paura*, il Mulino, Bologna 1997, pp. 169 ff.
42   Girard, *Violence and the Sacred*, p. 23.
43   Ibid., p. 40–41.
44   René Girard, *Things hidden since the foundation of the world*, Continuum, London-New York 2003, pp. 195–96.
45   Girard, *Violence and the Sacred*, pp. 41 ff.
46   Ibid., p. 42.

47 G. Carillo, *Vico: Origine e genealogia dell'ordine*, Editoriale Scientifica, Naples 2000.

48 Giambattista Vico, *The New Science*, trans. and ed. T. Goddard Bergin and M. Fisch, Cornell University Press, Ithaca, N.Y. 1948, Book II. Poetic Wisdom 221, par. 658.

49 Niklas Luhmann, *Social Systems*, Stanford University Press, Stanford, Calif. 1995, p. 374.

50 Ibid., p. 376.

51 Niklas Luhmann, *Ausdifferenzierung des Rechts: Beiträge zur Rechtssoziologie und Rechtstheorie*, Suhrkamp, Frankfurt am Main 1981.

52 Niklas Luhmann, "The Autopoeisis of Social Systems," in *Essays on Self-Reference*, Columbia University Press, New York 1990, p. 6.

53 Ibid., p. 7.

54 The immunitary semantics of the law in Luhmann is a central topic of the book by B. Romano, *Filosofia e diritto dopo Luhmann*, Bulzoni, Rome 1996.

55 Luhmann, "Autopoiesis," p. 12–13.

56 Luhmann, *Social Systems*, p. 140.

57 Luhmann, "Autopoiesis," p. 7.

58 Luhmann, *Social systems*, p. 372.

59 Regarding the complex question of the relationship between the autopoesis of living systems and that of social systems in Luhmann, see at least *State, Law, Economy as Autopoietic Systems: Regulation and Autonomy in a New Perspective*, ed. A. Febbraio and G. Teubner, Giuffrè, Milan 1991; and G. Teubner, *Recht als Autopoietisches System*, Suhrkamp, Frankfurt am Main 1989.

60 N. Luhmann, "Conflitto e diritto," in *Laboratorio Politico*, 1982, no. 1, p. 14.

61 In this regard see E. Resta, *L'ambiguo diritto*, Angeli, Milano 1984, pp. 34 ff. On Luhmann's relation to Talcott Parsons, see G. Marramao, *L'ordine disincantato*, Editori Riuniti, Rome 1985, pp. 30 ff.

62 Luhmann, *Social systems*, p. 371.

63 Ibid., p. 370.

64 Ibid., p. 382.

II The *katechon*

1 Jacques Derrida, "Faith and Knowledge: the Two Sources of 'Religion' at the Limit of Reason Alone," in *Religion: Cultural Memory in the Present*, Stanford University Press, Stanford, Calif. 1998, pp. 1–78.

2   Ibid., p. 44.
3   Ibid., p. 53.
4   Emile Benveniste, *The Indo-European Language and Society*, U of Miami P, Coral Gables, Fla. 1973.
5   Ibid., p. 472.
6   Ibid., p. 452.
7   Ibid., p. 454.
8   Ibid., p. 467.
9   Ibid., p. 455.
10 Ibid., p. 469.
11 Ibid., p. 391.
12 Ibid., p. 522.
13 Derrida, "Faith and Knowledge," pp. 34–36.
14 Benveniste, *Indo-European Language*, p. 452.
15 Ibid., p. 453.
16 Max Weber, *The Sociology of Religion*, Beacon Press, Boston, Mass. 1992.
17 Henri Bergson, *The Two Sources of Morality and Religion*, Mac-Millan and Co., London 1935, p. 109.
18 Ibid., p. 115.
19 Ibid., p. 132.
20 Niklas Luhmann, *Funktion der Religion*, Suhrkamp, Frankfurt am Main 1977 [Quoted from Italian version: *Funzione della religione*, Morcelliana, Brescia 1991, p. 36].
21 Walter Burkert, *Structure and History in Greek Mythology and Ritual*, University of California Press, Berkeley 1979, p. 50.
22 See E. Lévinas, *Du Sacre au Saint. Cinq nouvelles lectures talmudiques*, Minuit, Paris 1977.
23 For a different slant, see V. Vitiello, *Cristianesimo senza redenzione*, Laterza, Bari-Rome 1995; also by Vitiello, "La spada, l'amore e la nuda esistenza, ovvero: cristianesimo e nichilismo," in *Nichilismo e politica*, eds. R. Esposito, C. Galli and V. Vitiello, Laterza, Bari-Rome 2000, pp. 221–46.
24 M. Buber, *Reden über das Judentum*, in *Werke*, Kösel & Lambert Schneider, München-Heidelberg 1964, p. 152.
25 A. Badiou, *Saint Paul. La fondation de l'universalisme*, PUF, Paris 1997.
26 I am referring, naturally, to Karl Barth, *Epistle to the Romans*, Oxford University Press, Oxford 1933.
27 Jacob Taubes, *The Political Theology of Paul*, trans. Dana Hollander, Stanford University Press, Stanford, Calif. 2004.
28 Ibid., p. 131.

29 Carl Schmitt, *Nomos of the Earth*, Telos P, New York 2003.
30 Dietrich Bonhoeffer, *Works*, *Vol. 10. Ethics*, Augsburg Fortress, Minneapolis, Minn. 2008.
31 See Massimo Cacciari, *Dell'inizio*, Adelphi, Milan 1990, pp. 623 ff.
32 On this topic, see G. Meuter, *Der Katechon. Zur Carl Schmitts fundamentalistischer Kritik der Zeit*, Duncker & Humblot, Berlin 1994, as well as A. Scalone, " 'Katechon' e scienza del diritto in Carl Schmitt," in *Filosofia Politica*, 1998, n. 2, pp. 283–92.
33 Giorgio Agamben, *The Time that Remains*, trans. Patricia Dailey, Stanford University Press, Stanford, Calif. 2005.
34 On the various meanings of "political theology" see *Teologia politica*, eds. L. Sartori and M. Nicoletti, Centro Editoriale Dehoniano, Bologna 1991, but especially Carlo Galli, *Genealogia della politica*, il Mulino, Bologna 1996, pp. 333–459.
35 Erik Peterson, *Der Monotheismus als politisches Problem*, Kösel, München 1951. On the issues discussed by Peterson, but using a highly original interpretation in defining political theology, see R. Panattoni, *Appartenenza ed Eschaton*, Liguori, Naples 2001.
36 The reference is to Carl Schmitt's *Politische Theologie II* (Duncker & Humblot, Berlin 1984); English version *Political Theology II*, Polity Press, Cambridge 2008.
37 Carl Schmitt, *Roman Catholicism and Political Form*, trans. G. L. Ulmen, Greenwood Press, Westport, Conn. 1996, p. 12.
38 Henri De Lubac, *Corpus mysticum: the Eucharist and the church in the Middle Ages: historical survey*, University of Notre Dame Press, Notre Dame Ind. 2007.
39 Ernst Kantorowicz, *The King's Two Bodies. A study in mediaeval political theology*, Princeton University Press, Princeton, N.J. 1997.
40 Ibid., p. 13.
41 Ibid., p. 311–12.
42 Ibid., p. 438.
43 See ibid., pp. 269 ff. See also R. E. Giesey, *The Royal Funeral Ceremony in Renaissance France*, Droz, Geneva 1960.
44 Marcel Gauchet, *The Disenchantment of the World: A political history of religion*, trans. Oscar Burge, Princeton University Press, Princeton, N.J. 1997.
45 Ibid., p. 22.
46 See C. Lefort, "Permanence du théologico-politique?," in his *Essais sur le politique*, Paris, Seuil 1986, pp. 251–300.
47 For a phenomenology of current forms of the sacred, see G. Filoramo, *Figure del sacro*, Morcelliana, Brescia 1993.

48 Gauchet, *Disenchantment*, p. 4.
49 M. Richir, *Du sublime en politique*, Payot, Paris 1991.
50 Ibid., p. 97.
51 De Lubac, *Corpus Mysticum*, p. 84.
52 Ibid., p. 85.
53 Ibid., p. 123.
54 Immanuel Kant, *Über das Mißlingen aller philosophischen Versuche in der Theodizee*, in *Gesammelte Schriften*, Akademie Textausgabe, De Gruyter, Berlin-Leipzig 1969, vol. 8 [for English version see "On the Failure of All Attempted Philosophical Theodicies," in *Kant on History and Religion*, ed. and trans. M. Despland, McGill-Queen's University Press, Montreal 1973].
55 Odo Marquard, *In Defense of the Accidental*, Oxford University Press, Oxford 1991, p. 10.
56 Kant, *Über das Mißlingen aller philosophischen Versuche in der Theodizee*, vol. 8.
57 Odo Marquard, *Aesthetica und Anaesthetica*, Paderborn, Schöningh 1989. G. Marano, in *La parola infetta*, Nuova Editrice Magenta, Varese, 2003 treats the problem of immunity in terms of esthetics.
58 Marquard, *In Defense*, p. 12.
59 Hans Blumenberg, *The Legitimacy of the Modern Age*, MIT Press, Cambridge, Mass. 1983, p. 53.
60 P. Ricoeur, *Le Mal*, Labor & Fides, Genève 1986, p. 25 [English version: "Evil: A challenge to philosophy and theology," in *Journal of the American Academy of Religion*, Vol. 53/3, 1985].
61 Marquard, *In Defense*, p. 13.
62 Ibid., p. 15.
63 From a different perspective, see also P. Flores d'Arcais, *L'individuo libertario*, Einaudi, Turin 1999, pp. 41–42.

III *Compensatio*

1 Odo Marquard, *In Defense of the Accidental*, Oxford University Press, Oxford 1991, p. 23.
2 J. Svagelski, *L'idee de compensation en France*, L'Hermès, Lyon 1981.
3 See C. Appleton, *Histoire de la compensation en droit romain*, Masson, Paris 1895.
4 Odo Marquard, *Aesthetica und Anaesthetica*, Paderborn, Schöningh 1989, p. 131.
5 J. Svagelski, *L'idee de compensation en France*, p. 9.

6   See P.-H. Azaïs, *Des compensations dans les destinees humaines*,
    Garnery, Paris 1808.
7   Svagelski, *L'idee de compensation en France*, pp. 79–80.
8   By Theodor W. Adorno, see especially *Negative Dialektik*, Suhrkamp,
    Frankfurt am Main 1966 [Italian version: *Dialettica negativa*,
    Einaudi, Turin 1970, pp. 112–13]. See also M. Horkheimer, *Kri-
    tische Theorie. Eine Dokumentation*, Fischer, Frankfurt am Main
    1968 [Italian version: *Teoria critica*, Einaudi, Turin 1964, I,
    pp. 197–223].
9   See especially Martin Heidegger, *Ontologie. Hermeneutik der Fak-
    tizität*, Klostermann, Frankfurt am Main 1988 [Italian version:
    Ontologia. Ermeneutica dell'effettività, ed. E. Mazzarella, Guida,
    Naples 1992, pp. 29 ff.; Heidegger, *Kant und das Problemder
    Metaphysik*, in *Gesamtausgabe*, op. cit., III [Italian version: *Kant e
    il problema della metafisica*, Laterza, Bari-Rome 1981, p. 181];
    Heidegger, *Holzwege*, in *Gesamtausgabe*, V [Italian version: *Sentieri
    interrotti*, La Nuova Italia, Florence 1968, p. 98].
10 Michel Foucault, *Les mots et les choses*, Gallimard, Paris 1966
    [quoted from Italian version: *Le parole e le cose*, Rizzoli, Milan
    1978, p. 351].
11 Niklas Luhmann, *Gesellschaftsstruktur und Semantik*, Suhrkamp,
    Frankfurt am Main 1980 [quoted from Italian version: *Struttura
    della società e semantica*, Laterza, Bari-Rome 1983, pp. 205–6].
12 Ibid., p. 226.
13 On this topic, see my essay "Nichilismo e comunità," in *Nichilismo
    e politica*, ed. R. Esposito, C. Galli and V. Vitiello, Laterza, Bari-
    Rome 2000, pp. 25–40; and on Hobbes, see my book *Communitas*,
    pp. 3–31.
14 In this regard see R. Prandini, *Le radici fiduciarie del legame sociale*,
    Angeli, Milan 1998, and especially E. Pulcini's *L'individuo senza
    passioni*, Bollati-Boringhieri, Turin 2001.
15 See the entire issue of *Sociologia e politiche sociali*, 1999, no. 3—
    including an Italian translation of the manuscript by T. Parsons, *The
    American Societal Community. A General Outline*—ed. R. Pran-
    dini. In addition to the essay by Matteo Bortolini in the same issue,
    see also his "La democrazia associativa," in *Teoria politica*, 2000,
    no. 2, pp. 77–96.
16 Friedrich Nietzsche, *Gay Science*, Cambridge University Press,
    Cambridge 2001, pp. 212–13.
17 Friedrich Nietzsche, *Genealogy of Morals, Ecce Homo*, ed. Walter
    Kaufmann, Random House, 1989, III/13.
18 Ibid., III/13.

19 Ibid., III/21.
20 J. G. Herder, *Ideen zur Philosophie der Geschichte der Menschheit*, in *Sämtliche Werke*, Weidmannsche Buchhandlung, Berlin 1877–1913, (reprint: Hildesheim 1967–68), XIII-XIV [Quoted from Italian version: *Idee per la filosofia della storia dell'umanità*, ed. V. Verra, Zanichelli, Bologna 1971, p. 89].
21 Ibid., p. 118.
22 M. Scheler, "Die Stellung des Menschen im Kosmos," in *Gesammelte Werke*, Francke, Bern-München 1976, IX [Quoted from Italian version: "La posizione dell'uomo nel cosmo," in *La posizione dell'uomo nel cosmo e altri saggi*, ed. R. Padellaro, Fabbri, Milan 1970, p. 195].
23 M. Scheler, "Mensch und Geschichte," in *Gesammelte Werk*, op. cit., IX [Quoted from Italian version: "Uomo e storia," in *Lo spirito del capitalismo e altri saggi*, ed. R. Racinaro, Guida, Naples 1988, pp. 277, 279].
24 Scheler, "Die Stellung," p. 203.
25 Ibid., p. 204.
26 G. Anders, "Une interprétation de l'a posteriori," in *Recherches philosophiques*, IV (1934–35) [Quoted from the Italian version: "La natura dell'esistenza," in *Patologia della libertà*, ed. K. P. Liessmann and R. Russo, Palomar, Bari 1993, p. 43].
27 G. Anders, "Pathologie de la liberté," in *Recherches philosophiques*, VI (1936–37) [Quoted from Italian version: "Patologia della libertà," in *Patologia della libertà*, op. cit., p. 67].
28 G. Anders, "La natura dell'esistenza," p. 48.
29 G. Anders, "Patologia della libertà," p. 57.
30 Ibid., p. 58.
31 Ibid., pp. 71–72.
32 For a detailed reconstruction of Plessner's historical and cultural world, see S. Giammusso, *Potere e comprendere. La questione dell'esperienza storica e l'opera di Helmuth Plessner*, Guerini e Associati, Naples 1995; a broad interpretation of his thought placed in the framework of philosophical anthropology is provided by M. Russo in *La provincia dell'uomo. Studio su Helmuth Plessner e sulproblema dell'antropologia filosofica*, La città del sole, Naples 2000, with an introduction by V. Vitiello.
33 Helmuth Plessner, *Die Wissenschaftliche Idee. Ein Entwurf über ihre Form*, in *Gesammelte Schriften*, Suhrkamp, Frankfurt am Main 1980–85, I, p. 101.
34 Helmuth Plessner, *Die Einheit der Sinne. Grundlinien einer Ästhesiologie des Geistes*, in *Gesammelte Schriften*, op. cit., III, p. 314.

35 Helmuth Plessner, *Conditio humana*, in *Gesammelte Schriften*, op. cit., VIII [Quoted from Italian version: *Conditio humana*, in *I Propilei. Grande storia universale del mondo*, Mondadori, Milan 1967, I, p. 71].

36 Plessner, *Macht und menschliche Natur*, in *Gesammelte Schriften*, op. cit., V, p. 225.

37 Plessner, *Die Stufen des Organischen und der Mensch*, in *Gesammelte Schriften*, op. cit., IV, p. 385.

38 Plessner, *Conditio humana*, p. 72.

39 Ibid., p. 72.

40 Ibid., p. 72.

41 Ibid., p. 73.

42 Helmuth Plessner, *Grenzen der Gemeinschaft. Eine Kritik des sozialen Radikalismus*, in *Gesammelte Schriften*, op. cit., V [English version: *The Limits of Community: A Critique of Social Radicalism*, trans. Andrew Wallace, Humanity Books, Amherst, N.Y. 1999].

43 Plessner, *The Limits of Community*, p. 136.

44 Ibid., p. 144.

45 See Helmuth Plessner, *Diesseits der Utopie*, Diederichs, Düsseldorf-Köln 1966 [Italian version: *Al di qua dell'utopia*, Marietti, Genoa 1974, p. 130].

46 Friedrich Nietzsche, "On Truth and Lie in an Extra-Moral Sense," trans. Walter Kaufmann, in *The Continental Aesthetics Reader*, ed. Clive Cazeaux, Routledge, London 2000, pp. 53–54.

47 Plessner, *Limits of Community*, p. 134.

48 Ibid., p. 141.

49 Ibid. Quoted from Italian version: *Limiti della comunità. Per una critica del radicalismo sociale*, ed. B. Accarino, Laterza, Bari-Rome 2001, p. 93.

50 Ibid., p. 154.

51 Ibid., p. 162.

52 R. Kramme, "Antropologia politica. L'immagine antropologica della società in Helmuth Plessner," in *Ratio imaginis*, ed. and introduction by B. Accarino, Ponte alle Grazie, Florence 1991, p. 100.

53 Carl Schmitt, *Der Begriff des Politischen*, Duncker & Humblot, München-Leipzig 1932 [Quoted from English version: *Concept of the Political*, trans. George Schwab, University of Chicago Press, Chicago 2007, p. 59–60].

54 Theodor W. Adorno, *Minima Moralia*, trans. Dennis Redmond, 2005, http://www.efn.org/~dredmond/MinimaMoralia.html, part I, aphorism 16.

55 Plessner, *Limits of Community*, p. 184.

56   B. Accarino, "Le ragioni del mondo. L'anti-comunitarismo di Helmuth Plessner," in H. Plessner, *Limiti della comunità*, Laterza, Bari-Rome 2001, p. 167.

57   Ibid., 171.

58   See B. Accarino, "Contingenza. Il tatto come categoria delle scienze sociali," in *Le figure del consenso*, Milella, Lecce 1989, pp. 163–81.

59   See R. von Jhering, *Der Zweck im Recht*, Olmas, Hildesheim–New York 1970, pp. 569–93.

60   Plessner, *Limits of Community* [Quoted from Italian version: *Limiti della comunità. Per una critica del radicalismo sociale*, ed. B. Accarino, Laterza, Bari-Rome 2001, p. 101].

61   M. Merleau-Ponty, *Le visible et l'invisible*, Gallimard, Paris 1964 [Quoted from Italian version: ed. M. Carbone, *Il visibile e l'invisibile*, Bompiani, Milan 1994, pp. 265–66].

62   For a clear introduction to Gehlen's work see the essays that U. Fadini has contributed over the years, especially those collected in his *Il corpo imprevisto. Filosofia, antropologia e tecnica in Arnold Gehlen*, Angeli, Milan 1988. The monograph by F. G. Di Paola, *La teoria sociale di Arnold Gehlen*, Angeli, Milan 1984 is also still useful.

63   A. Gehlen, *Wirklicher und unwirklicher Geist*, in *Philosophische Schriften*, Klostermann, Frankfurt am Main 1978, I, p. 89. In this regard see W. Lepenies, *Melancholie und Gesellschaft*, Suhrkamp, Frankfurt am Main 1969 [Italian version: *Melanconia e società*, Guida, Naples 1985, pp. 235 ff.].

64   Ibid., p. 266.

65   See M. Scheler, *Wesen und Formen der Sympathie*, in *Gesammelte Werke*, op. cit., VII [Italian version: *Essenza e forme della simpatia*, Città Nuova, Rome 1980, p. 334].

66   Arnold Gehlen, *Man in the Age of Technology*, Columbia University Press, New York 1980, p. 14.

67   Arnold Gehlen, *Anthropologische Forschung*, Rowohlt, Hamburg 1961 [Quoted from Italian version: *Prospettive antropologiche*, ed. G. Poggi, il Mulino, Bologna 1987, p. 28].

68   Arnold Gehlen, *Man, His Nature and Place in the World*, Columbia University Press, New York 1988, p. 52.

69   Ibid., p. 28.

70   Ibid., p. 43.

71   Ibid., p. 55.

72   Ibid. [Quoted from Italian version: *L'uomo. La sua natura e il suo posto nel mondo*, Feltrinelli, Milan 1990, p. 379].

73 See M. Hauriou, "Théorie de l'institution et de la fondation," in *Cahiers de la nouvelle journee*, (1925), no. 4.

74 Arnold Gehlen, *Prospettive antropologiche*, p. 46.

75 Arnold Gehlen, *Urmensch und Spätkultur*, Athenaion, Wiesbaden 1977.

76 Ibid., p. 443.

77 Ibid., p. 90.

78 Ibid., p. 30.

79 Gehlen, *Prospettive antropologiche*, p. 90.

80 H. Popitz, *Der Aufbruch zur artifiziellen Gesellschaft*, Mohr, Tübingen 1995.

81 Ibid., p. 42.

82 Ibid., p. 55.

83 Ibid., p. 43.

84 A well-developed analysis of this statement by Heidegger is contained in Jacques Derrida, *Geschlecht I* and *Geschlecht II*, Galilée, Paris 1987.

85 See B. Stiegler, *La technique et le temps 1. La faute d'Épimethee*, Galilée, Paris 1994.

IV Biopolitics

1 This is the thesis put forward by D. G. Hale in *The Body Politic: A Political Metaphor in Renaissance English Literature*, Mouton, The Hague-Paris 1971; and then essentially reworked by E. M. W. Tillyard, in *The Elizabethan World Picture*, Pelican, Harmondsworth 1972; and by L. Barkan, in *Nature's Work of Art: The Human Body as Image of the World*, Yale University Press, New Haven 1975. Finally see J. Sawday, *The Body Emblazoned: Dissection and the Human Body in Renaissance Culture*, Routledge, London 1995.

2 See P. Becchi, "Meccanicismo e organicismo. Gli antecedenti di un'opposizione," in *Filosofia Politica* (1999), no. 3, pp. 457–72. But see the entire section on the "body politic" in *Filosofia politica* (1993), no. 3, which includes essays by A. Cavarero, D. Panizza, and S. Mezzadra.

3 See A. Cavarero, *Corpo in figure*, Feltrinelli, Milan 1995, pp. 187–217 (although it supports the thesis we argue against on the logocentric marginalization of the body in modernity).

4 Thomas Hobbes, *Leviathan (1651)*, Chap. 29.

5 Ibid., Chap. 19.

6   Jean-Jacques Rousseau, *Economie politique*, in *Oeuvres Complètes*, Gallimard, Paris 1959–69, III.

7   Jean-Jacques Rousseau, *The Social Contract*, Section 6, "The Social Compact."

8   Ibid., Section 7, "The Sovereign."

9   Emmanuel Joseph Sieyès, "What Is the Third Estate?" in *Political Writings*, ed. and trans. Michael Sonenscher, Hackett Publishing, Indianapolis, Ind., 2003, p. 162.

10 I am alluding to the important work by Antoine de Baecque, *The Body Politic: Corporeal Metaphor in Revolutionary France, 1770–1800*, Stanford University Press, Stanford, Calif. 1997.

11 J. Rogozinski, " 'Comme les paroles d'un homme ivre...': chair de l'histoire et corps politique," *Les Cahiers de Philosophie*, 1994–95, no. 18, pp. 71–102.

12 Ibid., p. 101.

13 M. Carbone appears to take a similar approach in a recent essay entitled appropriately "Carne," appearing in *Aut Aut*, 2001, no. 304, pp. 99–119. The political significance of the theme of "flesh" is also well delineated by E. Lisciani-Petrini in "La passione impolitica della politica. Merleau-Ponty tra 'filosofia e non filosofia'," in *Nichilismo e politica*, op. cit. pp. 55–73.

14 This is what Jacques Derrida also winds up admitting, although with many reservations, in *Le Toucher, Jean-Luc Nancy*, Galilée, Paris 2000, pp. 262 ff.

15 D. Franck, *Chair et corps. Sur la phenomenologie de Husserl*, Minuit, Paris 1981, p. 167.

16 Martin Heidegger, *History of the Concept of Time*, Indiana University Press, Bloomington 1992, p. 41.

17 See J. Schlanger, *Les metaphores de l'organisme*, l'Harmattan (earlier ed. Vrin 1971), Paris 1995, pp. 182 ff.

18 For more on this topic, see S. D'Alessio, "Tra la vita e la morte: declinazioni della libertà in Machiavelli e Hobbes," in *Tolleranza e libertà*, ed. V. Dini, Elèuthera, Milan 2001, pp. 41–66.

19 See S. Greenblatt, "Invisible Bullets: Authority and Its Subversion," in *Shakespeare's "Rough Magic": Renaissance Essays in Honor of C. L. Barber*, ed. P. Erickson and C. Kahn, University of Delaware Press, Newark 1985, pp. 276–302.

20 J. G. Harris, *Foreign Bodies and the Body Politic*, Cambridge University Press, Cambridge 1998, pp. 23 ff.

21 For more on this, see also W. Pagel, *Paracelsus: an Introduction to Philosophical Medicine in the Era of Renaissance*, Kargel, Basel 1968.

22 Paracelsus, *Paragranum*, trans. Nicholas Goodrick-Clarke, North Atlantic Books, Berkeley, Calif., Section 5.7, pp. 74–75 [Sentence in square brackets quoted from Italian version: *Paragrano*, trans. F. Masini, Laterza, Bari-Rome 1973, p. 105].

23 Ibid, *Paragrano*, Italian version, p. 105.

24 Ibid., p. 121.

25 Jean-Jacques Rousseau, *Rousseau's Social Contract, Etc.*, trans. G. D. H. Cole, J. M. Dent, Dutton, London-New York 1920, p. 149.

26 J. G. Harris, *Foreign Bodies and the Body Politic*, p. 73.

27 Jacques Derrida, "La pharmacie de Platon," in *La dissemination*, Seuil, Paris 1972. For a discussion on this aspect of Derrida—between *communitas* and *immunitas*—see the monograph by C. Resta, *L'evento dell'altro. Etica e politica in Jacques Derrida*, Bollati Boringhieri (coll. Saggi), Turin 2003.

28 For a look at this relationship see the very helpful study by A. Orsucci, *Dalla biologia cellulare alle scienze dello spirito*, il Mulino, Bologna 1992.

29 The reconstruction of this question by V. Cappelletti, *Entelechìa. Saggi sulle dottrine biologiche del secolo decimonono*, Sansoni, Florence 1965 is still useful.

30 T. Schwann, *Mikroskopische Untersuchungen über die Übereinstimmung in der Struktur und dem Wachsthum der Thiere und Pflanzen*, Verlag der Sander'schen Buchhandlung, Berlin 1839, p. 223.

31 R. G. Mazzolini, "Stato e organismo, individui e cellule nell'opera di Rudolf Virchow negli anni 1845–1860," in *Annali dell'Istituto storico italo-germanico*, vol. 9, 1983, pp. 153–293. But for more on Virchow's role see equally A. Bauer, *Rudolph Virchow – der politische Arzt*, Stopp, Berlin 1982.

32 Georges Canguilhem, *Knowledge of Life*, Fordham University Press, New York 2008, p. 48.

33 Rudof Virchow, *Cellular Pathology: as based upon physiological and pathological history*, John Churchill, London 1860, p. 14.

34 See A. Orsucci, *Dalla biologia cellulare alle scienze dello spirito*, il Mulino, Bologna 1992, p. 76.

35 Rudof Virchow, *Alter und neuer Vitalismus*, in *Archiv für pathologische Anatomie und Physiologie und für klinische Medicin*, vol. 9 (1856) [Quoted from Italian version: *Vecchio e nuovo vitalismo*, Laterza, Bari-Rome 1969, p. 137].

36 Ibid., pp. 163–64.

37 Ibid., pp. 167–68.

38 The texts by Virchow that are cited here are collected in an appendix to the essay by Mazzolini, cited above, pp. 282–90.

39 C. Bernard, *Leçons sur les phenomènes de la vie communs aux animaux et aux vegetaux*, Librairie J.-B. Baillière et Fils, Paris 1885, p. 356.

40 Virchow, *Die Cellularpathologie*, pp. 72–73.

41 Antoine de Baecque, *The Body Politic. Corporeal Metaphor in Revolutionary France, 1770–1800*, Stanford University Press, Stanford, Calif. 1997, p. 93.

42 Michel Foucault, *The Birth of the Clinic*, Routledge Classics, London 2003, p. 157.

43 X. Bichat, *A Treatise On the Membranes in General: and on different membranes in particular*, Cummings and Hilliard, Boston 1813, p. 22–23.

44 P.-J.-G. Cabanis, *Note touchant le supplice de la guillotine*, in *Oeuvres complètes de Cabanis*, Bosange Frères, Paris 1823, vol. 2, pp. 161–83.

45 For an overview of the concept see the article "Biopolitica" by L. Bazzicalupo, in *Enciclopedia del pensiero politico*, ed. R. Esposito and C. Galli, Laterza, Bari-Rome 2000, p. 70. More specifically on biopolitics in Foucault, see the issue of *Cites*, 2000, no. 2, *Michel Foucault: de la guerre des races au biopouvoir*.

46 M. Foucault, "The Birth of Social Medicine," in *Power, Essential Works of Foucault, Vol. 3*, Penguin Books, London 2002, pp. 134–156 [Quoted from the Italian version: "La nascita della medicina sociale," in *Archivio Foucault 2. 1971–1977. Poteri, saperi, strategie*, ed. A. Dal Lago, Feltrinelli, Milan 1997, p. 227].

47 Michel Foucault, "About the Concept of the 'Dangerous Individual' in 19th Century Legal Psychiatry," *Politics, Philosophy, Culture: Interviews and Other Writings, 1977–1984*, ed. M. Morris and P. Patton, Routledge, London 1988, p. 134.

48 On the phenomenology and crisis of the paradigm of sovereignty, see E. Balibar, "Prolégomènes à la souveraineté," in *Nous, citoyens d'Europe?*, La Découverte, Paris 2001, pp. 257–85.

49 Michel Foucault, *Will to Knowledge, History of Sexuality Vol. 1*, Penguin Books, London 1998, p. 143.

50 Among the many works that Foucault dedicated to the process of medicalization of modern society, in addition to the above-cited "Birth of Social Medicine" see also "La politique de la santé au XVIII siècle," in *Les Machines à guerir. Aux origines de l'hôpital moderne; dossiers et documents*, Institut de l'environnement, Paris 1976.

51 Michel Foucault, "The Crisis of Medicine of the Crisis of Anti-medicine?" in *Foucault Studies Journal*, 2004, no. 1, p. 9. On this topic see also *Reassessing Foucault: Power, Medicine and the Body*, ed. C. Jones and R. Porter, Routledge, London 1994.

52 Foucault, "Crisis of Medicine," p. 9–10.

53 This aporetic dialectic between risk and protection is central to interpreters of contemporaneity as well, among critics from such widely divergent schools as J. Delumeau (*Rassurer et proteger*, Fayard, Paris 1989), Niklas Luhmann (*Soziologie des Risikos*, De Gruyter, Berlin 1991), U. Beck, (*Risikogesellschaft. Auf dem Weg in eine andere Moderne*, Suhrkamp, Frankfurt am Main 1986) and Z. Bauman (*In Search of Politics*, Polity Press, Cambridge 1999).

54 Foucault, "Crisis in Medicine," p. 10.

55 Ibid., p. 11.

56 Michel Foucault, *Maladie mentale et personnalite*, PUF, Paris 1954.

57 See G. Le Blanc, *Foucault et le contournement du normal et du pathologique* and B. Cabestan, *Du regime: normativite et subjectivite, entrambi in Michel Foucault et la medecine*, ed. Ph. Artières and E. Da Silva, Kimé, Paris 2001, respectively, pp. 29–48 and 60–83.

58 For a comparison of the two thinkers see P. Macherey, "De Canguilhem à Canguilhem en passant par Foucault," in *Georges Canguilhem, Philosophe, historien des sciences*, Albin Michel, Paris 1993, pp. 286–94. On the topic of norm see also G. Le Blanc, *Canguilhem et les normes*, PUF, Paris 1998.

59 Georges Canguilhem, *On the Normal and the Pathological*, D. Reidal 1978, p. 159.

60 Ibid., p. 149.

61 See K. Goldstein, *Der Aufbau des Organismus*, Nijhoff, Den Haag 1934 (especially Chapter 8, "Norm, Health and Illness," and the section in it on "The tendency toward preservation as the expression of a life in decline").

V The implant

1 Donna J. Haraway, "The Biopolitics of Postmodern Bodies: Determinations of Self in Immune System Discourse (1989)" reprinted in *Feminist Theory and the Body: A Reader*, ed. Janet Price, Margrit Shildrick, Routledge, New York 1999, p. 204.

2 See Donna J. Haraway, *Modest_Witness@ Second Millennium: Female Man(c) Meets OncoMouse(tm)*, Routledge, New York 1995.

3 Donna J. Haraway, *Simians, Cyborgs and Women: The Reinvention*

of Nature, Free Association Books, London 1991, p. 245, footnote 4.

4   In addition to the previously cited introduction by R. Braidotti, see also B. S. Turner, *The Body Society*, Sage Publications, London 1996, pp. 63 ff. A margin of difference from Foucault's biopolitics is also traced out by Michael Hardt and Antonio Negri in *Empire*, Harvard University Press, Cambridge, Mass. 2000.

5   A particularly balanced stance regarding these dynamics is given in C. Formenti's, *Incantati dalla rete. Immaginari, utopie e conflitti nell'epoca di Internet*, Cortina, Milan 2000 and U. Fadini's *Sviluppo tecnologico e identità personale*, Dedalo, Bari 2000. But important observations on the transition between phases are also presented in A. Bonomi, *Il capitalismo molecolare*, Einaudi, Turin 1997; in M. Cacciari and G. Bettin, *Duemilauno. Politica e futuro*, Feltrinelli, Milan 2001; in N. Irti, *Norma e luoghi. Problemi di geo-diritto*, Laterza, Bari-Rome 2001; and in C. Galli, *Spazi politici. L'età moderna e l'età globale*, il Mulino, Bologna 2001.

6   See M. Dery, *Escape Velocity: Cyberculture at the End of the Century*, Grove Press, New York 1996.

7   Haraway, "The Biopolitics of Postmodern Bodies," p. 204.

8   See the substantial work on this topic by U. Galimberti, *Psiche e techne. L'uomo nell'età della tecnica*, Feltrinelli, Milan 1999.

9   Jean-Luc Nancy, *Corpus*, trans. by Richard A. Rand, Fordham University Press, New York 2008, p. 107.

10   Nancy, *Corpus*, "The Intruder," p. 168.

11   Ibid., p. 170.

12   For the history of immunology, in addition to A. M. Silverstein, *A History of Immunology*, Academic Press, New York 1989, A. M. Moulin, *Le dernier langage de la medecine. Histoire de l'immunologie de Pasteur au Sida*, PUF, Paris 1991 and B. Genetet, *Histoire de l'immunologie*, PUF, Paris 2000, see the highly informative anthology edited and with an introduction by G. Corbellini, *L'evoluzione del sistema immunologico*, Bollati Boringhieri, Turin 1990.

13   F. M. Burnet, *The Integrity of the Body*, Cambridge University Press, Cambridge, Mass. 1963 [quoted from Italian version: *Le difese organiche*, Boringhieri, Turin 1967, p. 82].

14   E. S. Golub, *Immunology: A Synthesis*, Sinauer Associates Inc., Sunderland, Mass., 1987, p. 515; second quote from the Italian version: *Immunologia. Una sintesi*, Zanichelli, Bologna 1989, p. 32.

15   J. H. L. Playfair, for example, in *Immunology at a Glance*, Blackwell, Oxford 1979 (5th ed. 1996), p. 12, describes the evolutionary

model of the immune system in these terms from the amoeba to the mammal.

16 M. Biondi, *Mente, cervello e sistema immunitario*, McGraw-Hill, Milan 1997, p. 1.

17 J. Klein, Immunology. *The Science of Self/Non Self Discrimination*, Wiley-Interscience, New York 1982, p. 3.

18 M. Kendall, *Dying to Live: How Our Bodies Fight Disease*, Cambridge University Press, Cambridge 1998.

19 P. Jaret, "Our Immune System: the Wars Within," in *National Geographic*, June 1986, pp. 702–35.

20 See W. Anderson, "Immunities of Empire: Race, Disease, and the New Tropical Medicine, 1900–1920," in *Bulletin of History of Medicine* 120, (1996), no.1, pp. 94–118 and D. Ogden, "Cold War Science and the Body Politic: an Immuno/Virological Approach to 'Angels in America'," in *Literature and Medicine* 19 (2000), no. 2, pp. 241–61.

21 See also D. Jacobi, "Quelques tendances ou effets de figurabilité dans la divulgation des théories immunologiques," in *Aster*, 1990, no. 10, pp. 129–53.

22 Susan Sontag, *Aids and Its Metaphors*, Farrar, Straus & Giroux, New York 1988.

23 P. Treichler, *Aids, Homophobia, and Biomedical Discourse: An Epidemic of Signification*, in *October*, 1987, 43.

24 J. Dwyer, *The Body at War: The Story of our Immune System*, Trade Division of Unwin Hyman Limited, London 1988 [all quotes are from the Italian version: *Le guerre del corpo umano*, Mondadori, Milan 1991].

25 L. Nilsson and Jan Lindberg, *The Body Victorious: The Illustrated Story of Our Immune System and Other Defenses of the Human Body*, Delacorte, New York 1987.

26 For this approach, see F. W. Timmerman, Jr., "Future Warriors," in *Military Review*, September 1987.

27 Nilsson, *The Body Victorious*, p. 24.

28 Dwyer, *Le guerre del corpo*, p. 59.

29 Ibid., p. 60.

30 Nilsson, *The Body Victorious*, p. 21.

31 Dwyer, *Le guerre del corpo*, p. 60.

32 Nilsson, *The Body Victorious*, p. 24.

33 Ibid., p. 25.

34 Ibid., p. 26.

35 Ibid., p. 31.

36 Ibid., p. 31.

37 Ibid., p. 20.

38 Martin A. Nowak and Andrew J. McMichael, "How HIV Defeats the Immune System" in *Scientific American*, Aug. 1995, p. 58.

39 Ibid., p. 62.

40 Jan Zita Grover, "AIDS: Keywords" in *The State of the Language*, University of California Press, Berkeley 1989, p. 143.

41 See Sandra L. Gilman, *Disease and Representation: Images of Illness from Madness to Aids*, Cornell University Press, Ithaca-London 1988 [Italian version: *Immagini della malattia, dalla follia all'Aids*, il Mulino, Bologna 1993, pp. 348 ff.].

42 Susan Sontag, *Aids and Its Metaphors*, Picador, New York 1990, p. 106.

43 See Patton, *Inventing Aids*, Routledge, New York 1990.

44 Dwyer, *Le guerre del corpo*, p. 61.

45 As L. Steinman expresses it in "Le malattie autoimmuni," in *Le Scienze*, no. 94, 1997, p. 86.

46 See P. Ehrlich, "Über Haemolysin. Dritte Mitteilung," in *Collected Studies on Immunity*, ed. C. Bolduan, Wiley, New York 1906, p. 27.

47 G. Nossol, *Antibodies and Immunity*, Basic Books, New York, 2nd ed. 1978, p. 243.

48 Nilsson, *The Body Victorious*, p. 187.

49 E. S. Golub, *Immunology: A Synthesis*, Italian version: p. 357.

50 Baruj Benacerraf, Emil R. Unanue, *Textbook of Immunology*, Williams & Wilkins, Baltimore-London, 1979, p. 275.

51 F. M. Burnet, "The Darwinian Approach to Immunity," in *Molecular and Cellular Basis of Antibody Formation*, Academic Press, New York-London 1965, p. 17.

52 D. J. Haraway, *Come una foglia (intervista di T. Nichols Goodeve)*, La Tartaruga, Milan 1999, pp. 92–93. For a similar perspective, see E. Martin, *Flexible Bodies: Tracking Immunity in American Culture From the Days of Polio to the Age of Aids*, Beacon Press, Boston 1994.

53 Polly Matzinger, "Tolerance, Danger and the Extended Family," in *Annual Review of Immunology*, 1994, no. 12, p. 991.

54 Moulin, *Le dernier langage de la medecine*, p. 14.

55 For the reference to Leibniz, see P. H. Caspar, *L'individuation des êtres. Aristote, Leibniz et l'immunologie contemporaine*, Le Sycomore, Paris 1989.

56 A. I. Tauber, *The Immune Self: Theory or Metaphor?*, Cambridge University Press, Cambridge 1997 [quotes from Italian version: *L'immunologia dell'io*, ed. G. Corbellini, McGraw-Hill, Milan 1999].

57 The expression from Burnet (in *Biological Aspects of Infectious*

Diseases, Cambridge University Press, Cambridge 1940) that Tauber refers to is "climax community."

58 P. B. Medawar, E. M. Lance and E. Simpson, *An Introduction to Immunology*, Wildwood House, London 1977.

59 N. K. Jerne, "Toward a Network Theory of the Immune System," in *Annales d'Immunologie*, 1974, no. 125 [quoted from Italian version: "Verso una teoria del sistema immunitario come rete di interazioni," in *L'evoluzione del pensiero immunologico*, op. cit., p. 252].

60 Golub, *Immunologia. Una sintesi*, p. 284.

61 F. J. Varela, A. Coutinho, B. Dupire, N. N. Vaz, "Cognitive Networks: Immune, Neural, and Otherwise," in *Theoretical Immunology* 2 (1988), p. 365.

62 Tauber, *The Immune Self*, Italian edition, p. 171.

63 Ibid., p. 154.

64 See W. H. Fridman, *Le cerveau mobile*, Hermann, Paris 1991. See the introduction by M. Daëron to M. Daëron, M. Fougereau, W. H. Fridman, A. M. Moulin and J.-P. Revillard, *Le système immunitaire*, Nathan, Paris 1995, pp. 56.

65 For a critique of the "appropriative" relationship between mother and child see the essay by A. Putino, *Amiche mie isteriche*, Cronopio, Naples 1988.

66 Dwyer, *Le guerre del corpo*, p. 104–5.

67 See B. Waldenfels, *Der Stachel des Fremden*, Suhrkamp, Frankfurt am Main 1990; and *Topographie des Fremden. Studien zur Phänomenologie des Fremden*, Suhrkamp, Frankfurt am Main 1997.

68 Edmund Husserl, *Cartesian Meditations*, trans. Dorion Cairns, Martinue Nijhoff Publishers, The Hague-Boston-London 1960, p. 114.

69 B. Waldenfels, *Cultura propria e cultura estranea. Il paradosso di una scienza dell'estraneo*, in *Paradigmi*, 1992, no. 30, pp. 647–48.

70 See N. K. Jerne, "The natural selection theory of antibody formation; ten years later," in *Phage and the Origins of Molecular Biology*, ed. J. Cairns, G. S. Stent e J. D. Watson, Cold Spring Harbor Lab., New York 1966, p. 301.

71 A. Mackenzie, " 'God Has No Allergies': Immanent Ethics and the Simulacra of the Immune System," in *Postmodern Culture* 6, 1996, no. 2.

72 C. Debru, "Grammaire du soi," in *Soi et non-soi*, ed. J. Bernard, M. Bessis, C. Debru, Seuil, Paris 1990, pp. 267–77.

73 Emile Benveniste, *Problems in General Linguistics*, trans. Mary

Elizabeth Meek, University of Miami Press, Coral Gables, Fla. 1978, p. 197–98.

74   Ibid., 198–99.

75   In this regard, see L. Sznajder, "Y a t-il un réfléchi en latin? Étude sur les conditions d'emploi de 'se' et 'suus'," in *L'Information grammaticale*, May 1981, pp. 17–22, as well as J.-C. Milner, "Le système du réfléchi en latin," in *Langage*, June 1978, pp. 73–86.

76   See A. Meillet, *Introduction à l'etude comparative des langues indoeuropeennes*, Hachette, Paris 1903 (1937), pp. 336–38.

77   Emile Benveniste, *The Indo-European Language and Society*, University of Miami Press, Coral Gables, Fla. 1973 [Italian version: *Il vocabolario delle istituzioni indoeuropee*, I, Einaudi, Turin 1976, pp. 253 ff.]

Index